**Sales P... ...mies®**

BUSINESS AND
GENERAL
REFERENCE
BOOK SERIES
FROM IDG

*Quick Reference Card*

# Things to Keep in Mind While Prospecting

## Learn to love the word "No"

If you earn $100 for each closed transaction and it takes five contacts to make a sale, you really earn $20 for each contact. Every time you hear the word "no," you should say to yourself, "Thanks for the $20!"

## The S.T.P. formula for prospecting

Make a daily commitment to See Twenty People every day and watch how your business grows!

# Turn Static Features into Emotional Benefits

| Benefit | How You Tout Benefit |
|---|---|
| Cheaper | "A more economical value for your money." |
| Green | "A relaxing shade of color that will blend nicely with the rest of your furniture." |
| Faster | "Will give you more free time." |
| Better quality copies | "Enhance your professional image." |
| More miles per gallon | "Generates income back to you with real savings in reduced fuel consumption." |
| Security | "Sleep better with true peace of mind." |
| Swimming pool | "Think of the fun memories you'll build with your family enjoying the cool waters together." |
| Barbecue grill | "Can't you just smell the steaks sizzling as you enjoy a relaxing dinner in the great outdoors?" |

*...For Dummies: Bestselling Book Series for Beginners*

# Sales Prospecting For Dummies®

BUSINESS AND
GENERAL
REFERENCE
BOOK SERIES
FROM IDG

Quick
Reference
Card

## Who Can Help You Find More Prospects?

1. Family members

2. Coworkers

3. Spouse's coworkers

4. Children's friend's parents

5. Church members

6. Club members

7. Neighbors

8. Anyone you are a customer of

9. Your local librarian

10. The Internet

11. Anyone you come within 3 feet of

12. Anyone you can help!

Remember to involve as many senses as possible in every client contact. The more you involve a client's senses, the more involved the client will remain.

*...For Dummies: Bestselling Book Series for Beginners*

# Praise, praise, praise for Sales Prospecting For Dummies!

"*Sales Prospecting For Dummies* is a concise, yet comprehensive, guide to getting and maintaining a salesperson's most vital lifeline: new prospects. If you want to succeed in sales, this book should be your daily activity guide."

—Michael Tove, District Sales Trainer, CMA

"Without a doubt, this is the most revolutionary book you will ever read on selling successfully. Tom Hopkins's wisdom has created boundless wealth in the lives of salespeople around the world."

— Glenna Salsbury, CSP, CPAE, President of the National Speakers Association 1997-98, author of *The Art of the Fresh Start*

"Tom Hopkins's sincerity and clarity permeate every page. His strategies empower me to defeat anything that defies success — not only in sales, but in life."

— Judith Ann Roberts, Personal Financial Analyst, Primerica Financial Services

"Every sale begins with prospecting. This book will improve your prospecting skills. As a multi-franchise car dealer who survived on sales for 25 years, I know the importance of prospecting. It keeps you in business. If you want to thrive, study this book, set your goals, plan your time, multiply your leads, and master the art of prospecting."

— Linda Brock-Nelson, Former Owner/Founder, Linda Brock Auto Mall

"I loved this book — and I hate to read! This book will help rookies and veterans alike learn how to sell to the customer of the '90s and beyond. Fun and easy to read, it's a must for anyone whose goal is incredible success."

— Ken Brockbank, Executive Vice President, Unishippers, Inc.

"The chief reason why most salespeople don't meet their sales quotas is because they make too few sales presentations. Read Tom Hopkins's *Sales Prospecting For Dummies* and your sales production will skyrocket. I recommend it to the novice salesperson as well as the seasoned pro."

— Robert L. Shook, author of more than 40 books, including *The Greatest Sales Stories Ever Told*

"Our readers look forward to Tom Hopkins's articles because of his ability to explain and illustrate his famous Champion selling strategies. Salespeople can easily understand and apply the strategies to increase their own sales. In this book, he incorporates the *...For Dummies* practical learning style to make all of his successful professional selling strategies even easier to acquire."

— Homer Smith, Editor, *Master Salesmanship*

"Tom Hopkins is the foremost authority today in the field and subject of sales closing and prospecting. Not since the days of J. Douglas Edwards has there been someone as astute in both of these arts as Tom Hopkins. This masterpiece of information will open new vistas and great horizons for all who read it. It is must-reading for everyone who desires the best that life can offer."

> — Larry W. Coyle, Executive Vice President, TeamUp International, Inc.

"*Sales Prospecting For Dummies* is a must-read for all new salespeople and seasoned salespeople looking to freshen their approach. The ability to find and develop new business sources is the key to long-term success in sales."

> — Diane Turton, Diane Turton Realtors

"If you are new to sales this is definitely the book to read. If you are an experienced sales professional, there's plenty of good solid advice and tips for you, too. Tom Hopkins is a master sales trainer whose vast experience is shared with you in an easy-to-understand and easy-to-use manner."

> — Louis O. Sepulveda, C.P.P.

"Prospecting is where most salespeople fail; Tom Hopkins has once again put together his unique blend of hands-on implementation, humor, and balance to make *Sales Prospecting For Dummies* mandatory reading for the professional salesperson.

> — Dave Ramsey, author of *The New York Times* bestseller, *Financial Peace*

"Utilizing the techniques from *Sales Prospecting For Dummies*, I've met thousands of people, grown a successful business, developed a continuous referral network, and had my company featured in over 70 news stories."

> — Roseann Higgins, President and Founder, S.P.I.E.S.

"This is a classic — clear, concise and filled with powerful principles that anyone can use to become a top-producing salesperson. I should know. Over the course of my 17-year financial consulting career, I've applied these proven sales strategies and have benefited greatly as a result. I know many other sales professionals — from all walks of life — who have enjoyed new levels of success by applying the insights in this informative book. If you want to increase your sales, read *Sales Prospecting For Dummies* now."

> — E. Anthony Reguero, Chartered Financial Consultant

"A precise, step-by-step, easy-to-understand sales manual that teaches and inspires the novice while sharpening the skills of the lifelong sales professional. A book, to be referred to again and again, by a master of sales."

> — Laura Laaman, sales speaker and author

# ABOUT IDG BOOKS WORLDWIDE

Welcome to the world of IDG Books Worldwide.

IDG Books Worldwide, Inc., is a subsidiary of International Data Group, the world's largest publisher of computer-related information and the leading global provider of information services on information technology. IDG was founded more than 25 years ago and now employs more than 8,500 people worldwide. IDG publishes more than 275 computer publications in over 75 countries (see listing below). More than 60 million people read one or more IDG publications each month.

Launched in 1990, IDG Books Worldwide is today the #1 publisher of best-selling computer books in the United States. We are proud to have received eight awards from the Computer Press Association in recognition of editorial excellence and three from *Computer Currents'* First Annual Readers' Choice Awards. Our best-selling *...For Dummies*® series has more than 30 million copies in print with translations in 30 languages. IDG Books Worldwide, through a joint venture with IDG's Hi-Tech Beijing, became the first U.S. publisher to publish a computer book in the People's Republic of China. In record time, IDG Books Worldwide has become the first choice for millions of readers around the world who want to learn how to better manage their businesses.

Our mission is simple: Every one of our books is designed to bring extra value and skill-building instructions to the reader. Our books are written by experts who understand and care about our readers. The knowledge base of our editorial staff comes from years of experience in publishing, education, and journalism — experience we use to produce books for the '90s. In short, we care about books, so we attract the best people. We devote special attention to details such as audience, interior design, use of icons, and illustrations. And because we use an efficient process of authoring, editing, and desktop publishing our books electronically, we can spend more time ensuring superior content and spend less time on the technicalities of making books.

You can count on our commitment to deliver high-quality books at competitive prices on topics you want to read about. At IDG Books Worldwide, we continue in the IDG tradition of delivering quality for more than 25 years. You'll find no better book on a subject than one from IDG Books Worldwide.

John Kilcullen
CEO
IDG Books Worldwide, Inc.

Steven Berkowitz
President and Publisher
IDG Books Worldwide, Inc.

*Eighth Annual Computer Press Awards* ≥1992

*Ninth Annual Computer Press Awards* ≥1993

*Tenth Annual Computer Press Awards* ≥1994

*Eleventh Annual Computer Press Awards* ≥1995

# SALES PROSPECTING FOR DUMMIES®

## by Tom Hopkins

IDG Books Worldwide, Inc.
An International Data Group Company

Foster City, CA ♦ Chicago, IL ♦ Indianapolis, IN ♦ New York, NY ♦ Southlake, TX

## Sales Prospecting For Dummies®

Published by
**IDG Books Worldwide, Inc.**
An International Data Group Company
919 E. Hillsdale Blvd.
Suite 400
Foster City, CA 94404
www.idgbooks.com (IDG Books Worldwide Web site)
www.dummies.com (Dummies Press Web site)

Library of Congress Catalog Card No.: 98-84877

ISBN: 0-7645-5066-7

Printed in the United States of America

10 9 8 7 6 5 4 3 2 1

1E/QR/QU/ZY/IN

Distributed in the United States by IDG Books Worldwide, Inc.

Distributed by Macmillan Canada for Canada; by Transworld Publishers Limited in the United Kingdom; by IDG Norge Books for Norway; by IDG Sweden Books for Sweden; by Woodslane Pty. Ltd. for Australia; by Woodslane Enterprises Ltd. for New Zealand; by Longman Singapore Publishers Ltd. for Singapore, Malaysia, Thailand, and Indonesia; by Simron Pty. Ltd. for South Africa; by Toppan Company Ltd. for Japan; by Distribuidora Cuspide for Argentina; by Livraria Cultura for Brazil; by Ediciencia S.A. for Ecuador; by Addison-Wesley Publishing Company for Korea; by Ediciones ZETA S.C.R. Ltda. for Peru; by WS Computer Publishing Corporation, Inc., for the Philippines; by Unalis Corporation for Taiwan; by Contemporanea de Ediciones for Venezuela; by Computer Book & Magazine Store for Puerto Rico; by Express Computer Distributors for the Caribbean and West Indies. Authorized Sales Agent: Anthony Rudkin Associates for the Middle East and North Africa.

For general information on IDG Books Worldwide's books in the U.S., please call our Consumer Customer Service department at 800-762-2974. For reseller information, including discounts and premium sales, please call our Reseller Customer Service department at 800-434-3422.

For information on where to purchase IDG Books Worldwide's books outside the U.S., please contact our International Sales department at 650-655-3200 or fax 650-655-3295.

For information on foreign language translations, please contact our Foreign & Subsidiary Rights department at 650-655-3021 or fax 650-655-3281.

For sales inquiries and special prices for bulk quantities, please contact our Sales department at 650-655-3200 or write to the address above.

For information on using IDG Books Worldwide's books in the classroom or for ordering examination copies, please contact our Educational Sales department at 800-434-2086 or fax 817-251-8174.

For press review copies, author interviews, or other publicity information, please contact our Public Relations department at 650-655-3000 or fax 650-655-3299.

For authorization to photocopy items for corporate, personal, or educational use, please contact Copyright Clearance Center, 222 Rosewood Drive, Danvers, MA 01923, or fax 978-750-4470.

is a trademark under exclusive license to IDG Books Worldwide, Inc., from International Data Group, Inc.

# About the Author

**Tom Hopkins** is the epitome of sales success. A millionaire by the time he reached the age of 27, Hopkins now is Chairman of Tom Hopkins International, the largest sales training organization in the world. Each year, he teaches professional selling skills to hundreds of thousands of students around the world.

Thirty-four years ago, Tom Hopkins considered himself a failure. He dropped out of college after 90 days and, for the next 18 months, carried steel on construction sites to make a living. Believing that there had to be a better way to earn a living, he went into sales — and ran into the worst period of his life. For six months, Hopkins earned an average of $42 per month and slid deeper into debt and despair. Pulling together his last few dollars, he invested in a three-day sales training seminar that turned his life around. In the next six months, Hopkins sold more than $1 million worth of $25,000 homes.

At age 21, he won the Los Angeles Sales and Marketing Institute's coveted SAMMY Award and began setting records in sales performance that still stand today.

Because of his unique ability to share his enthusiasm for the profession of selling and the selling techniques he developed, Hopkins began giving seminars in 1974. Training as many as 10,000 salespeople a month, he quickly became known as the world's leading sales trainer.

Hopkins was a pioneer in producing high-quality audio-and videotape programs for those who could not attend the seminars or who wanted further reinforcement after the seminars. Recognized as the most effective sales-training programs ever produced, they are continually updated and are now being utilized by more than one million people.

He has also written ten books, including the best-selling *How to Master the Art of Selling,* which has sold over 1.3 million copies in nine languages; and three ...*For Dummies* books: *Selling For Dummies, Sales Closing For Dummies,* and this book, *Sales Prospecting For Dummies.*

Hopkins is a member of the National Speakers Association and one of a select few to ever receive its Council of Peers Award for Excellence. He is often the keynote speaker for annual conventions and is a frequent guest on television and radio talk shows.

## Publisher's Acknowledgments

We're proud of this book; please register your comments through our IDG Books Worldwide Online Registration Form located at http://my2cents.dummies.com.

Some of the people who helped bring this book to market include the following:

*Acquisitions, Development, and Editorial*

**Project Editor:** Rev Mengle

**Acquisitions Editor:** Mark Butler

**Copy Editors:** Patricia Yuu Pan, Michael Simsic

**General Reviewer:** Bill F. Sadler

**Editorial Manager:** Leah P. Cameron

**Editorial Assistant:** Donna Love

*Production*

**Project Coordinator:** Valery Bourke

**Layout and Graphics:** Steve Arany, Cameron Booker, Lou Boudreau, Angela F. Hunckler, Drew R. Moore, Anna Rohrer, Brent Savage

**Proofreaders:** Kelli Botta, Melissa D. Buddendeck, Michelle Croninger, Rachel Garvey, Rebecca Senninger, Janet M. Withers

**Indexer:** Sharon Duffy

---

*General and Administrative*

**IDG Books Worldwide, Inc.:** John Kilcullen, CEO; Steven Berkowitz, President and Publisher

**IDG Books Technology Publishing:** Brenda McLaughlin, Senior Vice President and Group Publisher

**Dummies Technology Press and Dummies Editorial:** Diane Graves Steele, Vice President and Associate Publisher; Mary Bednarek, Director of Acquisitions and Product Development; Kristin A. Cocks, Editorial Director

**Dummies Trade Press:** Kathleen A. Welton, Vice President and Publisher; Kevin Thornton, Acquisitions Manager

**IDG Books Production for Dummies Press:** Beth Jenkins Roberts, Production Director; Cindy L. Phipps, Manager of Project Coordination, Production Proofreading, and Indexing; Kathie S. Schutte, Supervisor of Page Layout; Shelley Lea, Supervisor of Graphics and Design; Debbie J. Gates, Production Systems Specialist; Robert Springer, Supervisor of Proofreading; Debbie Stailey, Special Projects Coordinator; Tony Augsburger, Supervisor of Reprints and Bluelines; Leslie Popplewell, Media Archive Coordinator

**Dummies Packaging and Book Design:** Patti Crane, Packaging Specialist; Kavish + Kavish, Cover Design

♦

The publisher would like to give special thanks to Patrick J. McGovern, without whom this book would not have been possible.

♦

# Dedication

This book is dedicated with heartfelt thanks to all of my team at Tom Hopkins International. Without your loyal commitment to excellence, we could never have trained and positively impacted the lives of more than 3 million salespeople worldwide.

Special thanks to Laura Oien for her 20 years of contribution; to Spence Price for his loyalty and integrity; and to Judy Slack for her creativity and assistance in writing many of my books and helping me produce our audio and video training systems.

# Author's Acknowledgments

First and foremost, I acknowledge my lovely bride, Debbie, for giving me valuable input and feedback on all of my training. (By the way, another good place to prospect is at seminars. That's where we found each other.)

I so appreciate the dedication and friendship of John Kilcullen, the CEO of IDG Books Worldwide, Inc. Your inspiration for this line of books was definitely heaven-sent.

Kathy Welton and Mark Butler of IDG Books are appreciated for their continued interest in our training and how it can help their readers.

Thanks also go to Judy Slack, my director of research and development, for fine-tuning the material and researching the new content that was needed.

Bill F. Sadler, thank you for reviewing the content and giving us your professional opinion. Your feedback was excellent.

Thanks to my fellow speakers, trainers, and my wonderful students who provided valuable input and great examples.

And special thanks go to Dan Baldwin, the writer who worked with all of us at THI, twisting and bending my material into the ...For Dummies style, for his diligent research assistance, great sense of humor, and willingness to go the extra mile for us. Good job, Dan!

Last, but not least, I thank Rev Mengle and Patricia Yuu Pan at IDG Books Worldwide, Inc., for their persistence in keeping everything on schedule and up to the ...For Dummies standards.

# Contents at a Glance

# Cartoons at a Glance

*By Rich Tennant*

"I wouldn't qualify this one too long."

**page 53**

"Get names!"

**page 5**

"I met my husband when I sold him an air purifier. That's him over there with some of my referral-in-laws."

**page 179**

"I don't take 'no' for an answer. Nor do I take 'whatever,' 'as if,' or 'duh.'"

**page 207**

"He's a new breed of cop. Captain-smooth, cocky, a real salesman. He's getting names, addresses, contributions to the Police Benevolence Fund. ... it's incredible."

**page 251**

"I sell subscriptions to a heavy metal magazine, and believe me—it's not easy getting sales prospects in a mosh pit."

**page 103**

*Fax: 508-546-7747 • E-mail:* the5wave@tiac.net

# Table of Contents

# Introduction

*T*he professional selling cycle includes many steps, beginning with locating and meeting prospective clients (which we in this industry call *prospecting*), through qualifying, demonstrating, and addressing concerns, to the final closing of the sale. I cover each of these steps in great detail in *Selling For Dummies* (IDG Books Worldwide, Inc.). If you're new to selling, you may struggle with this first step. You may be uncomfortable talking with strangers about a product or service you're just learning about.

That discomfort is understandable. One of our greatest fears as human beings living in this ever-changing world is to be thought poorly of — to be rejected. Unfortunately, that single fear has kept millions of people from becoming high achievers in the field of selling. Many of those people have given up on selling and are living lives where their financial incomes are dictated (limited?) by someone else. Too bad. Don't you give up. If you're dedicated enough to achieving selling greatness to pick up a copy of this book, you'll find that the answers to many of your questions lie in these pages.

My goal in this book is to help you gain a solid perspective on what prospecting is and how to go about it; and to employ some simple, yet powerful ways to build a prosperous selling career by meeting and getting to know the right people.

## *Who Should Read This Book?*

This book is written with the traditional salesperson in mind — someone who earns his or her living primarily from moving products or services into the lives of end-users. This book is for you if:

- ✔ You're a career salesperson who wants to boost your sales income right now.
- ✔ You find yourself hesitating when approaching strangers.
- ✔ You have ever walked away from people not knowing whether or not they'd be good candidates for your product or service.
- ✔ You've already read my book *Selling For Dummies,* but want more information specific to prospecting.

> ✔ You're a small-business person struggling to grow your business.
>
> ✔ You're involved in network marketing and have discovered that it really is a numbers game, and that the more people you meet, the faster you'll find those who are like-minded enough to build an organization.

All of the material found within these pages is based on more than 30 years of personal experience and research, the experience of top professionals in many fields, and sound psychological principles. I won't show you something that has not been proven to work in the real world of selling.

## How to Use This Book

I have no way of knowing which chapters you will be drawn to first, but those are the ones I recommend you begin with. However, I also strongly suggest that you read the book from cover to cover to gain the maximum benefit from its contents. Keep a highlighter handy. Highlight the points that are most meaningful or pertinent to you on your first read. In doing so, you've turned this great little textbook into a handy quick-reference guide.

This book is small enough to tag along with you in your briefcase. However, I don't recommend you leave it there for long. The best place for this book is in your hands, opened to the very piece of information you need to help you find your next qualified prospect.

## How This Book Is Organized

*Sales Prospecting For Dummies* is organized into six parts. The chapters within each part cover specific topic areas in detail.

### Part I: Who Needs You?

In this part, you'll find out just what you need to know to be prepared to answer this question. If you don't know who needs you and your product, how will you ever find them? Discover how to make prospecting your hobby and how to build your image to the point where prospects seek you out.

### Part II: Resources of the Rich and Famous

Here's the meat of the book — the where-and-how-to-find-them part. This is where you find specific prospecting strategies with proven successful phraseology that you can master and begin using right away.

## Part III: Making the Contact

In this part, I go over methods for maximizing every meeting with every person. Learn how to speak so that others will listen. Keeping their needs in mind goes a long way toward putting others at ease as you attempt to discover more about how they will benefit from your product or service.

## Part IV: What's a Few Referrals Among Friends?

This part is filled with ideas for getting new prospects from satisfied clients and for keeping you and your product in the minds of your clients so that they'll continue to refer others your way.

## Part V: It's a Numbers Game

Every person you meet may not turn out to be a good prospect. And you won't get appointments with everyone who is. That's a fact of the selling game of life. So in order to stay on top of your game, you must face and overcome failure and rejection. This part is a great place to go to get your excitement back after one of those tough days of prospecting.

## Part VI: The Part of Tens

The brief chapters in this part are full of ideas for prospecting that you can implement quickly and easily into your current prospecting system. The chapters take only a few minutes to read and are a great way to get yourself pumped up for a day of seeking new clients.

# Icons Used in This Book

This icon highlights the crucial pieces of information and skills necessary for getting people happily involved with your product or service. I borrowed this idea for my teaching from a college professor who had a somewhat laid-back attitude about classwork. He said he didn't care what we did during class time as long as we learned the information he told us was Red Flag knowledge. These were the pieces of information from which he created his exams.

This icon is for personal stories from my years of experience or stories that have been shared with me by my students.

I use this to highlight little tidbits that sales champions should always keep in mind.

 We've all heard horror stories about the wrong thing said to the wrong person, or something similar. This icon helps you avoid these potential pitfalls.

 Other books in the ...*For Dummies* line also have valuable information to make you a more effective prospector. This symbol points out these books.

 These are strategies that most salespeople overlook, such as unusual methods or places for finding prospects. The items highlighted by this icon are the things champion salespeople do that average ones don't.

 This icon points out the hottest prospecting tips in each segment.

 This icon denotes actual scripted phraseology that other sales professionals and I have tested, used, and proven to be successful.

## Where to Go from Here

Go anywhere inside this book! I've tried to make every page count. Each page contains at least one practical piece of information that can assist you in improving your prospecting skills. I want you to be comfortable with the material, so please begin wherever you feel most comfortable.

# Part I
# Who Needs You?

The 5th Wave                    By Rich Tennant

"Get names!"

## In this part . . .

*H*ere's where I show you just what prospecting is all about. I cover how to watch for prospecting opportunities in everything you do, every day. Knowing just what your product can do for people will serve as something like a prospecting compass, showing you in which direction to seek out quality prospects.

# Chapter 1
# Prospecting Defined

*I*f you've been in the selling profession any length of time, you remember how challenging your first few weeks were. You found out more about your product or service than you ever dreamed possible. You may have had no idea of how to sell, but you knew if you could talk with enough people who were interested in the product, sooner or later you'd bring back one of those papers with an order on it or move one of those products from your car, briefcase, or store into someone else's hand. And, someone would pay you for doing so.

But finding just the right people isn't always easy. That's where the art of prospecting comes in.

## What is Prospecting?

*Prospecting* is finding the right buyer for your product or service. Prospecting involves two steps:

  ✔ Finding the people to sell. That's what this book is all about.

  ✔ Selling the people you find on their need for your product or service.

Simple, isn't it? That doesn't mean prospecting is easy or that you can take it lightly. You have to get organized, plan, stay motivated, and, most of all, you have to act.

There are almost as many different ways to prospect as there are types of prospects. But the methods break down into two general categories: cold calling and what I call warm prospecting.

Cold calling means contacting anyone and everyone with the hope that someone, somewhere will want your product or service. For some sales professionals, cold calling means getting out the telephone book and, starting with Aaron Aanderson, calling people at their homes. Others count on the Yellow Pages for leads. Still others must put on their walking shoes and start knocking on homeowners's doors, or entering lobbies at businesses, seeking prospects. These methods usually lead to conversations like this one:

*CHAMPION STRATEGY #1*

| | |
|---|---|
| **You:** | Good morning. My name is Tom Hopkins. I'm in business in the community. Who in your company is responsible for the training of the fine sales staff you have here? |
| **Them:** | That would be Jake Carlton. |
| **You:** | Is Mr. Carlton in? |
| **Them:** | Yes, he is, but he's in a meeting. |
| **You:** | By the way, what is your name? |
| **Them:** | My name is Anne. |
| **You:** | Thank you for your help, Anne. May I ask when the best time is to reach Mr. Carlton? |
| **Them:** | Probably first thing in the morning. He spends a lot of his day in meetings and training sessions. |
| **You:** | That's perfectly understandable and probably why he does such a great job. I'd like to leave my card, Anne. Would you please give it to Mr. Carlton with a message that I'll contact him early in the day tomorrow? I need only two minutes of his time. I have some information to share with him that could greatly enhance the training he is currently providing, with the end result being increased sales and a great amount of time saved in his current efforts. Again, I thank you for your assistance, Anne. You're doing a great job here! |

Using cold calling, as in this scenario, you didn't get to meet Mr. Carlton because your timing wasn't convenient for him. You did, however, gain a bit of knowledge about him that will bring you one step closer to meeting him tomorrow — even if the meeting takes place over the telephone. You can bet that when you call in and address Anne by name in the morning she'll remember your courtesy toward her and try to continue to help you by getting you through to Mr. Carlton.

This may be the hard way of reaching Mr. Carlton, but if you currently have no other means of getting yourself in front of him, go for it!

Cold calling can be an overwhelming endeavor, one that can easily dishearten you if it's not done properly. That's why so many salespeople avoid it like the plague. It's a good part of the reason that the mere mention of the term *prospecting* in general elicits groans from salespeople the world over.

*Warm prospecting,* on the other hand, involves contacting people who you have good reason to believe will become clients and with whom you have some sort of connection. Your connection could be a referral from someone else or you could already have met your warm prospect through a social or business situation. Your contact with him would go something like this:

CHAMPION STRATEGY #1

> **You:** Hi, John, I'm Mary Doe with Worldwide Widgets. Sam Smith at Acme and I have been working on some projects involving our products, and he said that you're a lot like him: Always on the lookout for ways to do things better.
>
> **Them:** Yeah, Sam and I go way back. We've been known to browse a few trade shows together.
>
> **You:** Well, we have a new widget that Sam is putting to use on their Alpha project, and he thought it would interest you. Is there some time next week I can stop on by and show it to you?
>
> **Them:** Hmm. If Sam's using it, it's probably something I'd want to know about. Sure, let's get together.

Warm prospecting brings about far better and faster results. But how do you get from cold calling to warm prospecting? This book has lots of ideas for finding qualified prospects. But before you become a prospecting professional, you have to recognize the need to prospect.

## Where Prospecting Fits In

If you ask 100 sales professionals what their favorite aspect of selling is, I'm willing to bet that 95 of them will *not* mention prospecting. In my one-day seminars, I teach selling skills, ideas, and techniques for all aspects of the selling cycle, which I have broken down into seven areas:

- ✔ Prospecting
- ✔ Original contact
- ✔ Qualification
- ✔ Presentation
- ✔ Addressing concerns
- ✔ Closing the sale
- ✔ Getting referrals

When I bring up prospecting the first time at a seminar, there may be an audible groan from the audience. Many students shift in their seats, telling me with their body language, "Prospecting? Yuck!" I have to believe they have that reaction because they don't have the right attitude about prospecting.

Besides prospecting, I teach a little about how to make a positive first impression with your original contact. I talk about the value, ways, and means of qualifying prospects to determine if you have the right solution for them. I cover methods and styles of delivery for presenting or demonstrating your product or service. I talk about many methods of addressing client concerns and several ways to close a sale.

When I get back around to the end of the selling cycle, which involves a type of prospecting called *referrals,* students have a different attitude entirely. They listen more intently. They lean forward in their chairs. They nod. They take more notes. Obviously, they don't mind this perspective on the subject. That's because I have given them effective skills they can begin applying on their very next sale, so I've gained some credibility with them.

Students have another reason to pay attention: I begin talking about referrals by telling my students how high the closing ratio is on a prequalified, referred lead versus a cold call.

As your career progresses, you'll find most of your prospects come from your satisfied clients. This is what I mean by referral prospecting. Make getting referrals a major source of your new business by asking for them after closing every sale. The request can be as simple as this:

> Well, Mr. Smith, you probably know another boating enthusiast who could benefit from ownership of a new boat, someone in your circle of friends, perhaps a family member. I sure would appreciate the opportunity to serve them as well. Who comes to mind?

The customer probably knows several people and may be willing to provide names, addresses, and phone numbers. Sometimes the happy customer even contacts the referral for you. Studies indicate a poor 10 percent closing ratio with nonqualified leads, yet with qualified referrals, that closing ratio jumps to a whopping 60 percent! Your credibility jumps sky high with good referrals, too, because the individual knows and trusts the person making the referral. You ride in on the waves of those feelings. Your goal should be to build an endless chain of satisfied customers who are delighted to refer business your way. By my fifth year in sales, literally all my business was from referrals. Satisfied clients become interested in your success and continue to send people to you if you handle them properly.

High closing ratios grab the attention of anyone who sells a product or service for a living. In order to begin getting any kind of closing ratio, you need to prospect. You must see enough of the right people at the right time and with the right presentation to make sales — and the only way to do that, my friend, is to prospect. This book shows you what prospecting is all about and how to fall in love with it.

## Gaining Competency in Prospecting

The education process — learning product information and gaining selling skills — is the beginning of your career in sales. Getting to know your product is essential. If you don't know what your product will do for people, how will you know when you've found the right people to talk with about it? How will you know what to tell people to build their interest in it? Once you understand the wonderful benefits your product will bring to its new owners, then you're ready to start earning an income. You begin that income-earning process with the first step in the selling cycle — prospecting. But very few of the people who need to prospect enjoy doing it, probably because they haven't found out all the fun ways to prospect. They don't have the right attitude about it. Maybe they don't completely understand the critical importance of prospecting in the selling cycle.

Those salespersons who don't understand the vital importance of prospecting are in a state that I call *unconscious incompetence* — one of four levels of competency that apply when learning anything new. Unconscious incompetence is the level you begin with whenever you're introduced to anything new. It could be that you've never had a need to know before now. Yesterday, you were just happily tripping along through life completely unaware of the need for or skills involved in prospecting. But now you're in selling.

Being aware of something but not knowing much about it is the second level of learning competency — *conscious incompetence.* At this level, you know you don't know everything you need to know about the subject, whether the subject is prospecting or the composition of gases on the surface of Pluto. However, if you're intent on selling acreage on Pluto to just the right prospects, you recognize the need to know about both of those subjects. At this level, you may be curious. You may be anxious about how much you don't know. You may be intimidated by all the study ahead of you. Never fear. You can find out almost anything if you have the desire and discipline to do so. By reading this book, you've taken the first step toward competence in prospecting. You've sought out expert advice. You've already jumped to level two. My goal with this book is to help you get to level three.

Competency level three is *conscious competence.* At this point, you're learning new information, skills, and ideas that will eventually help you master the topic of choice — in your case, prospecting. You're reading. You're listening to others. You're experimenting with strategies and phraseology. You're winning a little, losing at times, but analyzing everything so you can tweak it and make it better.

Now, my ultimate wish for you is for you to move to level four, *unconscious competence.* At this point, everything you've learned has become smoothly integrated into your overall selling skills package. You are operating primarily on reflex. The right words and deeds simply flow from you with nary a thought. Being a professional prospector has become second nature. You continue to study, but no longer have those anxiety feelings when the topic of prospecting is brought up. You have a million ideas on where and how to contact new prospects and you're acting on them in a well-thought-out manner. You've become one of the top 5 percent of professionals in selling.

# Getting the Prospecting Mindset

Unless you sell some unique product for a very exclusive or narrow market, everybody is a prospect. I call this realization the *prospecting mindset,* and if you're going to build a successful referral business, you must acquire it. That little "idea" light bulb above your head needs to flick on and shine brightly. Everyone is your prospect.

Although prospecting is a matter of discussion that most sales-people would just rather not think about, prospecting is the key that opens the door to your success. If you don't acquire the prospecting mindset, you're slamming those doors in your own face, bruising your nose, chipping a tooth, and developing a great big bump the size of an apple on your forehead — none of which is conducive to closing a sale. You must begin to look at the world differently, to develop a new attitude.

Take a look at a downtown street during the noon hour. All of those people are your prospects. They need what you can provide. Get excited about that! "But, Tom," you say, "I'm an automobile salesman. I surely couldn't sell a new car to that man in the wheelchair, can I?" Others have. A client of an associate built a fine business creating transportation for disabled citizens. One of his customers had lost the use of his legs, fingers, and thumbs. The company rebuilt a van for him, installing a wheelchair lift, lockdowns for the chair behind the steering wheel, and attachments allowing him to steer and shift with just the force of his arms. My point is simple: The men of that company didn't see a man in a wheelchair. They saw a man who needed transportation. They saw a prospect.

Look at all those folks! Virtually every one of them has car keys in a pocket or a purse. They write with fountain pens, wear clothes, need insurance, want a pool, are saving for a trip, and they are just waiting for your product or service, too. If for some reason some don't need what you have at the moment, they will in the future, and they probably know someone else in need, too! Every time you see a crowd, a group of people, a club, a family, or even a single person, know in your heart that they really are your prospects. Make yourself look at life this way every chance you get. Make it a habit, a good one.

## Turn prospecting into dollars with STP

The key to success with prospecting is what I call *STP*. In fact, I used to put cans of STP oil around the office I managed: on desks, in the lunch area, even in the bathroom. Why? So my salespeople would be constantly reminded of the need for continued prospecting. What's the STP stand for? No, I wasn't selling oil additives. The STP was to remind my salespeople to *See The People*. Dogs and cats aren't going to invest in your product or service, are they? Will vending machines invest with you? Nope. You sell products and services to people only. So you must get yourself, your voice, your ad, your letter, whatever, in front of them in order to make sales.

Some of my students have translated the STP into See Twenty People or See Thirty People, if they know that's how many they need to meet to close

the number of sales necessary to reach their monthly income goals.

I strongly recommend that you research your prospects as much as you can to prequalify them. Even if you're canvassing a neighborhood making cold calls, you can still take time to take a look at the city directory in the reference section of your library. A wealth of information is available; for example, you can find out whether the prospect rents or owns a home, as well as the prospect's marital status, place of employment, and often job title. You can use all this information in evaluating the prospect and in your sales presentation. Pay attention to ads and articles in the local newspapers that can tell you of changes in people's lives. Changes, such as a promotion or a move to another location, mean opportunities. Early on, realize that your prospects are everywhere.

Once you develop the prospecting mindset, you have taken a giant step toward becoming a master prospector, a master salesperson — a champion.

## *Yes, You Can Sell Ice to an Eskimo*

A couple of years ago I was interviewed for an article in a major metropolitan newspaper. We were discussing the fact that a good salesperson can probably sell just about anything to anybody. Right then and there, the reporter challenged me to show him how I'd sell ice to an Eskimo. Enjoying the challenge and wanting to provide an interesting sidebar for his story, I thought for a second and then provided both sides of the following role play.

**Tom:** Hello, Mr. Eskimo, my name is Tom Hopkins and I'm with the Arctic Ice Company. I'd like to show you the many benefits Arctic Ice can offer you and your family.

**Eskimo:** That's real interesting and I've heard a lot of good things about your company, but ice really isn't a problem here. It's free. I mean we even live in the darn stuff.

**Tom:** Well, sir, quality of life is one of the reasons so many people are turning to the Arctic Ice Company, and I can see that you are a man who cares about quality. You know as well as I do that price and quality are usually related. Could there be a reason the ice you're currently using is free?

**Eskimo:** Well, it's just there, all over the place.

**Tom:** You're exactly right. The ice you use is just sitting around, day and night, unprotected. Don't you agree?

**Eskimo:** Well, yeah, there's an awful lot of it.

**Tom:** Yes, sir. Us. You and me. Your neighbor over there cleaning his fish on it, that polar bear tromping through it, and have you seen that mess the penguins made down by the water's edge? Would you think about that, imagine it for a moment?

**Eskimo:** I'd rather not.

**Tom:** Maybe that's why all this ice is so, shall we say, cost-effective?

**Eskimo:** Excuse me, I suddenly don't feel so well.

**Tom:** I understand. You know, before you could really feel good about serving your family that, uh, unprotected ice in their beverages, you'd have to sterilize it wouldn't you? How would you do that?

*(continued)*

*(continued)*

| | |
|---|---|
| Eskimo: | Boil it, I guess. |
| Tom : | Yes, sir. Boil it all the way through and then what would you have left? |
| Eskimo: | Water. |
| Tom: | And you have wasted your time. Speaking of time, if you'll just give me your autograph on this agreement, your family can enjoy their favorite beverages with clean, safe Arctic Ice tonight. Oh, I was wondering about your neighbor with the fish guts, do you think he might enjoy the benefits of Arctic ice? |

A little fanciful, perhaps, but I hope you get the idea. If you can get your prospect to like and trust you, if you see things and present them as to his benefit, you can turn prospects into satisfied customers. Even at 60° F below zero!

# Chapter 2

# Just Exactly What Is It You're Selling?

*W*hat do you sell? If I ask 100 professionals this question, I will receive close to 100 different answers. I've done this in my seminars, so I know this to be true. The answers come to me as, "financial services," "health and beauty products," "business opportunities," "computers," "real estate," "luxury automobiles," and so on. I prefer to hear answers like these: "peace of mind with regard to financial matters," "enhanced self-esteem through effective self-care," "the freedom to make your own choices in a profitable business," "methods for saving time and money while enhancing your company's image," "places where memories are made," and "comfort and security on the road."

Can you see the difference? As a sales professional, you must realize first and foremost that you do not sell products and services. You sell what those products and services will do for the people you serve.

Marketing experts use words, phrases, and images that show their clients how their products do one or more of the following:

▶ Save money

▶ Save time

▶ Improve their status

▶ Improve their looks or health

▶ Are easy to use or comfortable

▶ Allow them to have better sex lives

I bet you don't know anyone who doesn't want at least two of these things. Take a moment now and think about the product, service, or idea you represent. How do you tell people what you do? How can you use these six ideas to make people more interested in what you sell?

Think about it: Janitorial services don't sell office or home cleaning. They improve the image of businesses. They help families find more time to devote to leisure or other more important activities.

Whatever your product and whatever your level of experience in selling it, you can develop a thorough product knowledge. By seeing things through your customers' eyes, you can turn your awareness of its many features into real benefits. Forget the "what's in it for me" attitude, and think about what's in it for the other guy. That's when you both start winning.

## *You Are What You Represent*

You've undoubtedly heard the phrase, "be a product of the product." This means that you not only represent the product or service, but that you, personally, use it as well. Your statements regarding features and benefits gain tremendous credibility if your potential client knows that you speak from experience. You see, if you try to sell people a Ford truck but drive a classic Chevy, you'll lose credibility with them — even if they also love classic cars. You sell yourself and your company as much as, if not more than, you sell your product or service:

Mr. Clark, I could have chosen to represent any one of several companies that market laptops. I chose my company because I, personally, have benefited from its products. I firmly believe they are the finest laptops available in today's marketplace, and I'm proud to be on their team.

When you prospect, you need to make your potential clients want to be involved with you, too, not just want to buy the product or service you sell. After all, a relationship with you is part of the bargain with most product sales. You are, in essence, the agent for the product. Your personal integrity is as important to the sale as the history of the company and quality of the products. Products and services can't speak for themselves until *after* the client owns them and uses them.

How do you sell yourself? You begin by taking a sincere, serious look at yourself in a full-length mirror. Do you look like someone you would want to trust? Do you carry yourself with confidence? Do you dress appropriately for the industry you represent? When you can answer yes to these three questions, you can move on. If you need to improve in any of these areas, get cracking. In fact, you may want to flip to Chapter 11 and read about this topic more in depth.

Your attitude sells you, too. Do you begin every contact — even those on the phone — with a warm smile? Believe me, people can feel smiles over the telephone lines. Are you enthusiastic about your product? Don't be afraid to let the world see that you're excited about what you do. Excitement builds curiosity, especially if your prospects don't have much excitement in their lives. Your attitude is more critical to your success than you probably think.

How's your level of confidence? If you're confident about what you do, your potential clients think that you know what you're doing. You're in control because you've done your homework. You've learned how to move from finding people to selling the people you find and then selling to the people they know by referral. You're a pro and it shows.

What about the company or product you represent? You may work for a large firm that has a marketing department dedicated to presenting an image of its product to the public. You then have it easy when it comes to brand knowledge. However, many people may not want to do business until you prove that your product meets the expectations created for it by the marketing department.

# The Equilateral Triangle of Sales

I often draw a triangle with equal sides when I discuss the fundamentals of championship selling. (See Figure 2-1.) Notice that the triangle's base or bottom side is *attitude, enthusiasm, and goals*. That combination is a common denominator for life, not just sales. Our attitudes, enthusiasm for what we do, and goals for achievement in any area are what keeps our boats afloat. Without a positive attitude or enthusiasm for what we're doing, we'll spend most of our time bailing ourselves out of one leaky mess after another. On the left side of the triangle is *product knowledge*. Let's face it, if you don't know your product, you won't know how to sell it. The right side is *selling strategies and tactics,* otherwise known as people skills. All three sides are equally important in a successful selling career. You penalize yourself if you do not develop all three with equal dedication, enthusiasm, and energy.

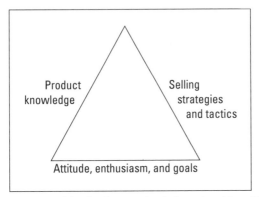

**Figure 2-1:** The fundamentals of championship selling.

We've all heard stories of the businessman who struggles all his life, neglecting his health and physical well-being, ending up with a fatal illness just when he should be enjoying his "golden years." You probably know someone so "dedicated" to his career that the long hours, weekends at the office, and night-after-night networking have led to broken relationships, families, and hearts. Almost everyone has encountered someone in business so focused on the nonspiritual side of life that when you look into his eyes, you see nothing there.

An audio recording engineer's success/near-failure/success story illustrates the importance of having balance in your professional life. The man is an expert in his field. You may have seen, or rather heard, his work on network television, in the movie house, or on cable specials. He has traveled all over the world for some of America's top corporations.

Many years ago his area was hit by a recession, and his local and regional business began to suffer. He became concerned, and then worried. As the recession deepened, so did his depression. Everyone who dealt with him heard only a constant barrage of comments about the bad economy. The recession affected everyone else, too. People could still find work, but they had to work harder, longer, and charge less to get it. His attitude made him resent that hard fact of life.

Unfocused, he forgot his goals and lost his enthusiasm, and that caused him to get sloppy. He began to miss important business appointments and recording sessions. He stopped marketing himself, and within three years he faced business and personal bankruptcy. Now that man just about talked himself out of business!

Here's the point. He had two sides of the triangle. He had excellent skills and strategies, and he had a thorough knowledge of his product. But he lacked the third side, the foundation of attitude, enthusiasm, and goals. When, after a difficult struggle, he rediscovered that side, he recovered his business and his personal life.

A triangle cannot stand with only two sides. When one falls, the entire structure comes crashing down. That is a law of math, science, and of sales.

# You Can't Prospect If You Don't Know Your Product

You really can't talk to people and determine whether they're good prospects if you don't know your own product inside, outside, top to bottom. You don't have to work on the manufacturing line or pursue a degree in design and engineering, but you have to know what you're selling so that you can relate it to your customers' needs.

A couple of salesmen for a large telecommunications firm called on a company that needed an increase in the number of its telephone lines because of an increase in its telemarketing force. The reps made a number of calls, showed the owner of the company lots of shiny, four-color brochures, and invested a lot of time and energy — and a lunch or two. Toward the end of the long selling cycle, the owner asked a series of questions about the installation of the new lines, such as how much downtime it would create for his business, what the construction and installation requirements would be, and other related matters. As it turns out, the control box would have been far too big for the space allowed, so a wall would have to be knocked down and extra cable would have to be installed. So the firm's downtime would be a few days longer, and the estimated investment would surely have to go up.

Those salesmen lost the sale.

The salesmen concentrated on selling the attractive telephones, the convenience of additional lines, the internal messaging, and other features, with no thought, and apparently no knowledge, of the other components of their package. If they had known the product better, they would have asked where it was to be installed or how much space was available for the equipment. They could have evaluated their prospect's needs and found a different unit more matched to its facility. If they did not have an appropriate unit, they could have at least thanked the owner for his time and moved on to the next prospect, instead of wasting all that time.

## Make a List, Check It Twice

You can't possibly know every darn thing about your product. But you need to know a lot about it. Start by making a basic list. Get out that pen and paper. For the purpose of this example assume you sell color copiers. Start with the most obvious:

- ✔ Name of the product? Models available? Most current model? Differences between models?

- ✔ Speed? Color or black and white? Collating capability? Easy to operate or do you need a degree from MIT?

- ✔ How long does the toner last? Cost of replacement toner? Upgrades available now or in the near future?

- ✔ Price ranges? Financing and terms?

That's pretty basic, isn't it? You may be surprised at the number of eager beavers who charge into the marketplace without even this amount of information. When you finish the list, stop and think about it again. Think twice. What other important information have you forgotten?

- ✔ Is the product available in different colors and sizes?

- ✔ What does the warranty cover?

- ✔ Is local service available?

- ✔ Does the company offer a customer hot line? Available 24 hours a day?

Put yourself in your prospect's shoes. What is important to him should be important to you. If you wonder whether you've covered all your bases (true professionals never assume anything — they always seek tidbits of information that may help them gain someone's interest in their product or service), ask a friend or loved one this question: "If you were in the market for a brand new Whatzit, what would you need to know about it? What would your concerns be?"

## Training Sessions: Sign Up

If you work for a wise organization, your management provides company training sessions for new employees. The manufacturer or distributor of the product you sell may also offer training sessions, at least on new products. Attend every training session you can, especially if you are new. You should receive information from someone who is highly knowledgeable and skilled.

Take the list you just compiled and see if you can add to it. Always take a list of important questions, and don't be shy about asking them. If you have to, make a real effort to "buttonhole" the speaker before he gets out of the room. You don't want to waste the opportunity to mine a valuable resource for information that may help you. The question you don't ask could be the very one your prospect asks the next day. "I'll, uh, get back to you on that," has lost an awful lot of sales.

 By the way, if you do ever have to say, "I don't know," be sure to follow it quickly with, "but I'll find out for you." And then let your prospect see you write a note to yourself to do just that (if you're meeting face-to-face). Two good things come from that little practice. First, you show an eagerness to serve your prospect's needs by promising to answer all of his questions. This may be your first opportunity to prove yourself. Second, if you know you're not going to make the presentation or sale today, you have an excellent reason to meet with your prospect again.

You also may want to ask the expert what types of businesses use the product or service. This is to help you explore other potential sources of business than those you know about, not to make you sound ignorant.

What's the most unusual business you know of that uses our Jimjammer? Who is the largest client for the Jimjammer IV?

If this person conducts in-house training for clients, ask him what questions clients frequently ask. Ask about the biggest challenges with training client staff. Which is tougher — teaching clients to use the equipment or changing the clients' thinking about how to use the equipment?

## Get the Most Out of Product Literature

Most companies recognize the value of printed literature. Someone may even have tossed a bundle on your desk with a "Here, kid, study these and then go get 'em." Do what the man says. Pick a time of day for serious study of your company product literature and read it as homework, not as a customer flipping through the pretty pictures.

 Some clients read every detail of those brochures, so you'd better know what the material says. If the brochure lacks vital information, make sure you have that additional information at your fingertips.

You'll be amazed at what you can learn. And, while reading the material, a particular feature may bring to mind a certain industry or type of client you hadn't previously considered. Study this material every day for three weeks. Have someone in your family ask you questions from the material until you can pass the most rigorous test.

Sad to say, and I hate saying it, but some companies send new salespeople out into the world with a handful of brochures and a "don't come back till you get a sale." In the old seafaring days of yore, this was called "walking the plank." This is no way for a manager to build a team of champions, and certainly no way for an individual to become one. If you'll pardon the pun, walking the plank just keeps you wet behind the ears.

My point is serious, however. If your company is of the seafaring legacy, then you must make it your responsibility to build a thorough knowledge of your product, even if you have to do it on your own time.

Many kinds of other materials can increase your knowledge.

- ✔ **Fact sheets.** Many companies prepare these, especially for news releases. They consist of simply stated facts about the product, the service, the manufacturer, or the company.

- ✔ **Video brochures.** Very popular in the past few years, these are often highly professional presentations of important information.

- ✔ **Audiocassette demos.** Many companies send out news release-type information to top clients on professionally produced audiocassettes. If the product you represent is sales training, for example, a condensed version of the program may be used in its promotion. Find out what the marketing department is promising that you'll bring to potential clients.

- ✔ **Video training sessions.** Often more technical and less professionally produced, these sessions can contain a wealth of information about the workings of the machine, construction techniques, installation methods, company history, and other facts of possible interest to a buyer.

- ✔ **Recent newspaper or magazine articles,** especially those from trade journals. You also can use trade journals to research your competition. Favorable product reviews by trade publications are excellent sales materials. If you market something to consumers, be sure you know what *Consumers Digest* thinks of it.

✔ **Technical data,** such as the MSDS (Material Safety Data Sheet). Technical data is often very dry reading and very, well, technical, but you may discover a few good bits of valuable information.

 Always treat your sales materials with respect, especially in front of prospects or clients. Brochures, videos, and fact sheets represent your product, your company, and all the people working there. If you trash your sales material, your prospect begins to wonder, "If that's how he feels about his company, how the heck does he feel about me?"

## Touchy-Feely

If you can't find any additional sources of information, you can still learn more about it. If you represent a tangible product, play with it. Take it out for a drive. Boot up the system and run the software. Drink it and see if it really offers "zesty, tingly flavors of freshness." Try one on for size. Sit in it. Toss it to your kid. Get to know it inside and out, what it does, how it does it, and how it compares to the competition.

Okay, but what if your product isn't a product — it's a service. If you represent a bus line, take a trip or two. See if you can get from here to there "on time with friendly service from people who know that you are Number One." Talk to clients. How does it make them feel? Listen especially for the adjectives they use to describe it, and then use them with potential new clients.

While you're kicking all those tires and experiencing all those services, think about how the customer fits into the picture. A lot of good customer-service ideas come from people just looking around the company with a fresh viewpoint. In his book *Up The Organization,* Robert Townsend provides terrific tips on how sales and customer service people can improve telephone service. He challenges managers to call their own offices to see what kind of nightmares are built into their own systems!

## Link with Coworkers

Look around your company and pick out the top salespeople. They already have the information you need, so ask them about the product. Be polite and don't monopolize all their time. They're in business to sell, not to teach. Most people, however, are flattered by attention and are more than willing to show you the ropes. Besides, they know that at some point, in some way, you'll be in a position to return the favor. That's good business.

Here's how a conversation may go between you and Bob Champion.

CHAMPION STRATEGY #1

| | |
|---|---|
| You: | Hi, Bob. How are you doing today? |
| Them: | Just great. |
| You: | Hey, Bob, I'm working on a sale of the XRG Model and my client has asked about its capability to defrickle. Do you have a client that uses that feature? |
| Them: | Sure do. K-O Industries defrickles all the time. The only thing you've got to watch out for is that the speed of the machine is set between 20 and 24 rpms. That's the optimum defrickling speed. Slower, and it jams up. Faster, and the frickles don't separate properly on the other end of the line. |
| You: | Wow. That's good to know. Any other advice? |

Keep the topic of conversation in focus during these product interviews. Top producers in the organization probably know an awful lot of information you just can't get from standard product literature. "Look, kid, I know the brochure says this, but out in the real world it's gonna do that!" Such information is invaluable.

Companies sometimes partner a veteran with a new employee for a short training period. If your company doesn't do this, go ahead and ask for one anyway. Explain that you think having such a resource will help you know your product better and thus better serve your clients. When you go out with veterans, use this valuable time to really study. Observe how they prepare or "gear up" for presentations. Pay attention to their attitudes, body language, and manner of greeting and handling people. Learn how they create moods by using word pictures and how they work through the seven-step selling cycle (discussed in Chapter 1) one element at a time. Note how they address concerns, present visual aids, use trial or test closes to see if the prospects are ready to go ahead, and thank the customers for their orders.

# Client Feedback

People who already use your company's product or service and are familiar with its pluses and minuses can be an excellent resource of product knowledge. If at all possible make a list of candidates, create a product survey, and give them a call. Ask them their honest opinions of the product, how has it served them, what they like most and the least about it, what they tell their friends about it, and so on.

In addition, a friendly call and a few questions is an excellent way to keep you, their salesperson, in mind. We don't live in a static world. Other salespeople could be, and probably are, calling your customers. And, you just may learn how you can serve their needs.

| You: | Good morning, Mr. Hanson. This is Kevin McNally. I'm just making a quick call to see how you're enjoying the Thingamabob 3000 that we installed a month ago. |
|------|------|
| Them: | Hi, Kevin. Well, it's pretty well integrated into our work flow now. I think everyone's been trained on how to use it. The staff members seem to like the speed of it over the 1500 model we had before. |
| You: | So the speed of the machine is the best advantage? |
| Them: | Well, I know the R & D people are talking up the quality of the output. I guess they figured out a way to adjust the settings to give them even better results for their specific needs than what the training recommended. |
| You: | Really? I'd sure like to learn what those settings are. Who would I ask? |

# Can You Have Too Much Product Knowledge?

Yes. Of course. Absolutely. Remember the sales triangle. Product knowledge is only one third of the total package. If you needed only product knowledge, you probably wouldn't be in sales. Who would? The inventor, the designer, the engineer, and the assembly people on the line, that's who. Everyone would be a top producer. You don't see this happening very much because those talented and hard-working people don't have the enthusiasm, attitude, and goals, or the skills and strategies to be in sales.

The designers and engineers in sales positions or management positions that I have seen generally have not done very good jobs. It's not that they don't try hard, or that they don't want to or that they can't learn. Unfortunately, they try to build with only one side of the triangle. These folks are oriented to the product and not to the customer. That's the nature of their background. They generally use so many facts, figures, and statistics that the prospects are too bloodied and beaten to make a buying decision. After a while, all the prospects can think about is getting the heck outta Dodge.

I knew a brilliant engineer who was promoted to a plant manager position that required a lot of selling skills in certain areas, particularly community relations. He had a great idea: Create a short video on the facility to tell the plant story to the community. (A vote on an important tax measure was scheduled for later that year.) The program was to be targeted to the "chicken n' peas circuit," the Rotary, Kiwanis Club, and similar organizations. He hired a professional video crew, an experienced writer, and a well-known narrator. And the program bombed. Totally.

The engineer/plant manager overloaded the video with information. He wanted every facet of the story told — how the equipment worked, the physics behind the processes, the nature of the atom, and so on. He produced a beautiful, if highly technical, video that was 45 minutes long. Those of you in service clubs are already going "uh-oh."

Why? Because service clubs don't generally have 45 minutes. Most club members have time to meet and mingle, eat their chicken and peas, hear a 15- to 20-minute program, and get back to work. In short, no one wanted to see the video because no one had time to see it. The plant manager concentrated on the product rather than the needs of his prospects.

The amount of product knowledge you need depends on your product or service and the needs of your prospects and customers. Get enough valuable information to answer all their questions, but draw the line somewhere before you get to the nature of the atom.

# Chapter 3
# Doing Your Homework

**In This Chapter**

▶ Joining the top 3 percent of the population

▶ Obtaining valuable free information

▶ Promoting yourself

An acquaintance in the public relations industry was attending to business in Nashville, Tennessee, one afternoon. While being escorted down that city's famous "Music Row," home to some of the nation's most famous music writers, producers, and publishing houses, he noticed a striking young woman standing on a street corner. She was dressed head to toe in a circus clown suit. She wore full-face clown makeup, including the obligatory bulbous red nose and wild purple hair. She was beating a bass drum.

"What the heck is that all about?" he asked.

"She's a songwriter," replied another man who was watching her.

"How long has she been doing that?"

"Every day for about a year and a half."

"For goodness' sake, why?"

"She wants to get noticed."

"She's certainly doing that."

"Yeah, but getting noticed ain't getting published."

The young woman set and achieved a goal. She wanted and did get noticed, but clearly her goals were skewed. She equated a realistic short-term goal with achieving a long-term goal. "If I get noticed, I'll get published."

That's very flawed thinking. You must always keep your mind on your real long-term goal and not become lost slogging through the long list of smaller achievements that you must pass through to reach your goal. It also seems that this young woman could have gotten a lot closer to having her songs on the Top 40 by finding ways to demonstrate her songwriting ability rather than just making a loud noise. Was her goal to be recognized or to be recognized as someone with a unique talent?

Remember the adage, "Be careful what you wish for." Wishes can come true, so be sure about what you really want.

The young woman was working awfully hard, but hard work doesn't guarantee real success. She should have explored the two avenues to success covered in this chapter: the incredible wealth of free information that can help people define, research, and achieve their goals; and effective promotion that generates a positive response rather than an amused and indulgent chuckle.

# Join the Smart 3 Percent of the Population! No Charge!

In his *Confessions,* St. Augustine commanded, "Take up. Read! Take up. Read!" Although he lived about 1,600 years ago, his words of wisdom are more applicable today than ever before because there's more information available than ever before. An embarrassingly small segment of the population, about 3 percent, owns and uses library cards. That's a real shame, but it doesn't have to be your shame.

If you don't have a library card, go out and get one today. Don't dawdle, just go get it and start using it. Where else can you join the top 3 percent of any group so easily and for free?

## Book it

Obviously, your local library is full of books — hardbacks, paperbacks, brand new, used, and nearly worn-out ones. You can probably find a book or two or ten about the subjects that interest you at your library. I think that poor young woman with the clown suit and bass drum could have structured her personal marketing program with a greater chance of success if she'd spent some time in the library looking up "publishing: music."

## Important issues

Many libraries carry a variety of current magazines, from mainstream publications such as *Parents, Time, GQ,* and *Cosmopolitan* to more specialized offerings such as *Photo, Variety, Popular Mechanics, Horse Breeder's Journal,* and the *New England Journal of Medicine.* Libraries can also carry a surprising number of trade journals for specific businesses and industries. These publications offer a vast wealth of specialized information that may not appeal to the general public but may be especially significant to your program of prospecting. You can probably find back issues for the past six months or year stored nearby. If you need more information, ask your librarian to see additional back issues.

## Good references

The reference section is a treasure trove of information for a variety of subjects. Want to learn how to write a great business letter or book, give a spellbinding speech, file a patent, locate a spot on the map, get the amount of yearly rainfall in Nova Scotia, or the tons of copper mined in Arizona, or any of a thousand other facts and figures? Find it or at least a solid lead to it in the reference section. You also can often consult *Moody's, Dun and Bradstreet,* the *Thomas Register, Contacts Influential, Standard and Poor's,* the White and Yellow Pages, or a city directory for a community miles away. You also may find numerous newsletters, research papers, statistical abstracts, working papers, works in progress, diagrams, maps, and charts.

## High-tech tomes

Many libraries have placed their catalogs of material on computer. Compared with card catalogs, computer versions help you search for materials more easily and quickly, and with more focus. Also, you may be able to print information that isn't available in hard copy.

Libraries are also expanding their audio/visual resources. You can check out audio books, video programs, and even slide shows just as you can check out *Selling For Dummies, Refrigerator Repair Made Easy, The Decline and Fall of The Roman Empire,* and *Cujo.* In addition to popular fiction, you can often find a fascinating selection of how-to or informational programs.

You can research other materials, particularly newspapers, at your leisure on microfilm viewers. Who was present at that ribbon-cutting or ground-breaking ceremony for the new plant back in 1963? Where did people go for entertainment during World War II? Why was the new city park built on Elm Street instead of Oak? How did city leaders feel about the 1992 federal tax proposals? If you want to know, all you have to do is load, crank, and watch.

## Living resources

An often overlooked source of information found in the library is the person pulling books out of the same section as you. People with similar interests may have sources of information or personal experiences that are as valuable as those books on the shelves. Don't hesitate to quietly and politely introduce yourself, noting that you have similar interests. Just keep the conversational level down, lest you face the dreaded librarian's fear-inducing *shushhh!*

### Daily delivery

You have other valuable resources at your disposal. One of the finest is something you probably use along with your morning coffee. Take up your daily newspaper and read it with a student's eye:

> "ABC Co., specializing in imported pencil holders, announces the opening of a second outlet at . . ."

Analyze the article. What's the story behind the story? How can it apply to you? If ABC Co. is opening a second outlet, business must be booming or it's expecting a boom. If you represent a product that it can use, you need to get in touch with its decision maker ASAP!

The newspaper or the broadcast news programs aren't just a source of information. They can also be valuable sources for putting your story in front of your prospects.

## Positive Press

How do you think all those notices get in the paper or on the TV or radio anyway? News organizations can't cover all the events, pound every street, or attend even a fraction of the meetings that occur in any town. Smart people and organizations don't wait for reporters to come to them. They deliver the goods to the news media themselves.

You can do the same thing too — it's called public relations. You need to remember two key facts about this field:

- ✔ The news media publishes/broadcasts the news.

- ✔ No news organization can possibly cover, much less report, all the news that's out there.

If you make the job easier for reporters/editors/producers, you stand a good chance of getting your story told. You don't have to have a degree in journalism, a friend on the paper or news station, or a big advertising budget, either. All you need is a respect for the medium and an understanding of how to get the information to them in a format that they can use, a willingness to promote yourself or your business, and a bit of information about how the system works. That's what the last part of this chapter is all about.

### The medium for the message

Take a moment to change your thinking about the news media. From now on, the local news outlets are no longer sources of information; they are prospects for prospects! Work with them, and they can be an amazing source of leads, potential customers, and positive images within your community. Figure out what each news medium needs and how you can meet that need.

Each of the following sections details different kinds of news media that you're likely to have in your area. The media can cover short notices such as promotions, transfers, expansions, and new product lines. They may also be good places for interesting articles about you, your product or service, or some fascinating fact related to your business. But to work with the media, you need to understand how each medium works.

## Radio

Some stations are all news; others use large blocks of time, such as the noon hour, for expanded news coverage. Most stations provide only five minutes of news and weather and traffic once an hour. Much of that time has to be devoted to the big stories of the day. That leaves precious little time to tell the world that you've added another sales representative down at the old shoe store.

## Television

Television stations generally devote more time to news. Don't neglect the special programming opportunities such as public affairs shows, even if this means you have to wake up with the chickens to be on the air. Your prospects may be watching television at that time.

Television is a visual medium, and the producers, editors, and reporters think about what makes for "good video." Why do you think fires receive such great coverage? Smoke and flames and scurrying firefighters in bright yellow suits make for interesting pictures, even if the blaze is in an old house abandoned in 1942. When taking a news story to TV stations, you're more likely to find yourself flying through the airwaves toward your prospects' living rooms if you deliver a visual hook.

Good visual hooks include action — lots of it. Show your product in action. Show people using it, preferably happy people. Include testimonials. Show graphics of statistics. Talk as if this is the most exciting news of the day. If you're married to the idea of yourself or someone else in your organization delivering a simple message in a "waist-up" shot, choose the most animated person you can find. If it's you, project yourself by almost exaggerating your expressions. Gesturing is action and action is good. If in doubt, watch your local newscasts with these ideas in mind. Which news stories held your attention? What were the elements? Can you provide similar elements for your story?

Always smile while delivering your message unless you're selling cemetery services. The smile carries over as enthusiasm in your voice.

## Newspapers

Newspapers carry more news word for word than any other medium. The size of the paper and, therefore, the amount of news, is strictly determined by the amount of advertising sold. The amount of news in the average half-hour TV news program doesn't fill up a single page in the average newspaper.

Contact the newspaper before pulling together your story. Find out if it has a particular format or style it prefers used for submissions. Some newspapers have forms you can fill out. These forms get them the basic information in the same order from every prospective story, making their jobs easier and increasing your chances of getting into print.

Remember that newspapers want news that's timely. Always send your information in to them in advance of your event so they can be prepared to cover it with a reporter if they feel the story warrants that level of attention.

Have a current, clean and clear, black-and-white photo of yourself (maybe in front of your place of business), your product, and maybe the two of you together that can be included with the news item. Don't rely on the newspaper to dig up a shot. That's how people end up with their high school photos or, worse, mug shots on the news. Don't count on having these photos returned. Make sure you clearly identify what's in the photo: the names of the people and/or product. Keep a supply of the photos handy if you're involved in an all-out news campaign.

## Magazines

Many larger cities have local or regional publications devoted to the business community, the arts and entertainment, homes and gardens, and the general public. These publications often carry short notices such as promotions, transfers, expansions, and new product lines. They may also be good places for interesting articles about you, your product or service, or some fascinating fact related to your business.

The magazines may also be monthly or quarterly publications so timeliness isn't quite as important as in other media. However, on the plus side, many such publications use full-color photographs, which will always present you in a better light. Magazine editors may also be more selective in the information they print, which can give you an added bit of celebrity status just for getting in the issue — especially if you're in a feature article.

## Please release me

The news that fits is generally the news that reporters and editors can use with the least amount of hassle. The fact that you or your boss was honored by the Visiting Firemen's Association is an important achievement in your life, but put yourself in editors' minds. They sit at their desks, green eyeshades low over their brows, cigars clamped between their teeth, and bright red pencils in their hands. Before them is a pile, a real pile, of news, every bit of it of equal value in their minds. Which items will they choose: the hand-written notes taken from a phone call to the new junior reporter, the poorly worded fact sheet with all those misspellings, or that ready-to-go release in proper format, correct spelling, and the king's own English?

Editors are just like detective Joe Friday of *Dragnet,* who used to say, "Just the facts, ma'am." So Table 3-1 shows the kinds of facts you need to include in your press release.

**Table 3-1**      **Checklist of Media Information**

| *For the Individual Prospector* | *For a Small Business* |
| --- | --- |
| Name | Name |
| Occupation/job title | Contact name and phone number |
| Number of years in sales | Location |
| Sales volume | Number of years in business/in the community |
| Type of industry represented | Number of people employed; annual payroll |
| Particular product represented | Sales volume |
| Family | Brief description of major product |
| Community involvement | Community involvement and/or impact |
| Accomplishments | Awards won |
| | Future growth plans |

You can also write up this information like a story, but be careful. Write your release in what is called the *inverted pyramid* style. That means that you place the biggest, most important news at the top of the page and the least important news at the bottom. News editors often trim stories by starting at the bottom and moving up. Consider this sad attempt:

---

IMPORTANT PRESS RELEASE

One of the city's most prominent citizens has been made president of his company this week. Mr. Beauregard Parish, vice president of the Acme Deluxe Ink company for the last ten years, has been promoted to president. Mr. Parish is married to Brunehilde Parish. They have some nice children named Cecily Anne and Bergstrom, who is in kindergarten. He has won a lot of awards, including the State Businessman of the Year Award, the Model Racing Trophy for six years, and Ink Man of the Year. Mr. Parish is famous because he invented color ink for underwater writing and printing.

THE END

---

How can this press release be improved? Several ways:

✔ **Be careful what title you use.** The term "Important News Release" raises the hackles of any editor. Editors decide what is and isn't important. Use the phrase "For Immediate Release" instead. If the information should not be published until a certain date, simply write "For Release On [fill in the blank with the correct date]." And use "News Release" instead of "Press Release." As a radio news executive once said to a friend of mine, "We don't have any presses."

✔ **Include a contact.** What if the editor gets excited about the story and wants to expand it or follow up on it? Whom should he call? He may find the right number in the phone book, but is that how you really want to treat a prospect? Always place the name of a contact person and a phone number at the top of your releases.

✔ **Leave out all the fluff.** Mr. Parish may actually be one of the area's most prominent citizens. However, that is really a subjective matter open to interpretation, and unfortunately, you aren't going to be the one doing the interpreting. Flowery descriptions may please Mr. Parish when he glances over the release, but they won't please the editor who will cross them out or, worse, toss the whole release into the round file.

Also leave out information that isn't relevant to the story. For example, the fact that Mr. Parish has earned a number of model airplane trophies has nothing to do with his current business achievement. However, the fact that he invented a breakthrough in his industry is very significant, as is the State Businessman of the Year award.

✔ **Do not write "the end" at the end of the release.** Just center the word "end" at the bottom or use the journalist's symbol for the same thing (—30—) centered at the bottom.

With all of this in mind, take a look at how the same information about Mr. Parish should look.

---

Contact: Johnette Doe (555) 555-5555

FOR IMMEDIATE RELEASE

Beauregard Terrebonne Parish was elected president of Acme Deluxe Ink, Inc. during the company's monthly board of directors meeting on June 10. Parish has served as vice president for ten years. The inventor of colored underwater ink, he was selected State Businessman of the Year for 1997.

—30—

---

All right, the release is now short and sweet and hard to beat. Sure, a lot of information was left out, but the story contains everything of importance. This is a release that editors can read once, approve, and then move on to the next piece of paper on their desks. If editors or reporters think the story needs to be expanded, they can pick up the phone, dial the contact number on the release, and ask questions.

Hand-deliver your news release to the proper reporter or editor whenever you can. Again, news people face a stack of equally important stories, features, and articles everyday. Your promotion, new product, or news item is no more important to editors than the other 30 or 40 promotions, new products, or newsworthy items on their desks. Anything you can do to make your story stand out from the crowd increases your chances of more and better coverage. Hand delivery also helps build stronger relationships and puts you in position to possibly be in the right place at the right time for a lucky break. If the reporters and editors know you, they are more likely to call you for a quote or an opinion when doing an article on something related to your business.

## Successfully dealing with the media

With rare exceptions, news people are professionals just as you, and just like you they deserve professional treatment. Keep these tips in mind to help build and maintain successful media relationships.

Try to develop a relationship with the reporter assigned to your "beat." In most cases, that should be the business page reporter. Build a relationship so that when he sees you coming he doesn't duck into the restroom because he knows you're bringing legitimate news. Keep in mind that reporters move on to other positions or other papers or become editors. Get to know the assignments editor, city desk editor, or the editor of the section of concern to your business, whether it's arts and entertainment, sports, or farm news.

Deadlines are virtually absolute unless Martians show up on the White House lawn. Deadlines vary from one news medium to another. A hot news item that makes the 10 a.m. radio news may have to wait a day to get into the newspaper (if at all) because the paper already has been printed. Find out and respect the deadline for each medium. Allow the media enough time to do right by your information.

Your advertising budget is irrelevant, and bringing it up will do more harm than good. You can actually see the "Oh yeah, I'll show you!" mechanism click into gear within the editors' heads. The news and advertising departments are separated by walls of journalistic ethics, tradition, and common sense. You may be king in the ad department, but over in the news side you're probably just "Who's that?"

Accuracy is impossible 100 percent of the time. You will be misquoted, and mistakes will creep into stories. It's all part of the game. Screaming and shouting do not get you very far, but common sense and a cool head may do you some good. If the error seriously harms your business or personal life or your story contains gross errors, ask for (don't demand) a correction or a retraction. Talk with the editor. Just like everyone else, news people are loath to admit mistakes, and they often can't even generate a second or follow-up story that makes up for the error.

Once you've sent off your most professionally prepared news release with appropriate and eye-catching photos, half your job is finished. What, you say. Only half? Yep. Now, you need to persistently and professionally follow up your submission to ensure that it lands in the right hands and is actually seen. There are Do's and Don'ts in this area of follow up, just as there are in any other aspect of business:

✔ Do make a quick call to the intended recipient, "just checking to see if the release was received and offering to be available to answer any questions that may arise."

✔ Do send a thank-you note after this contact — even if the contact was made by voice mail.

✔ Don't call daily, don't call the intended party's superior, and don't complain if your information is not published.

✔ Do update the information and send it again in about a month.

When promoting yourself through the news media, observe the rules of the media and consider what's in it for them. Remember the young songwriter in Nashville. Learn from her mistakes so that you too do not end up looking like a clown.

# Chapter 4
# Make Prospecting Your Hobby

> *The simple inherit folly; but the prudent are crowned with knowledge.*
>
> —Proverbs 14:18

This chapter is all about learning, and I don't mean sitting under the awful eye of old Miss Crabtree reciting "a-e-i-o-u." I mean real learning, specifically, the act and art of understanding and retaining information, a skill that many have lost.

I'm reminded of a story about President John F. Kennedy told by one of his college classmates. The man noted that he and JFK came from wealthy backgrounds, attended prestigious schools, knew all the right people, and had the doors of business and politics thrown wide open for them. The classmate then noted that he had gone on to a successful career and that JFK had gone on to become the leader of the free world. The major difference in the heights each attained was simple, he said. "After college I stopped learning and Jack never stopped learning."

A good salesperson never stops learning about life, about the world, or what goes on inside his or her head. That's how you sharpen, hone, and maintain your prospecting skills. Your brain is the best tool in your toolbox. Remember, if you don't use it, you'll lose it.

## Listen Up

First and foremost, I want you to recognize the real, true key to all learning: *listening*. In many quarters, listening is a lost art. Nobody ever learned anything while talking, so listen up.

The difference between hearing and listening is much like the difference between looking and observing. Dale Carnegie said that you become a good conversationalist by being a good listener. You also learn by being a good listener. If you ask the right questions and then really listen to the answers, your prospect will at some point say how your product can benefit him. Prospects may make statements such as, "I'm looking for something that is comfortable but that gets really good mileage." Or they may ask, "Will it seat two adults and four children comfortably?" And they will almost surely express concern with something like, "I really don't think I can afford it."

Astute listeners gather that information, turn it around, and tell prospects why they should buy from them. How do you learn to listen? I've broken down the process into four basic stages:

- ✔ **Hearing with your whole head.** Concentrate all your senses on the other person. Pay strict attention to every word being said and more. Notice body language, pauses that indicate concern or interests, shifty eye movements that may mean nervousness, levels of vocal stress, sweating, head shaking, toe tapping, finger rapping, scratching behind the ear, and anything else that communicates information. See the next section, "Show That You Are Listening," for more.

- ✔ **Translating what prospects say.** Translation is the art of distinguishing between what is said and what is actually meant. Some call this "reading between the lines." No matter how many words prospects say or how long it takes them to say those words, they always express a core of truth. You usually can boil down the words to 25 words or fewer.

- ✔ **Evaluating your translation.** Interpret your translation of your prospects' needs and wants into the benefits provided by your product. Evaluation is the connective tissue between what the prospect says between the lines and what you have to offer.

- ✔ **Following up with prospects by responding to them.** If you have practiced stages 1, 2, and 3, this response should be appropriate and should get you the desired results. Your goal may be to gather more information, cinch the individual as a prospect, or to get referrals. You must be specific and focus on your prospects' real concerns.

To be a successful prospector, you must practice all four of these principles every time you meet with anyone. Otherwise, you will miss what prospects are really saying and will miss opportunities, prospects, and sales.

# *Show That You Are Listening*

People who write screenplays are always being admonished to show something rather than to merely tell it, to make the audience experience the story visually. You can do the same thing when listening to a prospect.

✔ **Be conscious of your body language.** Your body language says, "I'm listening" when you make eye contact (without getting into a staring contest), when you lean slightly forward, nod in the affirmative, or even stroke your chin with your hand.

✔ **Taking notes shows interest,** especially if you break periodically to make eye contact. (Doodling a German Messerschmitt going down in flames below a P-38, however, doesn't count as note-taking.)

✔ **Ask a question.** Something directly related to the heart of the matter under discussion is best.

> Of course price is a concern, but if I could show you how a significant increase in fuel economy can offset that cost over the lifetime of the vehicle, well, wouldn't you be interested in hearing that?

✔ **Let the prospect finish.** People don't like to have the end of their sentences chopped off by someone overly eager to jump in with his or her own words of wisdom. Such amateurish rudeness builds massive walls between the salesperson and prospect. The Great Wall of China is nothing compared to the structure you can put up with inappropriate behavior.

✔ **Show interest with nods, uh-huhs, and go ons.** Sometimes all it will take for a client to tell you more is a simple nod. Hmms and uh-huhs work well, too. An occasional "I understand" will get you great mileage.

✔ **Repetition is the heart of learning.** Never hesitate to use it in conversation. "Now, let me make sure I have this absolutely straight . . . ." Repeating shows you've been listening.

✔ **If you're easing the conversation into a different direction, make sure you note and respond to what your prospect has said.** Suddenly jumping into a separate topic may totally disrupt the flow of conversation and may generate a bit of resentment or even hostility. As always, put yourself in your prospect's shoes.

> ✔ **Show respect and interest even if you don't feel it.** If the old boy is prattling along about the delphinium beds down at the old homestead, just remember that patience and good technique will allow you to bring him around to the subject of your 8-cylinder, turbo-charged, special-bonus-from-the-sales-manager-if-it-sells-today deluxe automobile. Eyes that continually glance out the window, a tapping toe, or comments that are just a tad off base show disrespect and will probably send your prospect or customer to someone more appreciative of delphiniums.

## Become a Lifelong Student of Life

You must embrace learning to be a successful prospector. How can you prospect if you don't learn your prospects' wants, needs, and desires? More than that, learning makes you a better salesperson and an all-around better human being, too.

Why should you shut off the learning center in your brain once you become an adult? I've never found that rule carved in stone, etched in a sacred book, or written up as the law of the land, yet after most people graduate from high school, they seemingly remove that part of their brain concerned with learning and put it in a box to be brought out only under emergency conditions. "In case of thought, break glass." That's a real shame because only after we reach adulthood and have at least a touch of real-world experience behind us are we in a position to really start learning. Perhaps the stress of family and career shuts down the process, but those are two of the best reasons ever to power up your learning center.

Learning is, or should be, a process that lasts a lifetime. I urge you to make the effort, take the time to keep on keeping on with your education. As Captain Picard of the Starship Enterprise says, "Make it so."

### Education is all around you

If you live in the U.S., you live in a country with extraordinary educational opportunities. The American library system, open and accessible to everyone, is the envy of the world. New and used bookstores are everywhere. State and community colleges offer a staggering array of adult education courses on everything from computer skills to self-defense to local archaeology, painting, writing, sculpting, and fixing a water heater. With just a quick scan of today's newspaper, I found a tremendous variety of learning opportunities: gold prospecting, cooking, writing fiction and nonfiction, a blues concert, a magic workshop, Dixieland jazz, short stories on video, a pops concert by a local symphony, and that's barely the first column!

During lunch today an associate of mine plans to attend a concert of Japanese taiko drums in a local mall. Why, you may wonder. "Because I've never attended a concert of taiko drums," he said. He may come to love the music, hate it, or be indifferent to it, but by the end of the lunch hour he will know something he did not know this morning. He will have increased his knowledge.

Stopping the learning process is almost criminal. Make the time to experience new people, places, and things, and you will become a lifelong student of life with repercussions that will benefit every area of that life, including your ability to prospect.

## *Does not compute*

The computer voice in *Star Trek,* the old version (now you know how old I am), would drone out the phrase "Does not compute" whenever confronted with an unsolvable problem. The same thing happens with the human mind when you try to take in too much information at one time. You experience an information overload, and the brain basically goes on strike. "Does not compute." I call it getting a brain cramp.

Usually a person — studying the skills and strategies of prospecting, for example — tries to absorb too much information in too short a time. The brain finally says, "Whoa, enough of this," and progress grinds to a painful, embarrassing halt. "Why can't I get this? There must be something wrong with me. I give up." Don't let a natural learning process overwhelm you. Remember that everyone at some time faces the conscious incompetent level. No one can do it all at once. If you feel the onset of an "I just give up" attitude, recognize that learning takes time and just take a break. Make a cup of coffee. Walk around the block. Get your mind off the matter for a while, rest the old brain cells, and then tackle the subject again a little at a time.

You may think, "Here I am, a grown-up, intelligent, educated adult. I should be able to figure out prospecting in no time at all." Figuring out prospecting may be simple, but that doesn't mean mastering it is going to be easy. You will get there, but at your own speed. Don't allow yourself to become frustrated if others make faster progress or if you just can't quite get the hang of it. Time will pass, and your skills and abilities will improve. Take everything one step at a time, and sooner or later you'll find yourself exclaiming, "Hey, I can do this!"

# Learning in Five Easy Steps

I've often thought that schools should put far more emphasis on how to learn as opposed to what to learn. You know how it goes. You show up at school, the teacher hands out your history/math/ English book, and says, "Read this, I'll give you a test in the morning." Great! I know how to read, you say. But how the heck do I learn this stuff? Unfortunately, many teachers can't tell you because no one took the trouble to teach them.

I'm going to correct that situation and show you how to learn almost anything in five basic steps:

- ✔ Impact
- ✔ Repetition
- ✔ Utilization
- ✔ Internalization
- ✔ Reinforcement

Master each one of these steps, use them together at all times, and you will learn.

## Step 1: Impact

Impact means that you cannot just read or look at new information and then forget about it. You must use your knowledge constantly. An associate of mine took a business/pleasure trip to Scotland recently and decided, in spite of his misgivings, to drive through the countryside, despite the Scottish way of driving on a different side of the road than in America. He was acutely conscious of his incompetence as he eased into the right-side driver's seat of his rental car, started shifting with his left hand, and then pulled into the correct lane. Within a day or so, he says, driving on the "wrong" side of the road was as natural as ordering breakfast. Aware of his incompetence, he had absorbed the necessary information, made it a part of him, began using it unconsciously, and moved on to more important things like making his appointments, touring the big castle, and getting to the pub in time for fish and chips and the local brew.

Impact itself is broken down into four steps:

✔ **Hear it.** Before you can learn something, you have to hear it, and that means you have to put yourself in a position to learn. Don't wait around hoping that information will fly in through the window. Go out and get it; expose yourself to the information you want and need every chance you get.

✔ **Write it.** When attending a seminar, presentation, or lecture and you hear something you want to learn, write it down. The same applies when reading something important. If you want, outline the material, or at least list its key elements. Sure, it takes time. But instead of breezing through the material and quickly forgetting it, you will be on your way to knowing it. Hey, remember the tortoise and the hare? Who crossed the finish line (who got the prospect) first?

✔ **Read it.** Study your notes, and I don't mean just glance over them so you can say, "I have studied!" Read the words and concentrate on what they mean. Think about what you have written down and commit it to memory.

✔ **Say it.** Say what you have heard and written. Practice makes perfect!

I know this process is a bit more time-consuming than skimming through a textbook, but think back to your real goal. You're not trying to be the first kid on your block to make it to "the end." You're in business to learn, and this is how you do it.

## Step 2: Repetition

I call repetition the "mother of all learning" and the key to mastering any new skill, technique, facts, or figures. For decades advertising and marketing studies have proven that people don't even realize they have seen advertisements (radio, television, newspapers, magazines, whatever) until they have seen or heard them six times.

If you make yourself repeat the words, scripts, and techniques of prospecting covered in this book a minimum of six times, you will, on average, have retained 62 percent of the material, based on studies of people with average intellect. This is not magic. This is not super-secret science, wish fulfillment, or fairy dust from the Good Witch of the North. This is simply the mastery of basic learning techniques. That's all.

## Step 3: Utilization

Utilization is where you actually start saying the words in front of potential clients, when you actually apply what you've learned so you can test its results. You get to try it on for size and see how it feels. You'll do a lot of analysis at this time, adjusting the words to fit you. For many, this is the toughest step because trying something new in a make-it or break-it situation can cause fear. However, if you keep doing today what you've always done, you can expect nothing more than the same results. In order to change for the better, you first have to change!

## Step 4: Internalization

Try to make the new information a part of you. Absorb it totally, think about it, and use it. As you do, learning will start to become virtually automatic. Your confidence in knowing and using the material will grow, as will your drive to learn even more. As you become better at internalizing, you will also notice a slight shift in your attitude. Learning actually starts to become fun because, for the first time in your life, you are doing it right.

## Step 5: Reinforcement

Make a genuine commitment to retrain yourself, right now, even before you're fully trained in prospecting. At least once a year take sufficient time to review your study books, workbooks, and your notes from the subjects you have learned so that you continue to retain what you have learned.

True professionals never think for an instant that they know it all. Several years ago, the people of Phoenix got a good look at a professional attitude following a disappointing playoff game by the Phoenix Suns basketball team. Charles Barkley, who played for the Suns at that time, had a bad night at the free-throw line. After the game, while the fans filed out and his teammates headed to the showers, "Sir Charles" moved over to the sidelines and began practicing his free throws. Imagine that! A superior athlete, at the top of his form, after an exhausting game, takes time to practice his skills. That's the sign of a real champion.

As you progress through the steps and stages of learning, please give yourself permission to fail and forgive yourself for failure. Trying to achieve excellence means that you will fail more than a few times somewhere along the trail. That's all right. Failure is part of the process. Don't fear failure.

Mistakes are just part of the game. Learn from them and take the lessons to heart. You're a lifelong student of learning. Instead of kicking yourself for some error, study what happened and move on. Find someone who can help you see where you went wrong or study some of your course materials for life, such as *Sales Prospecting For Dummies*. You can't have an up without a down, and you can't have success without failure. Admitting that to yourself is a big step in the learning process, something that not everyone can handle.

## Fake it till you make it

Visualization is one of the essential ingredients of any kind of success. If you have problems being a student of life, just fake it. I don't mean that in a negative way. Far from it, picturing yourself as a success is one of the best ways to achieve success. Think about someone who has already made it to the places you want to go. Visualize his attitude, traits, and skills, and put yourself in his place. See yourself reading or listening, getting and retaining the message, and using that information every day.

The motion picture comedy *Major League* has a scene of visualization. Right before the big game the Wesley Snipes character is sitting off to the side in the locker room. His eyes are closed, and his only movement is the flicking of his right wrist. In his mind that hand is guiding him through a home run, the smack of ball against bat, the mad dash around the bases, and the triumphant slide into home plate. Visualization works just as well for professionals in any field, especially for the salesperson in search of prospects.

## *Change How You View Prospecting*

I am constantly amazed by the number of people who look at prospecting as if it were a chore or a drudgery a step or two below chopping wood, cleaning out a stopped-up drain, or plowing the north forty. It's as if someone programmed these folks with the notion that work and play are mutually exclusive. Nothing can be further from the truth. Life just isn't supposed to be that way.

### *Tom's definition of work*

*Work is anything you do when you'd rather be doing something else.*

You can quite easily substitute the word "prospecting" for "work." Not for a second do I intend that statement as a criticism of work. You need to work to put bread on the table, to contribute to society, and to have the all-important feeling of self-worth that work creates. So what do I mean? Your work should be fun, something you really enjoy doing — just like prospecting.

"Ughhh!" you say? It's not that difficult. You don't have to change jobs, enter a new career, or move out of state to search for new opportunities. Just change your attitude. Make prospecting your hobby, a skill to be studied, improved upon, and most of all enjoyed.

When you treat prospecting as a hobby, your life changes. You gain more satisfaction from your job because you enjoy it more because you are better at it; you look at so-called obstacles for what they really are — exciting challenges and opportunities; and your higher level of achievement enhances your inner well-being. Changing your attitude to make prospecting a hobby may take a little time. Visualize it, act it out, play the part, fake it till you make it, absorb it, and before you know it, prospecting will actually be a hobby. Prospecting will be what it's supposed to be — fun.

Attitude is everything, and a change in attitude changes everything.

## It's time to quit working

Yep, you read that right. I want you to quit working, today if you can. Notice I didn't say quit your job, although some folks may have to do it. Turn your fear and dread of prospecting into an attitude of pleasure and achievement. This change requires learning. That's why the first sections of this chapter are so important. If you're still intimidated by the thought of prospecting, start studying the people who are masters of the technique. Watch how they do what they do and copy them. Learn and adopt their skills and techniques, and then put your own personal stamp on the process.

Work should bring you two basic rewards: money, which provides you the ability to put bread on the table with the occasional jars of peanut butter and jelly at bonus time; and joy. If you're not getting both, something is amiss. Take a few moments to objectively examine your job and your career. If you're really dissatisfied and unhappy, you probably aren't earning the amount you'd like and/or aren't having any fun on the job. Reading and studying this book, as well as *Sales Closing For Dummies* and *Selling For Dummies* (all published by IDG Books Worldwide, Inc.), can help raise your level of competence so that you become a more successful, profitable salesperson.

You don't quite believe me, eh? Have faith, my friend. Study, learn, and practice the techniques in this book with a passion to succeed, and you will experience a transformation. Somewhere down the road, not too far I think, a sudden realization will strike you: "Hey," you'll think, "ol' Tom was right. This is fun!"

## Hobbyhorsing around

To prove my point, think about this: Have you ever noticed how people act and talk when discussing their favorite hobbies? They're animated, active, and enthusiastic. Their voices flow like quick-time melodies, and their hands flutter around like butterflies. That's because they're excited and filled with fun. Contrast that with how they talk about prospecting. You'll hear that, "People are a drag, man." "Nobody's buying anything these days." "Door almost slammed in my face." "Wouldn't give me the time of day." "Hate this part of the job." And, as they say on *Seinfeld,* "yadda yadda yadda."

Okay, now take a close look at the salespeople who make prospecting a hobby. They are full of energy, enthusiasm, excitement, dedication to the job, and a joyful anticipation of the next opportunity to meet someone. They say things like, "I met the most fascinating people today," and "I learned the most interesting thing today." They can't wait to get back out there and mix it up with new people. The words *intimidation, fear,* or *hesitation* just aren't in their personal dictionaries. Why? Because they have turned the process of prospecting into a hobby that brings real pleasure and self-fulfillment.

Sure, they regale you with the latest triumphs in their other hobbies. The difference, however, between this top 5 percent of the achievers and the other sales folks is that these folks talk with equal joy and excitement about the successful prospecting trip, the way a difficult prospect came around and became a valued customer, the sheer pleasure of getting that third referral, or the new prospecting technique that worked far better than anticipated.

These people are champions. For them work is no longer something they do when they'd rather be doing something else. They do exactly what they want to do. Prospecting isn't work. It's a hobby, and a darn good one at that.

That's the kind of feeling you want to have about prospecting. If it's just not happening for you (yet), try to pick something, anything, about the process that you enjoy. Focus on that action and the positive feelings it brings. As you continue to reinforce that feeling, start looking for others. You'll soon have an expanding collection of positive feelings toward prospecting. Here are areas of prospecting in which you may find simple pleasures:

- ✔ Meeting interesting new people
- ✔ Handing over a professional business card
- ✔ Working outdoors on a beautiful day
- ✔ Dressing for success
- ✔ Seeing a new part of your community
- ✔ Contact with friends and relatives
- ✔ New learning opportunities
- ✔ Benefiting people with your product or service

Just pick something you enjoy about prospecting and focus your attention on it. Then find other things you enjoy about prospecting. Little things really do add up. Before you realize it, prospecting will become your newest, most exciting, most fulfilling hobby. Practice the skills and techniques, and it will happen.

# Part II
# Resources of the Rich and Famous

The 5th Wave    By Rich Tennant

"I wouldn't qualify this one too long."

## In this part . . .

1 show you the best, proven-successful strategies of top prospectors worldwide in these chapters. Getting the ball rolling with a new prospect is critical. I show you ways to start conversations and keep them going in a manner that will help your prospects see that they just can't live without your product — and they have to tell all their friends about it.

## Chapter 5

# Prospecting Is Just Like Fishing

*In This Chapter*

▶ Prospecting among friends and strangers

▶ Using 11 strategies for finding the right people

▶ Approaching prospects

*S*elling and fishing have quite a few things in common. You need the proper equipment such as hook, line, and sinker to fish. You also need the proper equipment such as product knowledge, selling skills, and motivation to sell. You need a fishing hole to fish, and you need your market to sell. To be a good fisherman, you need to find where the fish are biting. Skilled anglers call this last step the true art of fishing. People in sales call it prospecting.

This chapter helps you find the people, families, businesses, and organizations that can benefit from your product or service.

## Okay, Tom, Where's the Fishing Hole?

Captain Ahab searched the world over for the giant white whale, Moby Dick. I have an associate who may not be as insane as the good captain, but he was just as intense in his search for an Arkansas trout named Big Ralph. Before setting out on their quests, both men studied the object of their search well. They learned the animals' habits, feeding and spawning grounds, where they frolicked, and where they slept. The men did their homework.

Everyone new to sales faces a common dilemma: How can I spend time prospecting when I need to be learning my product and practicing my selling skills? The answer depends upon your level of product knowledge and sales experience. If you're new to sales, you should invest 75 percent of your time prospecting, and the remaining 25 percent learning about your product and developing your presentation skills. After all, as a newcomer, you don't have a lot of prospects to qualify, present to, close with, or follow up with, so invest most of your time fishing for good prospects.

Where should you go fishing? The following sections give you 11 effective ways to find the people or organizations willing and able to pay for your product or services. Believe me, all the hard work pays off. You can ask the associate from Arkansas I mentioned, the one with Big Ralph mounted in his den.

## Strategy 1: Cast a line at friends and relatives

To become a successful prospector, you don't have to begin by calling on the biggest, meanest hombre west of the Pecos. Start with people you know, people with whom you are at ease and who are at ease with you. Start with your friends and relatives. I call this the *warm*, or *natural*, *market* because you can work on your presentation before a receptive, friendly audience.

Friends and family members are in your corner. Unless you're the black sheep of the family, they already like and trust you. They are much less likely to say no, especially if you sell a product or service that can truly benefit them. Give them a call or stop by (at a time that's convenient for them) and tell them about your new business or career. Share your enthusiasm for the new opportunity and tell them about it. The technique can be as simple as the following:

| | |
|---|---|
| You: | Hi, Ted. This is Sally. |
| Them: | Hi, Sally, how are you doing? |
| You: | I'm doing great. In fact, I've just recently learned about a new way to avoid the consequences of my poor eating habits. It's very exciting and simple to do. |
| Them: | You sound pretty excited, what is it? |
| You: | I'd love to tell you more about it, Ted, but to tell you the truth, it's one of those things that's better experienced than heard over the phone. What are you doing tonight? I'd love to pop by and show you just what this is. It'll only take a few minutes. Would 7:00 p.m. be okay? |
| Them: | Well, I have some errands to run after work, but I could be home by 7:30 p.m. You've piqued my curiosity. Let's meet then. |
| You: | That's great. I'll pop by your place at 7:30. |

## Just say the magic words . . .

I want to share a key phrase that works extremely well in getting friends and family to allow you to present your new product or service:

*Because I value your judgment, I was hoping you'd give me your opinion.*

Examine that beautifully crafted sentence. "Because I value your judgment" says to them, "You are an important, experienced, and wise individual." The words "I was hoping" shows concern for them, that you won't pressure them. The phrase "you'd give me your opinion" says, "You and your thoughts are important, and I value them." Understand that sentence. Use it and watch a willing world place itself in the palm of your hand.

Never, never forget that the first rule of prospecting is to never assume that someone cannot help you build your business. What about dear old Aunt Gertrude? Okay, at 78 she's not much of a candidate for the washboard abs video, but what about the young people she teaches at church, or the joggers and speed-walkers she meets at the park, or cousin Fred in Illinois who just can't get enough of that deep-dish Chicago pizza? Aunt Gertrude knows people! She knows people who need the product or service you provide.

## *Strategy 2: Move on to acquaintances*

So the last time you drove dear old Aunt Gertrude down to her aquatic aerobics class you noticed that she has already developed some awesome washboard abs. That means you've probably exhausted your list of friends and family and now it is time to move on and to start prospecting your acquaintances (the *cold market*). Acquaintances include business and social associates, people with whom you do business such as the dry cleaner or the clerk at the video store, anyone with whom you have a relationship, even the guy next to you in the buffet line.

Stop for a minute and think about all the people you meet every day or week who may benefit from owning your product. If they can't benefit, they probably know someone who can. You probably can at least get a referral. Remember that prospecting is not selling. Just have a pleasant conversation and let people know what you do. If you use your day-to-day contacts and take advantage of the opportunities that step right up and say "hello," you'll be amazed at the doors that will swing wide open for you.

# How many people do you meet in a day?

You may be surprised at the number of prospects or referrals you can get just from casual conversation with the people you run into on a given day. Take a look at the following list of people you can meet while doing your daily business:

- Getting the morning paper: Neighbors, joggers, people walking pets

- Taking the kids to school: Teacher, coach, other parents, crossing guard, schoolbook salesperson

- Getting a haircut: Stylist, other customers, styling-product representatives

- At your annual physical: Doctor, nurses, people in waiting room

- At the civic group luncheon: Businesspeople, guest speaker, waiters, and waitresses

- During a trip to the bank: Teller, people in line, loan officer, man you help with flat tire in parking lot

- At the grocery store: Checkout clerk, stock clerk, woman demonstrating new product, more people in line

- At the fast-food restaurant: Clerk, neighbor from down the street, and everyone else in line

- While picking up baby-sitter: Sitter's parents and, of course, the sitter

- At the church meeting: Pastor, deacons, church members

- While at home: Call best friends, old friends, ex-girlfriend/boyfriend, long-lost cousin Ed

You encounter many others, such as the washing machine repair person, gas station attendant, members of your softball team, your accountant, and dentist. You also come upon the pet groomer, cobbler, librarian, insurance salesperson, carpet cleaner, antique dealer, golf pro, tax consultant, and taxi driver. Don't forget the travel consultant, and all those people in all those other checkout lines all over town!

Get the picture?

## Strategy 3: Tap business contacts

Even if you're just out of school, the service, or a lifetime on the farm, at some time you have worked for someone in business. Maybe you baby-sat for the neighbors, mowed lawns after school and summers, worked as a laborer in construction, sacked groceries, or sold magazines door-to-door. You know people who can use your product or service. You may have solid relationships with these people. They may appreciate your hard work, admire your ability to stick with it, and note your honesty. You may even find it easier to get to the heart of the matter with these folks than with people you know socially. After all, they're in business to do business and expect to hear sales presentations.

Become an active member in one or more of the business clubs and organizations in your community. (See Chapter 7 for details.) Join one of your local Chamber of Commerce committees that organizes semi-social events designed to help businesspeople. Beware that you don't overcommit yourself, though, and perform poorly. Nothing's worse for your selling career than a blight on your reputation in a volunteer or civic organization.

Check out your own industry to see if it has any trade associations. These groups can provide up-to-date information about business trends, valuable notices of who's who and who's doing what, classes and seminars, and a variety of opportunities for you to increase your networking efforts.

Many cities also have a number of networking clubs where people in noncompetitive businesses meet informally to exchange business cards and actively seek new business in a relaxed atmosphere. Usually, one member of the club makes a presentation about his or her business or service.

Toastmasters, an organization dedicated to the fine art of public speaking, is one of the most wonderful organizations to which you can belong. You will continually find their meetings to be fun, challenging, and enlightening experiences. Check your phone book and make the call.

## Strategy 4: If you're a client, talk to your salespeople

Who meets more people and who has more potential leads than a salesperson? If you are a client of several salespeople and aren't in competitive businesses, why not get other salespeople on your team? Find an appropriate time to discuss sharing leads. Or ask them to keep you in mind the next time an opportunity to recommend your product or service comes along. Naturally, you offer to provide the same service in return.

# Searching the wide, wide world of contacts

You have a wide variety of prospecting techniques at your disposal. Try them all. Find out which methods are best suited for your personality and style. Practice them. Use them and polish your skills until you are a master at finding the trophy prospects and reeling them in.

Use the astounding amount of resources and information available at your fingertips. Start with the good old Yellow Pages. You already have the local book. You may be able to find the Yellow Pages for cities around the state and for many major cities at your local library. The Yellow Pages contain the names, addresses, and phone numbers of potential clients organized by category for your researching convenience.

The world of business offers a staggering variety of reference materials. You may subscribe to or purchase most of the reference materials. However, you can find many of them at no charge at the library or your Chamber of Commerce. Chapter 3 includes an in-depth look at additional invaluable resources at your local library.

Following are a few highlights of how business references can make your prospecting chores much easier:

- ✔ Explore directories and registers of manufacturers, businesses, industries, charitable groups, and other organizations. A directory of toll-free numbers may prove invaluable if you're expanding your territory.

- ✔ Narrow your search. Businesses are categorized by type, geographic region, memberships in professional and trade groups, and other valuable categories.

- ✔ Stay up to date with the latest facts and figures. Reference resources get published yearly, quarterly, or sometimes monthly, and are updated frequently.

Newspaper and magazine ads, radio and television commercials, and other forms of mass communication can provide additional sources and information. Always keep your eyes and ears open, and never pass up an opportunity to locate a prospect. They're everywhere!

The Internet has taken the world by storm, and you should take advantage of this remarkable information resource. The Internet can provide you with the opportunity to deliver information about your own product or service and to conduct in-depth research and prospecting efforts at the same time. For more on prospecting on the Internet, see Chapter 6.

The world is wide, but don't be intimidated. Rejoice! That vast size just means you can tap into more proven methods and exciting new techniques to help you cast your nets and haul in the prospects.

You can soon build a small army of allies by making and aggressively working these contacts.

## Strategy 5: Prospect through other businesses

People in business love to be appreciated, to have their skills, abilities, and services praised by their customers. Smart businesspeople display letters of praise on bulletin boards, in frames on the walls, in portfolios that they show their prospects, and even in their advertising and promotional materials. When you receive excellent service, draft a well-written letter to the owner or manager expressing your satisfaction. Other people will probably see that letter, take note of your professionalism and courteous attitude, and perhaps remember you when they require your services.

If nothing else, you will have made a positive impression on someone doing business in your community, someone who will at some time be in a position to make an enthusiastic referral.

## Strategy 6: Benefit from the itch cycle

Every product has what I call an *itch cycle,* a predictable time in which owners of the product yearn to replace the product. The itch cycle centers on the fact that every product has a limited life span. Product life spans vary radically. Computer software may be out of date within a matter of months. Household appliances last for years; furniture may be passed from generation to generation. The length of the cycle is not really important. You just need to know how you can use the itch cycle to increase your sales.

Suppose a couple of newlyweds bought a new computer from your company two years ago. As an informed salesperson you know that the computer is now outdated. Instead of waiting and hoping for the happy couple to arrive at your store, give them a call. Ask how the computer is meeting their needs. Ask them if they have been satisfied. Maybe they're already thinking about replacing it and your call may get them off the fence and into your showroom. Maybe they haven't even considered buying a new computer, but your call plants the seed. They may turn to you, the courteous and concerned salesperson, for their next purchase.

If you don't know the replacement cycle of your product, ask the people in your company who know, or make a few phone calls to customers who use your product or service. Place the call as a brief survey and ask no more than three or four simple questions, such as:

> Are you still using your Triple X copier as the primary unit for your business?

or

> Is it still meeting your copying needs effectively?

or

> What unit did you have before investing in the Triple X?

Most people are willing to help out if the call isn't a major interruption. Unless the customer is a first-time buyer, you should get a pretty good idea of your product's life cycle and, more important, its itch cycle. Thank the customer, file your notes, and put that follow-up call on your calendar. Look for an opportunity to "pop in" with literature or information on your newest, most exciting trends in your product or service.

Consistently being in the right place at the right time to make a replacement sale is more than a matter of luck. Remember the itch cycle. Use it and never forget that some of your best prospects are the people already using your product or service.

## Strategy 7: Ride the wave of technical advancement

Never underestimate the importance personality plays within the itch cycle. Many people buy new products for reasons that have nothing whatsoever to do with a real need for replacements. I know several people who owned perfectly good television sets but who purchased wide-screen sets the moment they debuted. They replaced the wide-screen sets with even wider-screen sets with stereo sound. Then they added large satellite dishes, and now they are champing at the bit to own the first high-definition TV they can get their hands on.

With some folks, having the newest product is a matter of ego. They don't want to just keep up with the Joneses, they want to run circles around the Joneses and leave them eating their trail dust. These people are driven by status, which is okay. Some people just want to be on the cutting edge. They just have to have the the latest and greatest, or their lives are in shambles. How many people do you know who define themselves by logos? They don't wear any old suits; they wear Armani suits. They don't wear any old scent, they wear Joy or Calvin Klein. And they don't drive just cars, they drive "B-mers." That's okay, too. People naturally want to improve the quality of their lives. You succeed by providing them with the latest and greatest of whatever brand they crave. (If you don't have their favorite brand, you compare your brand to that one and show how yours will better serve their needs.)

Your approach is critical. Don't call them and say, "I've got something better than the whatchamacallit I sold you last year." If you do this, you belittle your company and product and your customers' intelligence. You run the risk of alienating good customers who may have been delighted with their (then) state-of-the-art purchases. You may not only lose Bob as a customer; you may also lose any referrals he could have provided.

Try a smarter approach:

**CHAMPION STRATEGY**

| | |
|---|---|
| You: | Bob, this is Larry down at Stereo City. I'm calling to see if you're still enjoying that SuperBoom stereo system you got last year. |
| Them: | Hi, Larry. Oh, yeah. It's great. I have it on all the time. |
| You: | That's great. I know you invested a lot of your time and effort into researching the equipment at the time to find just the right one for you. Because I value your judgment, Bob, I'd like to get your opinion on something new we may be offering. |
| Them: | What's that, Larry? |

You then describe the latest and greatest, getting Bob so excited that he can't wait to jump in his car and head down to Stereo City tonight.

Anything new — innovations, upgrades, new technologies — can trigger your customers' itches. Ring up good old Bob and ring up that sale!

## Strategy 8: Prospect your customer list

When salespeople change jobs or divisions or get promoted, some of their customers fall through the cracks and never get called on for repeat business. As companies grow and change, this happens far too often. However, this situation can also mean real opportunity for you. These customers are excellent sources of prospects.

Even if someone in your company dealt with a particular person and had great success, keep a close watch on personnel changes; the old contact may be gone, and the new person in charge may not know who did the last job. You can be the one to sell them again. Also, if you failed to sell them on your goods/services the first time, the new person may be more receptive.

How many times have you purchased a product or service that you were satisfied and happy with but then made your replacement purchase from another company? Maybe the first company just wasn't on your mind or a salesperson from another company called at the right time. Whatever the reason, the first company allowed, I said *allowed,* a sale to go to a competitor. That's not how you become a champion.

Any business in operation for any length of time should have a healthy customer list. Ask your manager if those customers were assigned to another salesperson. If not, ask for permission to contact them yourself. You should find a receptive audience. After all, these people have bought from your company before. They are familiar with the company's products, service, and employees. If your organization has lived up to its promises, these people will want to do business with a company they trust again and again and again.

Prospect your company's existing customer list, and you can very easily be the representative whom these satisfied customers request and refer other people to . . . again . . . and again . . . and again.

## Strategy 9: Read the newspaper

Millions of people sit down every morning with cups of coffee and their newspapers never realizing that they hold in their hands one of the greatest prospecting tools in the world. They tsk-tsk about kids today, send their blood pressure soaring over the latest government scandal, chuckle over the cartoons, and then toss a profitable day or week or month in the trash when they could raise their pressure with enthusiasm over the great leads they could find:

- ✔ Jane Doe, who was just promoted to vice president of XYZ company, is probably looking for a new wardrobe, maybe a more upscale automobile, and an advanced course in budgeting software. Perhaps the new job will entail significant travel, and she'll need airline tickets, hotel reservations, and an exceptional travel agent like you.

- ✔ John Doe, who just opened that little shop downtown, is probably going to need a computer, a copier, a delivery service, office supplies, and people!

- ✔ Mr. and Mrs. Smith and their brand new baby, Desmond, Jr., are surely going to need a nursery, a crib, baby clothes, a sitter, a minivan to cart the stuff around, and maybe even a new and bigger house. What about insurance, a college fund, and in a couple of months a quiet weekend just for the two of them in a great hotel not too far away from Junior?

All you need to do is drop the clipping in the mail with this note: "I saw you in the newspaper. I'm in business in the community and hope to meet you someday in person. I thought you might appreciate having an extra copy of your article to share with friends or relatives." Don't forget to include your business card.

Follow up in a week or two with a phone call.

| You: | Hello, Mrs. Smith, this is Suzanne Goodness at Lifelong Insurance. I sent you a little note a couple of weeks ago with a clipping of the good news about your new little boy. How are you doing today? |
|---|---|
| Them: | I'm getting used to a lot of new things these days. |
| You: | I'm sure you are, Mrs. Smith. I won't keep you long. I just want to introduce myself and congratulate you again on the new addition to your family. By the way, Mrs. Smith, have you and your husband made any plans yet for little Desmond's college fund? |

Marking, clipping, and sending these stories is a simple addition to your regular morning routine. This small service can lead to big rewards.

## Strategy 10: Know your service or support people

You can do a lot of successful prospecting right in your own company. Get to know the customer service and repair people because they're most often on the front lines of customer challenges. You may be in a position to turn those challenges into opportunities. For example, John Doe, the guy with the little shop, has called to have his copier repaired three times in the past four months. He's having challenges. He may be making more copies per month than the machine can handle. Maybe he has some new staff members who have mishandled the machine. Either way, John may be in a changing mode. Maybe he needs a brand new copier, one that has a one-year service warranty with a free inspection and cleaning every four months that just happens to be available at a highly affordable rate. The new copier is faster, makes sharper copies, and automatically collates so his staff is free to better serve their customers. An investment in a new copier solves a number of challenges at a cost that is comparable to those never-ending repair bills.

The people in your service and support departments can tell you about people like John Doe. They frequently spend extended periods of time with your customers, often in the customers' places of business. They may know about personnel changes, business expansions, and have a wealth of insights into your clients' businesses that you can use. Debrief service or support technicians after they visit any of your clients.

| | |
|---|---|
| Them: | Hi Anne. How's it going today? |
| You: | Fine. Steve, have a seat. Let's see, you were at the Hopkins account today, weren't you? |
| Them: | That's right. They were having some challenges with their copier. I made the repair and ran a full diagnostic. The machine's doing okay for their current needs, but I wouldn't be surprised if they need a second machine or something larger soon. |

| | |
|---|---|
| You: | Why *do* you say that? |
| Them: | Well, our service records show that we've been out there six times this year, and each time it was for a different reason. I think they're occasionally overloading the machine. Today, they were running a batch of 800 copies." |
| You: | Eight hundred? That machine isn't designed for that big a run. |
| Them: | I told Mary that, but she said this was a special project and they don't do this type of thing often. I suggested they research buying something with more capabilities. She seemed to have an open mind about it. |
| You: | I'll have to do some checking on the investment they're making now on the machine and service agreement. Did you notice what supplies they use? |
| Them: | They use Superior paper and toner, so obviously they're willing to invest in quality. |
| You: | That's great information, Steve. I appreciate it. Did you notice anything else while you were there? |
| Them: | I'm not positive, but I think the phone system was new. It was a brand I don't remember ever seeing before. |
| You: | That could be a sign they're growing. I think it's time to pay them a courtesy call. Steve, you've been real helpful. Thanks for debriefing me on this account. |

Invest some time making friends, and you'll be spending more time making sales.

## Strategy 11: Practice the 3-foot rule

Smart salespeople automatically classify anyone coming within 3 feet of them as a prospect. That's right. Unqualified, unknown strangers can turn into fully qualified, sold, and satisfied customers with remarkably little effort. All you need is the willingness to say "hello" and the ability to be a pleasant conversationalist.

What usually happens when you step into an elevator and someone is already there? The two of you probably spend the trip staring at the electronic light that reads 1-2-3-4-5 and so on. What an incredible waste of time and opportunity. Never be discouraged by the fact that the person next to you is a stranger. After all, the very fact that you know nothing of this person means it is impossible to write him or her off as a prospect. You just don't know, so find out.

I don't for an instant mean for you to go charging into a sales presentation, desperate, breathless, and fearful that your prospect will escape at the next floor. Take it easy and start a friendly conversation. Look for something to compliment: "If you don't mind my saying, that is a beautiful tie . . . lovely purse . . . interesting lapel pin."

Keep the conversation going, and soon the appropriate moment for exchanging names will arrive naturally. That's also the appropriate moment to politely mention your business, product, or service:

Have you been to John Doe's new store downtown? (Of course, you are John Doe or his number-one salesperson.)

or

Don't you wish you could get designer suits at an economical price? (Your new acquaintance can if he orders directly from the manufacturer through your catalog service.)

or

Wouldn't it be great to spend a couple of weeks on the beach/in the mountains/out of town?" (Your travel agency would be delighted to make the arrangements.)

The answers to the questions are almost always "yes." Then you have an opportunity to describe how your product or service exactly meets that need. You may be amazed at how much you can accomplish in a short time. You may not close the sale, but you will have planted a seed, made a potentially valuable contact, and perhaps even receive a call from a friend of the friend. "I heard from my neighbor that you can get a real deal on designer suits."

Sure, your sales average may not be very high with this approach, but it will be zero if you don't try. If you have time, even only a brief moment, what do you have to lose? If you don't make contact, the answer is "a sale."

# Three Ways to Approach a Prospect

You can approach people in many ways, but I have found that a combination of these three techniques works best:

- ✔ **The telephone.** You can make a lot of calls in a short period of time using the telephone. The phone is also easy on the annual budget. You can find one virtually everywhere, and almost everybody has one. The downside is that it is remarkably easy to say "no" over the telephone. Interruptions, real or invented, can cut short your presentation. Your prospect on the other end of the line has complete control of the situation and can hang up on you.

- ✔ **Direct mail.** Direct mail is efficient and cost-effective because you send the information directly to the person you want to receive it. Still, prospects have an easier time tossing a piece of paper in the trash can than actually reading it.

- ✔ **Face-to-face meeting.** A face-to-face meeting with a good prospect is ideal. It is simply the finest, most effective way to sell a product or service. Unlike a phone call or direct mail piece, it is difficult for someone to get rid of another human being. Increase the number of your face-to-face calls, and you will increase the number of presentations to people who need your product.

You may need to make several attempts before you determine the right approach for someone. Some may respond to mail, others may not respond until they hear from you three times. Each method reinforces the others.

When you go door to door, make sure you knock on the right ones. I believe in going out and talking to people. I know that if you say the right words and say them properly and pleasantly, you can meet people who want to learn about your product or service.

Here is how I put together a combination of approaches to make sure I'm not only knocking on the right doors but also that the doors will open wide for my presentation.

I mail a letter of introduction to my prospects. I say that my company has given me an assignment to conduct a brief survey to get feedback from people in the community. I thank them in advance for their help and note that I will be calling soon. I make sure that the letter is brief, simple, and polite.

> *Good morning, Mr. and Mrs. Sanders,*
>
> *My name is Tom Hopkins. I help people gain greater control over their financial future with the services provided by Champion Financial. My firm has asked that I contact 20 people in the area with a brief two-question survey to help us determine what services we might need to add to our current ones. I will call you next Thursday afternoon to ask you those two quick questions. I thank you in advance for your help in this matter.*
>
> *Sincerely,*
>
> *Tom Hopkins*

When I phone or plan to make a personal visit, I use the letter as an icebreaker. "Hi, I'm Tom Hopkins. Did you get my letter of introduction? I sent the letter because I didn't want to be like so many people in our business and just drop by unannounced." This letter is an exceptional technique because it sets you apart from the crowd. The simple courtesy makes you different than all the other salespeople who contact these prospects. It presents you in a positive light. Never forget that the number-one key to success in sales is getting people to like and trust you. You then ask permission to ask your survey questions, which will hopefully lead to a qualifying sequence, an opportunity to present, and then a sale.

Prospecting is a lot like fishing. Prospecting is fishing! It is an art that requires knowledge, skill, and infinite patience. When you master the techniques presented in this chapter, you'll always be in position to reel in the big ones.

# Chapter 6

# Prospecting by Remote

*In This Chapter*

▶ Setting up your own Web site

▶ Avoiding computer viruses

▶ Understanding the Internet's language

▶ Leveraging faxes, videotape, e-mail, and virtual reality

▶ Enterprising on the Internet

*F*inding people with the help of other people (see Chapter 7) is the most effective means of prospecting. And the trusty telephone — which you can read about in Part III — has long been a prospector's best friend. But new technologies allow the savvy sales professional to reach a much wider audience — an audience that doesn't even need to be seen! These salespeople prospect by remote, which includes the Internet; the convenience of faxes, virtual reality, and e-mail; and the staying power of videotape.

## Other sources to consider

This chapter can really give you only an overview of these "remote" topics as they relate to prospecting. Entire books can be written on some of the subjects in this chapter — and, in fact, entire books *have* been written on many of them. If you'd like more information on topics covered here, some of the IDG Books Worldwide, Inc. titles you may want to consider are *The Internet For Dummies,* 5th edition, by John Levine, Margaret Levine Young, and Carol Baroudi; *Small Business Internet For Dummies,* by Greg Holden; *Small Business Internet Directory For Dummies,* by Esau Barchini and Lee Musick; *Dummies 101: Creating Web Pages* and *CyberBuck$,* both by Kim Kommando; *VRML and 3-D on the Web For Dummies,* by David Kay and Douglas Muder; and *E-Mail For Dummies,* by Levine, Young, Baroudi, and Arnold Reinhold. Oh, and if you want more tips on how to close a sale by remote, check out *Sales Closing For Dummies.* I wrote that one.

# The Power of the Internet

I just heard a story that illustrates how far the Information Age has already taken us and how incredibly far we may go:

A man was tracing his ancient family roots and connected with an information source in Scotland via the Internet. "I requested a series of documents dating back several hundred years. The transfer of information took well less than a minute, but I remember thinking how frustratingly tedious that short wait was. And then I stopped and thought about what I was thinking. There I was, getting hard-to-come-by information from an obscure source located half a day and an entire ocean away in a foreign land. I had facts and figures delivered almost instantly and directly to my personal office right in my own home. And I was impatient about a 30-second wait. What a truly marvelous world we live in!"

The Internet is an integral part of the lives of millions of individuals, families, businesses, and organizations. Knowledgeable people predict that by the first ten years of the next century every person in the world will have access to the Internet. The phenomenally fast growth means you have more information at your fingertips, more contact with people all over the world, and, most important, more prospects within your grasp.

You don't have to be on the Net to be a successful prospector, but you should consider adding the Internet to your professional tool kit. A champion is always on the lookout for new and better ways to keep the prospect pipeline flowing.

As a prospector, think of the Internet as

- ✓ An incredibly huge and growing computer network made up of thousands of smaller networks, which consist of millions of computer operators (businesses, families, individuals, and the kid next door).

- ✓ A group of folks that uses the network for business, education, pleasure, and personal communication.

- ✓ An amazing assortment of easily accessible information.

If you're not around computers much, you may wonder what you need to get on the Internet. Basically, you need three things:

- ✓ **A computer.** File this under the Department of the Obvious. Make sure that the computer has a *modem,* which is basically a device that allows the computer to make a telephone connection. Most modems also serve as faxes, but your computer sales representative can tell you more about that.

📍 **Access to the Internet.** Most people log on to the Internet one of two ways:

- **Through an Internet Service Provider (or ISP).** An ISP doesn't provide any type of content; it just provides a connection to the Internet.

- **Through an online service (such as America Online, The Microsoft Network, CompuServe, Primenet, Prodigy, and so on).** An online service connects you to the Internet just as an ISP does, but also provides content such as daily news headlines, stock quotes, baseball scores, and information resources. Only those who subscribe to the online service have access to this information.

📍 **Internet software.** Often your ISP or online service provides you with connection software, or such software comes installed on your computer. If not, don't panic. The stuff is everywhere. You can find it at computer stores, in your mail, and on the Internet. You see ads for the software in magazines and catalogs. Examine everything carefully and decide what works best for you. Obtaining the software is the tough part; installing and using it is a breeze. Just follow the directions, or get your son or daughter or the kid next door to do it for you.

# Building Your Prospecting Information

Successful prospecting requires information. If you need facts and figures on gold mining in Alaska, a company's executive structure, or a street map of Dallas, head for the Internet. You can get the data (most often for free) with a few taps on the keyboard and clicks of the mouse.

More companies are maintaining Web sites, allowing you to access sources of data concerning their businesses. Company sites often link to specific pages relating to individuals, corporate divisions, or individual services. The sites usually include addresses for further information or for direct contact.

You can also consider the Internet as the world's biggest telephone company and postal system plugged right into your computer. You can contact businesses, organizations, and individuals as easily as you write letters. Just click the Send button, and in seconds, your letter, resumé, proposal, comment, idea, or documentation gets delivered across the street, across the country, or around the world.

# What exactly is the Internet?

The Internet began about 25 years ago as a project of the U.S. Department of Defense, which wanted a computer network that ran even if one or more computers within the system went down. The network soon became a network of networks, spreading to defense contractors and research universities, and, (I'm really compressing history here) eventually, to the U.S. public and, now, the world. As recently as the late 1980s, the Net connected only 33,000 computers worldwide. By 1995, the Net served more than 642,000 computers and 25 million people.

Telephone lines, fiber optics, microwave, and other state-of-the-art electronic means link all of the Internet's various networks. These networks permit users to contact each other via electronic mail and send and receive a variety of information such as text, photographs, drawings, programs, or anything that users can store in a computer file. Users can access banks of information for free or a fee.

So what's the *World Wide Web?* All you need to know is that the World Wide Web (also known as WWW, the Web, and 3W) is the system that lets anyone easily find or provide information on the Internet.

You can log on to the Web and quickly jump from subject to subject with a few clicks of a mouse. This swift movement is called *browsing* or *surfing.* For example, if you have a prospect interested in purchasing an aircraft, you can find the type of craft available in your area, the capabilities, and specs for the craft. That site may have *links* to other sites (or *pages*) that feature the schematics, photos, and even motion pictures of the plane in flight. Those pages may have further links to sites containing prices, upgrades, modifications of the aircraft, landing fees, and storage rates. You can even find maps of airports that your prospect is likely to use.

You can pretty much find whatever information you need on almost any topic. Don't worry so much about the technicalities of the Web, just enjoy what it does for you.

I don't believe anyone knows how many information sites are on the Net. For example, I just took a moment to log on to the Internet to see what there is to see. I looked up sites for telemarketing, retail, and sales. The search came up with the following number of information sources for each:

- ✔ Telemarketing: 173 sites
- ✔ Retail: 4,254 sites
- ✔ Sales: 3,567,585 sites

(By the way, pay a visit to www.tomhopkins.com if you're serious about your selling careers.)

Some Web sites will have become inactive and other, new ones will have appeared. I've found hundreds of thousands and even millions of matches for some of my searches. The amount of information available on the Net is truly staggering. I also searched for information on sales prospecting. Guess how many sites I found? Only 124, and that, my friends, is why I wrote *Sales Prospecting For Dummies.*

Anyone can put anything on the Net. As with all research and all communication, always consider the source.

## Searching, Searching . . .

Dozens of *search engines* can help you find your way around the Internet (and help prospects find their way to your page, too).

Each search engine is an Internet site that has its own features, benefits, and drawbacks. All you do is tell the search engine the topic you're looking for — you type in a word or phrase, and then click the Search button (more about *word searches* later in this section). The search engine speedily chugs through its database of sites and spits out a list of all the sites that match the words you typed. Click a site that interests you, and you link to that page. Easy, huh?

The following list shows a few of my favorite World Wide Web search engines, their Internet addresses, and highlights. Try out the following seven (and any others you may come across) until you find a favorite that closely meets your needs:

- ✔ **AltaVista.** www.altavista.digital.com. This comprehensive site can search through more than 16 million Web pages. A good search engine if you're looking for information as you prospect, but if people are looking for your page, they may get discouraged.

- ✔ **Excite.** www.excite.com. Excite not only lists sites that match your keyword or phrase, but also offers "similar sites" (sites that relate to, but don't match, the keyword/phrase).

- ✔ **HotBot.** www.hotbot.com. HotBot searches the full text of more than 50 million documents for your keywords. It also helps you fine-tune your search with built-in pull-down menus.

- ✔ **Infoseek.** www.infoseek.com. Infoseek has merged the resources of four other search engines and offers a full service Internet information source that contains the world's largest directory of categorized Web pages.

- ✔ **Lycos.** www.lycos.com. One of the oldest search engines, Lycos has its roots at Carnegie-Mellon University. You search the Internet by typing a key word.

- ✔ **WebCrawler.** www.webcrawler.com. America Online owns this site, but you don't need an AOL account to access it. WebCrawler automatically indexes every page it encounters.

- ✔ **Yahoo!** www.yahoo.com. Another oldie but goodie, Yahoo! organizes its information by categories and subcategories. Each site on its database has been personally screened by a Yahoo! employee.

To provide you with an example of how to best refine your prospecting on the Internet, I went to the experts. Michael Henderson, president of ADNet International (www.adnetintl.com) in Atlanta, Georgia, offers these tips for the following services.

## America Online

If you're a member of America Online, *America Online For Dummies,* 4th Edition, by John Kaufeld, has lots of good search tips. But you can do a simple search by using the Member Directory (located on the Members menu).

Say you represent a fly-fishing product and are seeking new clients. Go to the Quick Search tab and type fly fishing. Click Search. You now have 250 people or businesses that have expressed an interest in that subject. Wasn't that fast? Clicking any of the listed prospects gives you the entire prospect profile, as well as an e-mail address.

To further refine your search, such as individual state prospects, just go back to the Member Directory and type in the targeted state of interest. Other fields on the Member Directory page allow you to further refine your query with quite a bit of precision. You can target people by their sex, age, marital status, occupation, hobbies, and interests. This search can be very powerful!

AOL, like other online providers, also lets you get to the search engines mentioned earlier.

## Specialty directories

You can do a more targeted search with SIC (Standard Industrial Code) searches. These codes are available at your local library or from any number of sources online. WorldPages (www.worldpages.com), helps you find the SIC code and then helps you use it to prospect.

For example, say you're marketing fly fishing lures and you need to find retail fishing stores. On the WorldPages title page, click the words *SIC Find* to bring up a box where you can type in the SIC number and the appropriate geographical information. Don't know the correct SIC number? Then click the words *SIC Code,* and WorldPages responds with a list of the basic SIC codes.

Reading down that list of SIC codes, you'll discover that the basic SIC code 59 is for Miscellaneous Retail. Click the words *Miscellaneous Retail* and WorldPages pops up a more complete listing. Look under subcategory 594 (Miscellaneous Shopping Goods Stores) and you'll find 5941d (Fishing Equipment Stores Retail). You can then go back to the SIC Find page (on most browsers, simply hit the Back button a couple of times) and plug in the information.

Now, all you need to do is specify any city, state, province, or country that you're interested in to find particular fly-fishing retail-store prospects. For example, type in Dallas, Texas, United States, and hit the "Find It" button. You uncover names, addresses, phone numbers, and detailed maps. Yee-hah! In your excitement, don't skip over the fact that SIC codes 5941c and 5941b are related businesses (Camping Equipment Retailers and Bait Shop Retailers, respectively) that also can be great prospects for your fishing lures.

Another excellent source is Big Yellow (www1.bigyellow.com). Here, you can search for 16 million businesses under 7,000 different categories by city and state. Use the Category, City, and State boxes to enter the appropriate information — in my example, Fishing Tackle Dealers in Dallas, Texas. If you don't know the specific category, click the word *Category* and Big Yellow provides you with all the options in an alphabetical table. The results are similar to WorldPages, with alphabetical listings of the dealers, addresses and phone numbers.

## Classified directories

Literally thousands of areas on the Internet allow anyone to advertise products or services. The good news is that most of these Web sites are free. Sites such as Crecon (www.crecon.com) or Doornet (www.doornet.com) list thousands of free classified ads in hundreds of categories. Some of these free classified directories are designed for specific products or services while some are quite general.

These sites are great resources for testing your advertising copy because they cost you nothing. Unfortunately, only repetitive use of the free services determines which directories are more effective than others, so I strongly recommend multiple submissions to many services. Make sure that you track your advertisement with a code number or name to allow you to determine which of the services is giving you the most activity.

You can also use the classifieds in reverse. Identify several subject categories that could attract people who would want to own your products, and then contact the people who are placing ads in those categories. You may just find these people to be buyers as well as sellers.

# Your Very Own Web Site!

Numerous resources can help you create your own Web site. Check out computer-literate communications firms, your favorite computer store, your library, or a book (such as *Dummies 101: Creating Web Pages*) to get started. A number of special software programs that make creating Web pages easier (including Adobe PageMill, Claris Home Page, Corel Web.Graphics Suite, Microsoft FrontPage, and Netscape Composer, just to name a few) are also available.

You should place your site on a *Web server,* a computer that hosts your Web page. You may not want to use your own computer for your Web site's home because at some point during every 24 hours you probably want to sleep, eat a meal, read a book, or just walk around the block. (Monitoring and maintaining your Web site is not a prospecting activity. Defer it to an expert for pennies a day.) Your Internet Service Provider or your online service probably can allow you to place your own Web site on its server for a small fee or perhaps at no cost.

## How many pages do you need?

You can stuff as many pages as you want onto your Web site. Some individuals and companies get by with a single page, while other sites have untold numbers of pages. Use all the pages you need, but don't use one more than necessary. Remember that serious people "surfing" the Net want solid information at a glance. They may be impressed by fancy graphics, clever presentations, and page-after-page of text, but they really want information and they want it fast. That's what drives them. Try not to impress people with what you think is important. Rather, you should try to impress people by showing them how you can meet *their* needs. Constantly ask yourself, "What does my prospect really want to know?"

# Your computer is vulnerable

Computer crashes, data wipeouts, hackers, industrial espionage — they all cost money, money, money. No, you don't need to be like 007 or have a pal in the Pentagon if you want to have a Web site. However, you do need to know that your computer and its contents are vulnerable to some nasty forces. Keep these points in mind:

✔ You can never be certain that your e-mail messages are completely private. However, you shouldn't be paranoid about someone reading your personal messages. After all, the Internet was designed and built to be open and public, not to restrict the flow of information. You should, however, consider using secure channels for any proprietary information you wouldn't want the competition to know about.

You can use one of two methods to send information securely over the Internet: a secured protocol, or encryption. I won't bore you with the technical details. Consult with your Internet access provider if you're concerned about the security of your messages.

✔ Computers can catch viruses. In spite of all the media coverage, computer *viruses* — programs that infect other programs — are very rare. You can infect your computer with a virus when you download something from the Internet or stick a disk into your computer, so be careful about what you allow into your computer system. Some viruses are merely playful, placing an image or text message on your screen for a limited time and then disappearing. Others are downright deadly, wiping out every file on your hard disk. Get a good antivirus software program and install it on your computer.

✔ Remember to always, always back up any important files. There seems to be an unalterable law of the universe that whenever anything goes wrong it will go wrong at the worst possible moment. Like police officers on the beat, we all need backup!

Prospects are more concerned with content on your Web site than they are with the number of pages on your Web site. As always, the quality of information, not quantity, counts. Think only in terms of the needs of your prospects. What is important to them is what should be important to you. Period.

## What goes on the site?

Think of your Web site as a presentation. Experiment with different formats and presentations until you find the one that works best for you. If you need an idea starter, consider the following format:

- **Feature(s) and benefit(s).** List the features of your product or service and tie them to specific benefits for your prospect. If the vehicle you sell provides more miles per gallon than its competition, that fuel efficiency means more money in consumers' pockets or to corporations' bottom lines. If your consultation service provides education and training, prospects can receive more competent, qualified, and faster answers to their questions.

- **Proof.** You can provide a list of awards that your company and product have won, citations of excellence, diplomas, newspaper clippings, positive media coverage, and testimonials from satisfied customers. Keep the proof material short and sweet so visitors to your site can read it with a brief glance.

- **Call to action.** Because you won't be physically present during your "presentation," be sure to include a call for action and provide a means for the prospect to contact you. Don't forget to include your address, phone number, and so on, on every page.

Beyond this simple format for your Web site, do whatever you think can get the job done. You can use all text or text combined with other elements such as charts and graphs. You can use photos, moving or animated pictures, sound, sound effects, and music. Before you get too creative, take time to consider the likely computer systems that your prospects use. A sound message is useless if your prospects' computers cannot play it. So, if you include sound, also include text to cover both types of clients.

Beware of including too many graphic elements or animation items because they take quite awhile to download in to the recipient computer. If downloading takes too long, chances are good that your prospect won't wait and can possibly move on to a competitor's site.

# *Nine steps to a powerhouse Web site*

Whether you create your own Web site or hire someone to do it, keep in mind several important points:

1. **Keep the site simple.**

   During an in-person or telephone prospecting trip, you can often recover quickly from interruptions. You can't do that on your page, so make sure prospects can easily find their way back to your site following an interruption. If you need to present several concepts, place the simplest ones first and work your way through to the more complex ones.

2. **Make your site entertaining, interesting, and even fun.**

   People like being entertained, intrigued, and informed. Do that for them and they'll stay at your site longer and come back frequently.

3. **Present everything in terms that benefit your prospect.**

   If prospects see immediately that your primary concern is to communicate what's in it for them to read on, they will. What's the most common denominator benefit your happy clients have in common? Use that as your opening line on your site and you'll capture the attention of new prospects.

4. **Use relevant charts and graphs to spice up your page.**

   Use pie-type charts to show the relationship between the parts of a whole; use bar graphs to show the differences between two or more topics. Bright colors are good for important topics, but don't overdo it or you'll cause retina burn. Use shading, shadows, boxes, and ornaments to add a touch of depth and keep your page interesting. Caution: Don't go overboard. A page that's too confusing to look at or trudge through can turn off viewers. Photos are great but again, be careful about how long they'll take to download.

5. **Keep your text short whenever possible.**

   Try to keep paragraphs to 50 words or fewer, and don't use all uppercase letters.

6. **Be honest.**

   Exaggerations, half-truths, omissions of important information, and outright falsehoods may catch up with you at the worst possible time.

### 7. Step out from the competition.

Find positive ways to show that you, your product, and your company are a step ahead of your competitors. Testimonials are particularly effective.

### 8. Include your name and address on every page.

If someone finds an intriguing bit of info on your site, she may be motivated to contact you immediately. Prepare for that event by having your name and address as well as your e-mail address on every page.

### 9. Practice good netiquette.

From net and etiquette, *netiquette* simply means good manners on the Internet. In your communications, don't do anything through your computer that you wouldn't do in person. The key here is professionalism. Always, always maintain an air of professionalism in every contact that could bring you new business. Avoid slang. Don't send jokes until you know if the client likes them. Don't enjoy the accepted brevity of e-mail to the detriment of your presentation.

## *Promoting your site*

You aren't done working when your site is finally on the Net. You're just beginning. You can't sit around and wait for prospects to come through the telephone wires.

You need to promote your Web site so that prospects can find it. I just logged on to the Net and searched for "computers." On just one source, just one source, I found 817 categories and 23,645 matches for "computers!" If you are in the computer industry, how would I find your site?

Promote your Web site at every opportunity. Make it as easy as possible for your prospects and customers to find you. Print your Web site address on your letterhead and business cards. Include it in all your ads, flyers, brochures, and promotional literature.

Don't print your address on anything until you have thoroughly checked out your ISP or commercial online service and are happy with its performance. One business I know went through three ISPs in less than a month before finding the right one. If the business owner had started promoting his company's Web site before he was ready, he would have had an awful lot of useless business cards on his hands, not to mention irate prospects trying to connect to an out-of-date address.

# An Internet dictionary

The Internet is growing and evolving at a tremendous rate, and many of the features that are so exciting at the moment of this writing will be old hat by the time you read this book. The following short definitions give you a general idea of the many resources and tools currently available to the aggressive prospector.

**BBS.** Short for *bulletin board system*. BBSes work just like the corkboards you see in the hallways, kitchens, or recreational rooms in almost every business in America. Just as you would pin a note or read a note on the board, you can pick up a message of interest or leave your own.

**browser.** A computer program that enables you to access information on the World Wide Web.

**cybernaut.** If you use the Internet on a regular basis, you are a cybernaut.

**downloading.** The transmission of information from a source on the Internet directly to your computer and/or printer. You must pay to receive a lot of stuff, but the amount of free material out there will stagger you.

**e-mail.** Electronic mail is probably the most popular, most used feature of the Internet. You can instantaneously send friendly letters, "Hi, Bob," or basic memos, "Hi, Bob, I agree with your decision. . . .," or even long text materials, "Hi, Bob, here's the 200-page John Smith file."

**encrypted message.** A message that has the letters scrambled so that no one other than the desired recipient, who can unscramble the message, can read it.

**FAQ.** Frequently asked question.

**flame.** To send someone a nasty note. These frequently anonymous missives can be quite vulgar and are considered bad form.

**file.** Computer documents that you work with are called files. You can send files over the Internet to just about anywhere in the world.

**Gopher.** The Internet has so much information, you may need help digging through it all to find the specific items you need. Gopher services do just that. Think of a Gopher as a menu of stuff and a way to find your way to the right stuff.

**Internet address.** Just like a street address, e-mail requires an address so that the person or company at that address can be contacted. Addresses generally look like this one for the President: president@ whitehouse.gov.

**Java.** A computer programming language for the distribution of digital information. Because Java can "talk" to any computer operating system, it is ideal for something so wildly diverse as the Internet.

*(continued)*

*(continued)*

**logging on.** Connecting to the Internet.

**lurk.** Considered good and appropriate behavior, lurking is simply reading and understanding the posted messages in a newsgroup before posting your own. Jumping right in with your message before you know your audience is a good way to get flamed. (See *netiquette*.) Successful prospecting means knowing your market.

**mailing list.** Just as it sounds, this is an e-mail list of people who want to get information about a specific person, place, or thing. For example, if you're prospecting the timber harvesting industry, you can get on a list that will periodically send you information on the industry, specific regions of the country, selected businesses or organizations, individuals within the industry, or just about any type of fact or figure you need. You can respond, ask for additional information, or contribute to the flow.

**netiquette.** From *net* and *etiquette*, simply means good manners on the Internet.

**network.** A series of linked computers that allows enhanced communication or information exchange.

**newsgroup.** Like the office bulletin board, this is a place where individuals post and retrieve messages, except that these messages concern a single topic. Again, you can read or join the process with your own news, views, and comments.

**online services.** Companies that maintain a network of news, information, e-mail capabilities, games, files, and resources that you can access for a fee. America Online, The Microsoft Network, Prodigy, Primenet, and CompuServe are a few of the more prominent names.

**snail mail.** A derogatory term referring to the slowness of the postal system compared with the speed of e-mail.

**spamming.** Sending the same message to a lot of different newsgroups. It's considered bad netiquette.

**URL.** Uniform Resource Locator. Think of a URL as a street address or telephone number on the Net. It consists of two to five elements separated by specific characters, such as `http://one/two~three.com` or `th@primenet.com`. Note that you must enter the address precisely. For example, if you enter a backward slash instead of a forward slash, you have entered the wrong address. You can knock, but you can't come in.

**white pages.** Just what it sounds like, except that it lists e-mail addresses. Sometimes it contains additional material, such as a real address and telephone number.

**World Wide Web.** A worldwide resource of electronic documents linked by computers that you access through a browser. You move from one document to another with a swift click.

# *Other Remote Prospecting Methods*

Telephoning someone is a tried-and-true way to set up an appointment, but it isn't the only way to reach prospects. You also can reach potential clients through video prospecting, virtual prospecting, faxes, e-mail, and chats.

## *Video your way to victory*

Videotape presentations are the closest thing to an in-person presentation your prospect can get. You can show off your product and tell (in sight and sound) how it's put together, delivered, supported, cleaned, repaired, improved, and updated. Generally, the shorter the presentation the better. If it needs to be 15 minutes, then make it 15 minutes but not one second longer. If you can do the same work in seven minutes, do so. Padding doesn't make your company look bigger, just overweight.

Too many companies produce videos, send them out, and then sit back and wait for the orders to roll in. They've invested a lot of professional fees for the videos, paid for or developed a direct-mail list, written accompanying letters, and also paid the postage for delivery. A lot of time, expense, and effort goes into the project, and nothing happens. Why? These companies have forgotten one simple fact:

A video can't close the sale. You still need a salesperson to get the job done.

Salespeople can use videos to drum up good prospects. I recently came across an interesting approach developed by Doug Warren, president of Video Marketing Technologies, Inc., in Temecula, California.

Take a look at how his six-step program centers on three key elements: a video, three letters, and a bag of microwave popcorn:

1. **Develop a mailing list of prospects.**

2. **Phone the people on the list and offer to mail the video.**

   This step is a beautiful, no-pressure approach because the prospects get information they want without committing to the dreaded appointment. The salesperson doesn't mind because that foot is now firmly planted in the door.

### 3. Send a letter of confirmation within two days.

The letter acknowledges that the video is on the way and says thank you for the interest. You can add a short bit about the salesperson, but keep it very short. You're trying to qualify a prospect, not sell something.

### 4. Mail the video so that it arrives three days after the confirmation.

Include a bag of microwave popcorn. Say something like "enclosed is the video we promised you" and include a postscript about enjoying the popcorn. I love the popcorn because it is one of those wonderful, inexpensive, easy-to-do ideas that really sets you apart from the competition.

### 5. Send another letter stating that you will call to schedule a brief time to answer any questions she may have.

The letter should arrive three days after delivery of the video.

### 6. Phone the prospect.

Make the call three days after the last letter was received. By this time, the prospect has viewed the video, experienced your nonthreatening professionalism, and enjoyed some free popcorn. She should be ready for a face-to-face presentation. This method of prospecting breaks down some of the preconceived prejudices and barriers that typical prospecting creates.

Naturally, you want to get your videotape back. After all, it represents a sizable investment. Don't have a runner go pick up the tape, however; have a salesperson do it. If the prospect doesn't agree to an appointment, the salesperson has a second shot at getting one. The prospect isn't on guard because she's not expecting a presentation, and she may be in a more receptive mood. One-on-one, in the prospect's environment, you just may be able to schedule that appointment and, if luck is with you, make a presentation right then and there.

Doug Warren says that the extra work and extra touches are worth the effort because the plan generates very high quality leads with "educated prospects" who really want more information.

## *Virtual prospecting — really!*

Believe it or not, you can now surf the Net in three dimensions. I'm sure you've heard of *virtual reality*. Well, it's no longer just a 3-D game, it's a full-fledged prospecting tool. VRML (or Virtual Reality Modeling Language) enables you to take your prospect on a 3-D presentation. Suppose Ms. Prospect can't fly across the country for a tour of your plant. Well, now she doesn't have to. Using the program and the Internet, you can drive her through the opening gates outside the plant for a view of the exterior of the facility. You can guide her through an open door into the plant where she can see (in 3-D) every step of the operation from the arrival of raw material through manufacturing, quality control, shipping, and delivery. You can even take your prospect on a guided 3-D tour inside the machinery for a look you can't get any other way. How's that for supercharging a presentation?

Again, if you'd like more information on this technology, check out *VRML and 3-D on the Web For Dummies* (IDG Books Worldwide, Inc.).

## *Faxes*

Judging by what's received in my office, many businesses and salespeople think that a fax is a good stand-alone prospecting tool. It isn't. I regularly receive fax flyers addressed to no one in particular, and that's who receives them. No one in particular. I rarely make a follow-up call regarding such faxes. Some folks may compare those faxes to "junk mail" and not only discard them, but also gain a negative impression of the companies (and people) who sent it.

The fax machine is a wonderful tool to have in your arsenal of prospecting armaments; however, it is not a stand-alone tool. The fax machine is a complementary item. That means it should be used in conjunction with other means. I strongly recommend using faxed information and agreements, especially because faxed signatures are considered acceptable forms of commitment on purchase orders, agreements, and other sales-confirmation forms. However, they must be used properly. Here are the best suggestions when using faxes:

- ✔ Always send a fax to the attention of the appropriate party. That means you have to call first to get that name.

- ✔ Always include a cover page and indicate the number of pages in the entire document.

- ✔ Always follow up with a brief phone call to confirm that the fax was received in its entirety and given to the designated person.

✔ If sending a lengthy document, include a summary page indicating what is covered in the document.

✔ Always include a call for action or, at the very least, instructions as to what the next step is after the recipient reads the faxed information.

✔ Generate your cover page from your computer or typewriter unless you have exceptional handwriting.

✔ Don't send photos through the fax unless they've been screened just for this type of transmission; otherwise they'll come through mostly black and extremely unattractive.

✔ Try to contact a difficult-to-reach decision maker by fax after you've tried several times by phone. Consider a simple "fax-back" form where she can simply check off answers to your questions and pop the fax back into her machine.

Maximizing the benefits of your fax machine can take you closer to decision makers and demonstrate a concern for both detail and efficiency, if handled with these tips in mind.

## E-mail and chats

E-mail works pretty much like regular mail except that instead of licking a stamp, you click Send. Your message goes instantaneously to its destination where the message gets stored until the recipient retrieves it. In addition to speedy delivery, e-mail offers another interesting and valuable asset — brevity.

Writing a standard letter on paper can turn out to be an event. The writer feels inclined to include additional facts about the family, the dog, and the latest news down at the Rotary Club. People who write business letters have a certain formality to follow that requires at least a couple of paragraphs.

One of the biggest benefits of prospecting by e-mail is that those who use it regularly respond to it rather quickly, whereas a paper-and-envelope letter that arrives in the mail may sit unopened or get opened and moved to a "To Do" pile rather than being handled right away. If your potential prospect isn't interested in your offering, she most likely will ignore your message. Not too professional, but it happens. If she is interested, you'll hear from her rather quickly and move from prospecting to the getting-an-appointment stage.

E-mail has freed people from these customs. E-mail is instantaneous and, unlike a letter, it is not an "event"; it's just an exchange of information. The writer can afford to be extremely brief without offending the recipient. You can send just the information without the burden of having to include any additional facts, figures, or friendly banter. This doesn't mean that you should be less professional when using e-mail over regular mail, just that brevity has become the accepted style for e-mail messages. Also, be certain to check your spelling before pushing that "send" button. Having a spell checker is an advantage that e-mail has over old-fashioned mail.

Before embarking on an e-mail campaign with the addresses you acquired through your search, be certain that your message is delivered in a conversational style, getting right to the point, identifying why and how you are contacting this person. Don't risk your message looking and sounding like "junk e-mail." A good resource for understanding how to proceed on a good e-mail campaign is at www.hitstosales.com.

If you don't feel like typing up that three-page memo and waiting for a response, try chatting online. Chatting on the Internet is similar to talking on a telephone, except that you create text using your computer keyboard. (Note that technology now permits voice communication via your computer, too.) Unlike e-mail, chat occurs in real time. You communicate with the other party or parties at the same time they communicate with you. You can chat with only one person, or you can join or create your own chat group or chat room. The transmission of information, from short notes to entire documents, is remarkably fast, but may not be secure.

You don't want to be known as a chatting bore any more than you would want to be a bore at an in-person social gathering. While chatting, remind yourself to give before you get. Offer a valuable tidbit of information to those you're chatting with about the topic of conversation. Ask a question the answer to which would lead you to believe or not believe they would be a good candidate for your product or service. If you think they are, don't try to sell them while chatting in a group. Suggest the two of you make a connection at a different time and place — phone, fax, or e-mail. Or, at the very least, suggest they visit your Web site for more information.

# Chapter 7
# Making Connections

You can't do it all alone. Regardless of your talent, the fire in your heart, the depth of your experience, or the level of your skills and abilities, at some point (lots of points, actually), you're going to need someone else (or, more likely, lots of people) to help you. Somewhere along the line you will need a friend, a contact, an introduction, someone to urge you on or hold you back, or just an understanding heart and mind to listen to your own heart and mind. That's where building a network of friends and associates who can help you comes in. If you don't already have a network, I strongly suggest that you start building one, and I mean today.

## What's a Network?

A network is simply a group of people helping each other get where each wants to go as quickly, as easily, and as efficiently as possible. In sales, a network is a powerful way to get to a qualified prospect in the least amount of time and with the least amount of difficulty.

Harvey Mackay, in his book *Dig Your Well Before You're Thirsty* (Bantam Doubleday Dell Publishing Group, Inc.), describes a network as ". . . connecting the dots between A and Z without having to go through C, D, E. . . W, X, and Y." He goes on to add that ". . . a network is geodesic rather than pyramidal . . . the interconnecting links can be lateral, vertical, or diagonal. Each link is no more important than the other. The whole structure is designed to minimize the distance between any one point and another. Each part reinforces the other."

Mackay offers a pretty good, concise description of the ideal network.

A serious, fully functioning network offers many benefits to its members, such as

- ✔ Increased access to products and services
- ✔ Moral support
- ✔ Introductions to new people
- ✔ Friendships
- ✔ The opportunity to be of service to others
- ✔ Help in reaching goals
- ✔ Knowledge
- ✔ Power
- ✔ Fun

But remember what Mackay said about all links being equal. Most people think of networking in terms of receiving something from others: leads, prospects, customers, guidance, hints, techniques, or moral support. Starting your networking by first considering others is important. Remember, success is determined by the service you provide others, not by what others do to further your own goals. Take some time to carefully examine what you have to offer someone in your network. What capabilities, skills, information, talents, connections, and words of wisdom can you provide that can help build someone else's career?

Consider all that you have to offer:

- ✔ Education
- ✔ Job experience
- ✔ Skills and talents
- ✔ People you know
- ✔ People you're going to know
- ✔ Resources (books, video- or audiotapes, Internet access)
- ✔ Club and organization connections

Almost everything is useful to someone. For example, the fact that you're on a first-name basis with the owner of the local service station, flower shop, or antique mall may be a valuable asset at some point to someone in your network. Think!

A real network is not a group of acquaintances who might be able to help you out someday. Instead, a network is an association of individuals who have a solid relationship with each other and a strong commitment to the success of everyone within that group. And you can start your network with the people you already know.

## Thinking we (not me)

A champion networker is always thinking in terms of the good of others: What can I do right now to help out someone within my network? You have to give up the "I'm the only one who can do this right" mentality and realize that your efforts at prospecting are significantly enhanced as a member of a team. Ask yourself these questions to see if you are a "me" or a "we" personality.

✔ Do I always have to be the expert at everything?

✔ How often do I rely on the skills and abilities of others?

✔ Should I, can I, rely more on the help of others?

✔ Am I a loner?

✔ How good am I at delegating real responsibility?

✔ Can I admit that I don't have the answer to a question?

✔ Am I a team player?

✔ Do I willingly accept the assistance of others or do I resent it?

✔ Do associates ask for my assistance or do they hold off?

If you think about it, you have an awful lot to offer others. Realize that others have an awful lot to offer you. Accepting the team concept doesn't mean giving up your individuality or freedom of action. On the contrary, it enhances them.

## *Getting Centered*

Take out a pencil and paper and try this exercise. Draw a circle in the middle of a sheet of paper and write your name within it. Then start drawing lines, like spokes of a wheel. Add circles and place the names of people you know within them. This is a physical description of your network. Include the names of anyone and everyone who could possibly help you achieve your goals. Really think about all the people you know at work, at church, your civic club, the Chamber of Commerce, or at other organizations where you are active. Consider also the many people you see regularly and who may be of service to you or to someone within your network. Now draw more spokes from those wheels to the names of people they know who may also help develop your career.

I think you'll be surprised at the depth of support out there. Notice, too, that while you are smack-dab in the center of your own network you are at the same time a spoke on someone else's network. Teamwork! That's how you keep the wheels of progress turning.

---

## Meeting 'n' greeting

It's true that you only get one chance at a first impression. That's not to say that you can't overcome a botched first impression, but life is sure easier when you do it right the first time. Chapter 11 has some great suggestions on how to make sure your first impression remains a good impression.

---

How do you start networking? Here are four methods:

- ✔ **Become a copycat.** I mean this in the sense of a sincere study and emulation of a talented and skilled individual who is successful at networking. Observe how this person handles herself and then carry on the same way. If you're lucky, and if you pursue the matter properly, this individual may even take you under his or her wing and become a mentor. Imitation really is the sincerest form of flattery, and it isn't always a negative trait.

- ✔ **Get involved with organizations that provide opportunities to meet and interact with people and that will encourage you to come out of your fear-of-networking shell.** I mention Toastmasters more than once in this book because I firmly believe in that organization's proven capability to foster self-confidence, public speaking skill, and positive interaction among individuals. Check 'em out.

- ✔ **Play the part.** Shakespeare wrote, "All the world's a stage and all the men and women merely players." So why not get into the act by acting?

Film actor Nicolas Cage told an interviewer the story of how he discovered that his destiny was to become a performer.

When Nicolas was a kid riding the school bus, the school bully repeatedly picked on him. Frightened, but tired of the constant harassment, he one day donned cowboy boots, a cowboy hat, and dark sunglasses. He entered the bus not as Nicolas, but as Nicolas's cousin from the Wild West. He approached the bully and basically threatened to "punch out his lights" if he didn't leave his "cousin Nick" alone. For whatever reason (fear, intimidation, appreciation of a good scheme) the ruse worked. The bully left Nicolas alone, and an actor was born.

My point is this: Begin acting the role of a confident "networker," and before you realize it, a transformation will take place, and you will be a networker.

✔ **Become an interested introvert rather than an interesting extrovert.** Become interested in other people. Ask them questions about their interests, their concerns, their ideas. They will open up, and, before you know it, you'll have a group of new friends and acquaintances and a start on your network. Develop a sense of what is a comfortable question for the other party. Always start on light, noncontroversial topics and watch their body language responses to them.

Learn to recognize their slight resistance to a question they may deem nosy. An interested question may be, "Where did you get that lovely coat?" A nosy question would be, "And how much did you pay for it?"

## Building Your Network

Will Rogers used to say, "I never met a man I didn't like." That's a good way to approach life and a great way to approach networking. Everyone is a prospect; everyone can become a member of your network.

But while a network is not a formal organization with a written charter, bylaws, and weekend retreats in the islands, your network is a powerful tool and an important part of your career. So you want people who can help you, and — equally important — people you can help. Where will you find them? Here are two categories you should think about:

✔ **The obvious choices.** Certainly, if the corporate head of marketing at one of your city's largest companies asks you to golf, go. If you have the opportunity to serve on a service club committee with one of the prominent bankers in town, take it. Cultivate relationships with anyone who is in a position to know others in the business community. If you want to roll with the movers and the shakers, you have to be invited into their club.

✔ **The not-so-obvious choices.** If you are a white-collar worker, don't limit your network just to other white-collar workers. You never know who may be in a position to assist you. The auto mechanic may service the vehicle of someone you need to know or, better yet, he may be the good fellow's cousin. The receptionist or telephone operator can probably help you more than all the vice presidents in that tall building downtown.

Keep in mind that you don't look at the people you meet as people you can use. Rather, you look at them as valuable resources and, equally important, as people who you can help.

No matter how tempting or how easy staying close to home is, network with at least a few people outside your organization. Why? Getting important information from outside sources can be easier than getting that information from within your own organization. Many companies have a very regimented organizational chart that prohibits employee or manager A from talking to coworker G without first going through Mr. B, Mrs. C, Ms. D, and those two guys E and F over in accounting. Important news or views creep along this path at a frustratingly slow rate, especially if Mrs. C is on vacation or out reviewing the troops in Amsterdam. That's why your network is so valuable. If you have news for someone in the group, you just pick up the phone and call direct. The same happens to you. Instead of waiting for Mrs. C to return with her reports, memos, and wooden shoes, you get "just the facts, ma'am," from your friendly neighborhood network.

# Professional resources

You may be surprised at the number of resources available to someone new in business. Following is a sampling of the many sources that cater to small businesses and individuals.

✔ **Service Corps Of Retired Executives.** This government program, also called S.C.O.R.E., consists of retired or semiretired executives who donate their experience to help people and companies just starting out. Some of these executives may not be up to speed on the latest high-tech gizmo or the latest market trends (although some may really surprise you), but their advice on prospecting and people skills can prove invaluable. You can find S.C.O.R.E. in most midsize and major cities.

✔ **Sales and Marketing Executives.** This national business support group is an excellent source for a business *mentor,* an experienced businessperson in your field who agrees to be Merlin to your King Arthur, to provide advice and guidance through the battles and court intrigues of modern business. You can find Sales and Marketing Executives in most major cities.

✔ **The Small Business Administration.** This government agency is another resource worth exploring. It offers many free booklets on the various aspects of being in business.

✔ **Your organization's management.** Your organization may

assign an experienced veteran to show you the ropes. If your organization doesn't have such a program, ask. Explain that you want to be the absolute best you can be and that a short apprenticeship under an experienced instructor will benefit you and the company's bottom line. Phrased carefully, using the right words at the right time, you may find yourself an eager student under the guidance of an experienced (and flattered) professor.

✔ **A professional advertising, marketing, or public relations firm** can handle your prospecting if you have your own business and the financial strength. These companies work for an agreed fee, for a commission that is a percentage of the additional business it generates, or for a combination of the two. Most of these companies want long-term clients, but many of them are willing to take on short-term projects. You can also turn to professionals in mass media advertising such as radio, TV, or newspapers; targeted media such as direct mail or cable TV; and Internet marketing.

✔ **Contact a professor of marketing or graphic design at a local college or business school.** Some professors take on businesses as case studies for their students to get some experience. They may build you a complete marketing strategy or design materials for you as classwork. You may receive this service at no charge or for making a small donation to the school.

✔ **Graphic artist shops and freelance advertising professionals.** You can also deal directly with individual advertising or news media. Some copy shops and printers offer graphic design services at minimal fees if you guarantee to run your print job with them. Check out the people who work at your local copy shop. Some may be working their way through design school or toward a marketing degree in college and have some great ideas for you.

Research any individual or company carefully before you invest your time, dollars, and perhaps your future. Ask for references and check them out. You never know — the glowing tribute you receive may be from an investor in the agency, a relative, close friend, or someone who owes the company a favor.

When dealing with professionals in these fields always remember to keep your mind focused on your goals — solid gold prospects. Seeing your picture on television during your favorite prime-time serial can be exciting. However, if you're selling high-dollar boats, a direct-mail piece to the local yacht club membership list will probably net you a greater return on your investment.

# Working with Your Network

A network is no good unless you work it — no good to you and no good to anyone else in the group. Treat a network as you would an expensive, finely crafted instrument. Here are a few tips to help you make sure you and your associates are getting the most out of your association.

## Stay in touch

Obviously, pass along any valuable information to the appropriate member or members. Such information can be anything from a good lead, the fact that a new business is moving in or out of town, a warning about a shady member of the business community, encouragement about an upcoming presentation, or "Hey, what you do is totally your business, but I thought you ought to know. . . ."

Look for other ways to keep in touch just to make sure the lines of communication remain wide open and flowing. A member can easily feel neglected or even just fade away from the group. You can stay in touch in a hundred ways. Here are just a few idea-starters:

- ✔ Make a note of important dates such as birthdays or business or personal anniversaries and drop a card in the mail.

- ✔ Keep an eye out for appearances in the newspaper or magazines; clip and send the article with congratulations and a friendly comment. If you see an item in the paper or a magazine of interest to a member of the network, clip or copy it and drop it in the mail.

- ✔ When passing through a contact's town (come on, you don't think networks are limited to your hometown, do you?), see if you can arrange a breakfast, lunch, or dinner, or at least make a call from the airport.

- ✔ Use e-mail to stay in touch, and don't forget to pick up the phone just to say "Hi."

These contacts don't have to be lengthy or take on the appearance of an obligation; in fact, spontaneity often makes the contact more enjoyable. The main thing is to make contact and to keep on making contact.

Make a point of calling or visiting people you normally don't approach, especially a contact you haven't been keeping in touch with. Sometimes we're too shy or even embarrassed to contact the very people we need to contact the most. Go ahead. Pick up the phone, or better still, go pop by.

# Listen up!

Effective communication is a two-way street. When you're communicating with people in your network, make sure you really understand what the other person is saying. Repeat what she's saying if you have to, just to make sure you got it right. "If I'm hearing you correctly, you mean. . . ." You can't help someone out and she can't help you if neither party really understands the situation and the need.

## *Ask for help*

If you've kept the lines of communication open, don't hesitate a second to seek the support you need. You won't be considered a burden. Quite the contrary: People want to help other people. Asking for assistance helps you ease down the road of success and helps reinforce the fact that when the time comes, you'll be there to help the other party.

When you ask for help, keep two things in mind:

- **Say what you really mean.** Phrase your request in words that allow the other party to understand your real needs. "We've just added a new line of whatchamacallits. Who do you know that may need a new one?" That's a lot more effective than "Got any prospects for me?"

- **Be polite.** "I need you to help me get some prospects" borders on rudeness even if you don't mean to be so impolite. "I'm in need of a little help here and was wondering if you can spare a few moments of your time" is a better, more sincere way of opening the conversation.

Here's an example:

| | |
|---|---|
| You: | Sally, I could really use your help. |
| Them: | What type of help are you looking for, Joe? |
| You: | Our company is adding a new line that will serve larger businesses than our current line. I need to come up with some mid- to large-sized |

*(continued)*

*(continued)*

|        |                                                                                                                                                                       |
| ------ | --------------------------------------------------------------------------------------------------------------------------------------------------------------------- |
|        | businesses that might need these industrial widgets. Does anyone come to your mind?                                                                                    |
| Them:  | Hmm. Jobco is one of your clients now, aren't they?                                                                                                                    |
| You:   | Yes, they're not large enough for this product, though.                                                                                                                |
| Them:  | I know, but their parent company is CareerCo and their head of purchasing is on my husband's softball team. Let me do some checking on that lead for you.              |
| You:   | Thanks, Sally. That's great. I'd be happy to talk with your husband, too, to get some background before I make a call at CareerCo.                                     |
| Them:  | Let me see what I can arrange.                                                                                                                                         |

## Volunteer to help

Become known for the excellence of your service. Believe me, people talk and your career is most definitely influenced by word-of-mouth advertising. People talk about your level of service, be it good or bad. When you get a reputation for excellent service, people want to work with you. They want to introduce you to others who have need for excellent service, so they recommend you, your product, or service.

Be aggressive about providing prospects, information and service to the members of your network. Don't just pass along information that happens to come your way. Go out of your way to find ways to support your network. Don't wait for someone to ask for your help. Make a point of contacting the members of your network to see if you can be of service.

Even if there's no particular need at the moment, they'll certainly appreciate the thought and you will have further cemented a valuable relationship.

## Follow up

When you get a referral prospect, act immediately. Return phone calls, provide requested information, be on time, and deliver on your promises.

One other thing: Never forget to say "thanks" for any information passed down the pipeline. That one little word is the least-expensive, easiest-to-give, and most-neglected form of compensation on the entire planet. Captain Kangaroo was right on target when he said, *"Thank you* is a magic phrase!"

## Maintain your focus

A network is a living entity. Once or twice a year, evaluate the effectiveness of the people in your group to see if you need to add more support in a particular area. If you're all give and you're getting nothing back, you need to correct the situation or find a new network. But the opposite is also true, so honestly evaluate your own effectiveness to the other group members too.

When you do your network evaluations, also go through your list to make sure that it's up to date, that all addresses are current, and that important information is added. You can really be embarrassed and do great damage to your network by asking how little Abby is doing in grade school when she's just graduated college and is getting married next month. Ouch!

## Make networking an integral part of your lifestyle

Don't think of networking as an activity to be scheduled. "Today I will network between noon and 5:00 p.m." A champion at prospecting realizes that virtually every waking moment can offer an opportunity to use, build, or assist the network.

Remember the 3-foot rule: Approach anyone within 3 feet of you. Never hesitate to start a friendly conversation. It can lead to a prospect, a sale, or even a new and valuable member of the network.

By making your network more successful, you make yourself more successful. As the individuals within the network grow, succeed, and prosper, your range of contacts increases. Your connections with successful people connect you with an ever-growing circle of more successful people. The depth of your support group increases, as does your access to more and more powerful resources. All of this leads directly to more and more prospects.

# Part III
# Making
# the Contact

"I sell subscriptions to a heavy metal magazine, and believe me – it's not easy getting sales prospects in a mosh pit."

# In this part . . .

**T**hese chapters help you strategize and plan a
systematic approach to prospecting a particular market. I include how to get appointments
with prospects and how to get them involved
with your product so that they can truly consider its value to them. I discuss in detail the
benefits of your product or service to your
prospects and how you can help them realize
those benefits quickly.

# Chapter 8
# Getting Prospects Involved

*W*hen you approach people with your product, service, or idea, you must realize that they probably aren't looking for you, your product, or your idea. In fact, they may not know that you exist. How's that for a humbling realization? For that fact alone, you must approach prospects with the intention of finding out something about them, such as their needs, before you tell them anything about yourself and your offering. You have to be smarter than the average bear to be a champion prospector.

## No One Cares What You Sell

That statement is true. Prospects care only about how your product can solve their challenges. That's all. Those challenges can be a whole host of concerns beyond price and productivity.

Champion salespeople see things from their prospects' eyes. These salespeople know their products offer many features and benefits, but talk only about the benefits the customers really want to own. I've seen salespeople do it right and I've seen them do it wrong over the years. Real professionals always, always act according to a very simple rule:

*Don't sell what you want to sell; sell what customers want to own.*

I teach and lecture all over the world and am often involved in role-playing situations in which students and attendees act out realistic sales presentations. I am constantly amazed at the times I witness supposedly experienced salespeople rush into presentations by rattling off a series of features that may or may not be important to their prospects.

Consider these typical contact examples:

> **Them:** Hello, Mr. Prospect speaking.
>
> **You** Mr. Prospect, our new single-plate belt sander allows you to run more particleboard through your units at a higher rate of speed, thereby increasing your productivity within a single shift.

**Analysis:**

Naturally, Mr. Prospect wants higher productivity, but what if he is more concerned with producing a particleboard that requires only one coat of paint? Perhaps he is losing business to a competitor who produces a surface that does a better job accepting and holding paint or varnish. Suppose he has just lost a major order because of surface scratches due to faulty sanding belts. Could the quality of the surface you can help him produce supersede all other concerns at the moment?

> **Them:** Hello, Mr. Prospect speaking.
>
> **You:** Mr. Prospect, I'd like to introduce our new line of home roofing products that offer substantial savings over all competitive brands without sacrificing quality or, might I add, beauty.

**Analysis:**

Mr. Prospect, just like everyone else in the construction business, is terribly concerned with holding down costs while making sure that his customers always have roofs over their heads. However, what if a series of roofs that he installed begins peeling years before scheduled replacements because his current supplier cut back on quality? Suppose that Mr. Prospect has contracts to build half a dozen more houses (all need roofing materials, of course) and he's stuck with a supply of materials he knows he can't use.

Wouldn't the fact that your roofing materials were subjected to years of field tests in the deserts of western Arizona provide more immediate relief for his massive construction headache? Perhaps the fact that your company can deliver whatever amount of materials he needs wherever he needs them today may supersede his concern for the bottom dollar.

> **Them:**     Hello, Mr. Prospect speaking.
>
> **You:**     Mr. Prospect, my restaurant-grade food-processing unit utilizes a new, high-grade metal that lasts considerably longer, thus reducing the need for frequent blade replacement. You get higher productivity from a single unit at what amounts to a, heh-heh, cut in costs.

**Analysis:**

The owner of the restaurant chain could probably use reliable food-processing blades that require less frequent replacement and that would maintain his quality at a lower cost. But suppose many of his outlets hire undereducated workers as part of a companywide community outreach program. His real desire may be to have equipment that people can easily learn to use, is simple to operate, easy to clean, and simple to repair with basic tools. Could it be that the altruistic owner is more concerned with saving fingers than a few extra dollars? He also may be concerned about higher insurance premiums.

Okay, admittedly these three case studies are brief, but what was wrong with each presentation? All prospects and customers want to save money and deliver better products or services, *but that's not always what motivates them to buy.* They all have amazing, complex, and ever-changing series of challenges. Your product or service may offer the best solution to the specific challenge at hand, but you cannot afford to go into a call or presentation with a wrong set of assumptions. You can't sell the right product with the wrong approach.

Salespeople blow potential sales because they don't give potential customers what they want to own.

Whether you have a few moments on the telephone or a more extended period of time in an office, you need to research your prospects' concerns and start filling your memory banks with the ways your product can solve them.

All those questions and answers, all the interpreting and evaluating, and all the time and energy you invest help you answer this question: "What does this prospect really want to own?"

## TV or not TV

I met a director of television commercials who gave me an interesting illustration of why finding out what a buyer really wants to buy is so important. The director approached the owner of a large, well-known, regional western clothing goods store to produce the man's new series of commercials. They reached an agreement, an investment, and a time frame.

The director asked the owner whether he wanted sales commercials or image commercials. His client said that he wanted image spots. "Because sales volume wasn't our goal, we produced two excellent spots to help build his image over the long term," said the director. "One was a very funny urban cowboy spot, and the other was a beautiful fantasy with a beautiful model in elegant western clothing. They were excellent in every respect."

The director never got another job from that client again.

"We didn't sell a @#$@#% pair of blue jeans off either one of those spots," said the owner.

"It's my fault," said the director. "I just didn't take the time to find out what he really wanted."

As it turned out, the client really did want sales and had the misconception that image spots would do that for him. The director assumed the client understood the difference between the two types of commercials. Had the director discussed the difference in greater detail at the beginning of the relationship, he could have discovered what the client *really* wanted — sales!

Never assume your client knows how to get what she wants. You are the expert she has come to for advice. Do your job!

## *Two Hurdles for Champions*

Hey, nobody said prospecting was going to be easy! And you have two high, difficult hurdles to jump on your way to becoming a champion:

   ✔ **Take yourself out of the picture every time you meet with a prospect or client.** Why you use your product or how you would use your product if you were one of your customers means very little or nothing to potential clients. You sell the darn thing; you had better be using or recommending it, but they don't really care. Prospects aren't looking for your personal endorsement. They want the hard facts and figures on how your product can solve their challenges.

✔ **Get the dollar signs out of your eyes.** Always put your customers' needs ahead of your own natural desire for wealth. People who have experience with animals in the wild say that the critters can "smell fear." The same holds true with people in business. Customers can "smell" greed. If they see even the slightest hint of selfishness in your eyes, if they sense even the tiniest amount of desperation in your voice, you have planted a seed of doubt in fertile soil. Any solid rapport you may have felt quickly fades away. The good relationship you have so carefully built soon begins to sour, and the genuine interest in your product turns into a series of rather obvious glances at wristwatches.

Most salespeople have trouble clearing these two hurdles because they have to change the way they think about their profession and their customers in order to do it. You can't run down to the store for a book or tape with a 1-2-3 step plan. You can't buy it like a suit or a cellular phone, and you can't inherit it from a retiring coworker. You have to make it happen on your own, inside your own head.

As an exercise, put yourself in one of your prospect's shoes. Before trying this, make sure you know all you can about your prospect's company, its corporate history, its product line, possible plans for the future, and the personality of its management staff and your contact. Imagine that the salesperson (you) has just made a presentation, now ask your prospect (you, again) a series of questions:

✔ What will this product or service do to solve my immediate crisis?

✔ What will it do for the company in the long run?

✔ Will it increase profitability?

✔ Will it enhance productivity?

✔ Are any downsides balanced by equal or better upsides?

✔ What's in it for me?

That last bullet is always important. Sometimes you may work with an executive who doesn't have the power to give that ultimate "yes" and who must report to higher-ups for a final okay on making a purchase. By recommending to go with your company, this person may put his job on the line. In reality, this concern may outweigh all others. Even decision makers have to report to management staffs, presidents, or boards of directors. While you're wearing those prospect's shoes ask yourself, what will the big guns think of me personally if I recommend/purchase this product or service?

If you have any doubt about whether or not your product will do what the client needs, handle those doubts before the client recommends it to the higher-ups. If they go with your product and it's a poor choice, the client could lose his job over it. If you lose, you lose not only a sale, but your reputation with that client. And you can rest assured that the client will tell others about your poor performance and could cost you a lot of business overall. Don't take risks like that!

Play this little game seriously, and if you can't answer all the questions to the prospect's benefit, go back and do some more homework.

# What Do They Want from Me?

I've read surveys and the summaries of many surveys conducted to find out what businesses really want from suppliers and representatives of their suppliers. Price is often at or near the bottom of their concerns. Here, in no particular order, is a short-list of what your prospects want from you:

- To be there when needed
- Prompt return of phone calls
- Timely response
- Honesty
- Product knowledge
- Industry and market knowledge
- Sincerity
- A commitment to long-term service
- Consistent performance
- Interest in their success with the product or service
- Quality products at a fair investment

You notice there's nothing about being a technical wizard about the intricate workings of your Electro-Gizmo Deluxe. You don't see "sparkling personality" or "knows how to tell a good joke" either. Not everyone can tell a good joke, and few of us can ever take apart a gizmo. Every one of us, however, can return a phone call. That goes for the rest of the list, too.

---

## Staying the course

When champions call prospects or customers, the champions want to

✔ Maintain control

✔ Be professionals

As the saying goes, that ain't easy, folks. Your knowledge of how your product can meet the needs of your prospects — give them what they really need — can allow you to maintain control of the presentation. As prospects express concerns, you can knock 'em down directly by addressing those concerns.

Prospecting, providing customer service, and following up are intense enterprises. The outcome of any given situation is often frustrating, aggravating, and discouraging. Real champions take situations as they come, realize that victories are around the corner, and no matter what happens, act with true professional behavior at all times.

---

# *Interactivity Is the Key*

You must interact with prospects and clients when you meet with them. Whether you meet prospects in face-to-face encounters, over telephone calls, through the Internet, or by letters, you must get prospects involved.

Interact with prospects by engaging all their five senses. Find ways to use the senses to enrich your presentations, and you will enrich the lives of your prospects and your own, too.

The five senses are

    ✔ Seeing

    ✔ Hearing

    ✔ Touching

    ✔ Smelling

    ✔ Tasting

Seeing, hearing, and touching are generally considered the top three ways people experience the world, usually in that order. Everybody uses all five senses in varying degrees, but for most people one sense dominates all others. Make note of that. People don't choose to be seers or hearers. They're born that way, and that's the way they respond to the world throughout their lives. That's also how they respond to you.

The more you discover about the relative order of importance of the five senses, particularly if you can discover prospects' dominant ones, the better you can communicate with prospects.

You may be able to discover which sense dominates a prospect by paying careful attention to the way your prospect describes things. If the prospect talks in visual terms and says things, such as, "Let's take a look" or "Let's see what you've got," stress visuals in your presentation. If you notice that the prospect talks about color, clarity, brightness, or darkness, then you can pretty well assume that your prospect is focused visually. If you hear descriptions of music, the sound of the wind, the rustling of leaves, or the joyful laughter of a child, then you are dealing with a listener. The phrase "I hear what you are saying" is a clear and precise indicator that you have a listener on your hands. Other prospects speak of the world in terms of touching, smelling, or tasting. "I have a feel for that," or "My last car was a stinker," or "I really wanted a taste of that deal" can tell you which senses are most important.

Listen for the subtle clues about which sense dominates your prospect, and then talk in terms your prospect understands best and responds to.

## *Taking a look-see*

People whose world view is dominated by sight are those who create pictures in their minds and then make them come true. If you ever spend any time around professional athletes, you learn the power of visualization. Before a golf match or a basketball game, many players take time to play the round or the game mentally. They visualize making the putt or the long basket. When the time arrives in the real world, the action is half-done already. The action is mind-accomplished.

People who respond to the world visually have great memories for the way things look. They can call up the image of a golden sunrise, the color of a field of flowers, or the shape of that spot of gravy on your suit coat. When working with these folks, be conscious that they judge you primarily in terms of how things look. A wrinkled suit, improper makeup, a gaudy presentation packet, or sloppy visual aids make a far greater impression than the golden, pear-shaped sounds of your presentation voice.

Because these people view the world in pictures, you should present your product or service in visual terms. The more effectively you can do this, the better your prospects can start building pleasant images within their own minds. The more vivid, eye-appealing word pictures you create, the easier it is to bring those prospects to the point where they decide they'd like to see your product serving their needs.

## Hearing is believing

Some people get their "view" of the world by listening. They get the primary information for decision making by listening. Look for key words and phrases related to hearing.

- ✔ "That sounds about right."
- ✔ "I hear what you're saying."
- ✔ "Please, tell me about. . . ."

## The eyes are the window to the sale

Several years ago, human behaviorists Richard Bandler and John Grinder studied eye-movement responses of people dominated by the different senses.

Bandler and Grinder found that about 35 percent of the people studied were visually oriented and that distinct relationships exist between the way people think and they way the move their eyes.

The people who see the world do three things with their eyes that give you clues to what they are thinking.

- ✔ When people think about the future, they move their eyes up and to their right. They may be picturing the looks of admiration on their neighbors' faces when their neighbors see their new swimming pool, the excitement as the kids take their first splash, and the pleasant weekends with friends and family at barbecue and swim parties.

- ✔ When people think about the past, they move their eyes up and to their left. They may be reliving a sweltering summer when it was just impossible to enjoy their backyard or even get out of the house, the event that may have created the desire for a pool in the first place.

- ✔ When people's eyes seem to glaze over or become unfocused, they are collecting their thoughts, sorting out the images in their mind, and organizing the pictures in a mental slide show. If you see prospects do this, don't worry that you've lost your audience. On the contrary, you may have just gotten them to focus their attention exactly where you want it, on the benefits of your product or service.

If you'd like to read more in depth about the subject, try the audiotape *Sales Magic*, by Kerry L. Johnson (published by Simon & Schuster).

When you realize you're dealing with someone who interprets the world through sound, bring sound into your presentation. If you sell swimming pools, describe the laughter of the kids and the splash of the water as they cannonball in. Create a mental audio picture of the neighbors complimenting them on the new pool and all the fine days and evenings of pleasant, intelligent conversation they'll enjoy in the new environment.

You'll find it easier to use the telephone with these folks than with most others because they like to talk. They enjoy the sound of conversation and respond well to it. Often, they say things like, "No need to get together, just call me."

Some of these people also often talk to themselves. No, I don't mean crazy old Ernie down on the street corner. I mean the intelligent prospects who seem to mumble and mutter a lot. They're not absentminded; they just enjoy sound. Have you ever encountered someone who "speaks" to his automobile? Mechanical devices? The air?

- ✔ "Come on, baby, don't go out on me now."
- ✔ "All right, we're going to cut this sheet metal just so, aren't we?"
- ✔ "World, what are you doing to me?"

People who hear the world also do things with their eyes that indicate what they are thinking about.

- ✔ When these folks move their eyes to their right, they're thinking about the future, but in terms of sound. They're hearing the kids laughing and making big splashes.
- ✔ When they look to their left, they're hearing "images" from the past.
- ✔ When they look down and to the left, they're organizing sound bites into coherent patterns for analysis and decision making. Again, if you see prospects doing this, you may not have lost them; they may be lost in thought about using your product or service. Back off your presentation and allow them time to organize their thoughts before you continue.

## *Feels right to me*

People who get their primary information about the world through touching make buying decisions based on how they feel, and those decisions are often made quickly. How they feel about you or a given situation is more important than how you look or how the presentation sounds.

In meetings they will most surely shake your hand, but they may also pat you on the shoulder, grab your biceps to emphasize a point, or even thump your chest with a pointed index finger. This is how they interact with other human beings. They are not hesitant at all about reaching out and touching someone.

Again, look for clues and cues in their speech patterns.

- ✔ "Why don't we touch base next week?"
- ✔ "I've got a good feeling about this."
- ✔ "I'm under a lot of pressure here."
- ✔ "We'll hit a home run with this one."
- ✔ "I'm having a hard time grasping your point."

If you are a "touchy-feely" type, please note that physical contact in the workplace is a major source of litigation. One person's basic and innocent need for contact is another person's abuse of power or position. Be aware and be careful. Legal action for harassment will not build the reputation you want.

When people who assess their environments through feeling look down to the right and pause, they aren't ignoring you. They aren't avoiding eye contact or trying to hide something. It's just what they do when they're trying to organize their thoughts. As with the other eye movements that indicate thought, give prospects time to get their feelings in order.

## Taste the smell of success

A much smaller percentage of the population makes a connection with their environment through tasting or smelling, but you certainly run into some of them during your prospecting efforts, so you had better know how to sniff them out.

Again, look to your prospects for key words that indicate that they are dominated by their senses of taste.

- ✔ "I like a little spice in my life."
- ✔ "We can't go on an empty stomach."
- ✔ "I tell you I really relished the moment."

People oriented toward smells give other clues:

- ✔ "The deal just didn't smell right to me."
- ✔ "We knew we'd caught the scent of a good thing."
- ✔ "Before committing I thought I'd better nose around a little."

How do you sell a swimming pool with examples of taste? You can't very well rub your tummy and describe biting into a chlorine tablet. Yum-yum-yuck! Think about it, though, and I bet you can come up with a number of effective ways to bring taste into your presentation.

> Imagine, Mr. and Mrs. Prospect, the taste of all those fat, juicy hamburgers you'll be grilling at those neighborhood get-togethers around the new pool. Or the cakes and pies the neighbors bring over.

or

> Just think about that cold lemonade on a hot Saturday afternoon as you float away your tensions in that comfortable, cool blue water.

or

> I can just taste the fresh fruit in that homemade ice cream you make for your kid's birthday pool party.

## Good Sense Means Using All of Them

After you find and implement your prospects' dominant senses in your presentations, don't neglect the other four. If your prospect is visually oriented, paint beautiful word pictures throughout the meeting, but also sprinkle the conversation with sights and sounds, tastes and smells. Bring everything into play that you can, and use every powerful image you think appropriate.

The same image, the child cannonballing into the swimming pool, for example, can engage more than one sense. You may talk about the play of light on sparkling drops of water for visually oriented people. You can colorfully describe a child giggling and the big "whoosh" when she hits the water when speaking with people motivated by hearing. Try a word picture of the cold splash of water on a hot day with the touching/feeling people.

Champions learn how to use word pictures that engage all or as many of the senses as possible. Doing so helps to create a more complete image in their prospects' minds; it helps to make the images far more real.

Following is a sample of how the swimming pool presentation can develop for a visually focused prospect:

CHAMPION STRATEGY #1

| | |
|---|---|
| **Them:** | Can we get a colored pool or just the white plaster look? |
| **You:** | We have nearly 50 colors for you to choose from — soft blues, earthy browns, ocean greens, and a lot more. |
| **Them:** | I like blue. |
| **You:** | We offer ten shades of blue, plus, with the package you are looking at, you get tile edge at no extra cost. Most people choose a darker accent. |
| **Them:** | Wonderful! |
| **You:** | Just wait till you hear the giggles of those kids of yours splashing in the sun on Sunday afternoon. I suppose you'll have a lot of friends over, too. |
| **Them:** | We entertain a lot. |
| **You:** | There's nothing like sharing good conversation and a cold drink around the pool with friends and family. That's for sure. Why, I can almost smell those thick, marinated steaks grilling now. Wouldn't you agree that's a pleasant image? |
| **Them:** | Sure is. |
| **You:** | Can't you just picture yourselves on a cool evening, surrounded by the warm conversation of close friends? |

Well, you get the picture — and the feel, the sound, taste, and smell — and so will your prospects.

Take advantage of the five senses. Organize your presentation like a fine meal based on a delicious main course and wonderfully spiced up with side dishes and dessert. You can paint a much more powerful, emotional, and lovely picture using five brilliant senses than you can using only one.

(What did you think of the meal analogy in the previous paragraph? Could you see that it was a tasty image, or did it just smell and end up rubbing you the wrong way?)

# Chapter 9

# Choose Your Verbal Weapons Carefully

........................................................................

## In This Chapter

▶ Learning from the great conversationalist

▶ Working a room

▶ Avoiding Tom's Nasty Words

▶ Coloring the picture

▶ Asking questions that fly, not die

▶ Using Tom's questioning techniques

........................................................................

*D*ale Carnegie was widely regarded as a great conversationalist. People raved about the pleasurable experience of talking with this great man.

Mr. Carnegie had a secret: He asked people questions and then shut up and listened. He made himself an interested introvert rather than an interesting extrovert. I know you've heard, and many of you probably believe, that salespeople should be bubbly fountains of interesting talk and dazzle their prospects with their knowledge, experience, and brilliant wit. Folks, in prospecting and sales, it's just the opposite. The last thing in the world you want to be is an interesting extrovert. Smart salespeople never try to dominate conversations; rather, they try to draw out the people whom they talk with. You do that by becoming an interested introvert. You want to know what your prospects have to say because that's how you find out how you can serve their needs.

When prospecting, even the shyest person easily can become a great conversationalist by using Carnegie's proven technique. Don't try to overcome the prospect with your funniest joke, your product knowledge, your insights, or news about what's really going on down at city hall. Let prospects be the stars. Make your prospects feel important. (Because they are.) Become a quiet asker of questions. Draw out your prospects, and you (yes, even you shy folks) can become a great conversationalist. Carnegie's secret was to make the other person his main focus. People loved it because people love being the center of attention. People still love it.

# How to Work a Room Like a Champion

Informal networking at business or civic gatherings is a terrific way to use your abilities as a great conversationalist and to prospect. The key word here is *informal*. A lot of people object to the typical "talking salesperson" trying to push his product or service to people who aren't that interested. Many a potential sale has been scuttled by an overeager, pushy sales presentation at the wrong moment. In informal settings, you should merely strive to obtain enough information to determine whether a follow-up contact is appropriate and then to discover the best way to follow up with the prospect.

The same guidelines apply to social gatherings as well. Although talking business at your niece's wedding may not be good form, many good prospects for your business can be at the wedding. Don't just let them slip away. Be casual about what you do. If you think someone may be a good prospect, ask someone else who knows him to introduce you. Be sure to chat about the lovely couple and fun group of people attending, and then ask the other person what he does for a living. It doesn't matter if you already know. By asking, you're sort of obligating them to ask you the same question, thus opening that small window of opportunity you were hoping for.

Working a room can be broken down into six very basic, very effective steps:

- ✔ Prepare
- ✔ Greet
- ✔ Qualify
- ✔ Present
- ✔ Call for action
- ✔ Follow up

If you follow each of these steps, you'll be pleasantly surprised (perhaps amazed) at how much real prospecting you can do in an informal setting.

## Prepare for prospecting

You need to take an "M&M" approach — mental and material — when preparing to prospect. First, you need to have the right attitude. You must realize that you have a responsibility to create, maintain, and nurture a persuasive environment for you and your prospect. Whether on the telephone, door-to-door, or in an informal group, bring to the session all your energy, enthusiasm, curiosity, and interest. Be casual and nonthreatening in your appearance, manner, and language, but be genuinely interested in the other person. You have to create an environment that proves to prospects that they really are important and that you want to serve their needs.

But you also need some simple props. Always bring along a handful of your business cards. This may seem to be a no-brainer, but how many times have you seen salespeople desperately fumbling through pockets, purses, and wallets only to produce coffee-stained, half-torn cards with out-of-date addresses or phone numbers? How many times have you been that person?

## Take your business card seriously

Your business card is an advertisement for you, your company, and your company's products and services. Whenever someone receives a card, she immediately make a conscious decision as to whether or not the card is worth keeping. If she doesn't find a reason, the card can get either lost or tossed. Lynella Grant, author of *The Business Card Book*, has some tips on creating cards that prospects will choose to keep.

Avoid these blunders:

- ✔ Standard, prepackaged selections

- ✔ Cheap stock; basic, tacky paper

- ✔ Too much information packed on the card

- ✔ Type that's too small to read and/ or is in too many typefaces

- ✔ Grubby or marked-up cards

- ✔ Missing information (like e-mail or Web sites, new phone number, and so on)

Add these for spice:

- ✔ Simple humor or a witty or inspirational thought

- ✔ Eye-catching visuals — puzzles, illusions, images that challenge

- ✔ Useful information — data, formulas, maps, conversion charts

- ✔ Tactile sense — unusual embossing or texture of paper

- ✔ A miniature of your product as your card, if appropriate

- ✔ Uniqueness — something that sets you apart in your industry

Your visual identity is a vital business asset. Develop one that attracts those you want to serve, then display that identity with flair.

When working a room like a champion, always bring a pocket calendar to write down any appointments you make. In fact, add *pockets* to your list of valuable business tools. If you don't have a calendar with a notepad, bring some index cards so that you can jot down any important information you may need later. Be discreet with your jottings. You don't want to look a like a spy or someone mapping out a plan of imminent attack.

When asked the secret of success, Benjamin Franklin replied, "Plow deep while others sleep," meaning that a successful person works while others do not. If you're going to attend one of these functions, get all you can out of the experience. Arrive early, work the room, and leave late.

## Meet 'n' greet

Say hello and converse with people at informal meetings. Make sure to get out there and mingle with people you've never met. That's where the meat of prospects are. Don't be at all shy about introducing yourself to strangers. If a group is engaged in conversation, simply stand nearby and wait for an opportunity to enter. At some lull in the conversation, someone may make eye contact and acknowledge you. Step up and politely introduce yourself. You're not intruding; most people attend such gatherings to meet other people.

Make sure that you are casual early on. Talk about nonthreatening subjects such as the reason for the meeting, the weather, or a subject of common, local interest. Have a list of ice-breakers, good opening questions, already prepared: Where are you from? How did you hear about this group or meeting? Who else do you know? Could you introduce me? Of course, you can always improvise on the spot: I couldn't help noticing your lapel pin. What organization does it represent?

Don't forget to ask questions. People love to talk about themselves and the things they care about. Draw them out, and be comfortable in the knowledge that at some point you will be asked your profession. See the section "Dead-End Questions Lead Directly to Dead Ends" later in this chapter for more hints on how to ask questions.

## Qualify for quality

Not everyone is a good prospect; actually, most people aren't. But if you don't get out there and mingle, you'll never find the good ones. Wait for the right moment, and then informally ask a few, carefully phrased questions about the individual's specific needs as they relate to your product or service. Advertising/ media salespeople can ask something like, "What type of response are you getting from your advertising and promotional efforts?" If you sell home security systems, you can ask, "What are your biggest concerns regarding the safety of your family?" Try to find out what people need and when they need it, their plans, and who can say yes to a purchase.

## Start with an attitude of gratitude

Grab your cards and, in your best, neatest handwriting write "Thank you" across the front of each one. When you meet someone new, strike up a friendly conversation. Introduce yourself and start asking general questions. Ask why the person is attending the meeting, the nature of his business, or about something he is wearing such as an interesting lapel pin or piece of jewelry. Naturally, the person will respond to such pleasant conversation.

At some point this person will ask the nature of your business. That's when you hand over one of your cards. Unless his hands are full of cocktail weenies or chips and salsa from the buffet table, he'll take the card and give it a courtesy glance. People are curious, so people will ask you about the "Thank you" written on your cards. At that moment, say these words:

*I guess I'm thanking you in advance for, hopefully, the opportunity to someday serve your (insert the type of business) needs.*

Examine the beauty of that sentence. Using the word "hopefully" keeps you from sounding like one of those pushy salespeople. "Someday" is an undefined moment down the road, so your new acquaintance shouldn't be worried that you may start selling at any second. "Serve your needs" makes prospects feel that you view them as important individuals. Make it sound as though the sentence is coming off the top of your head, not as though you've practiced it, and you'll be pleased at just how well it works.

If the prospect is at all interested, you should now set a time to discuss further how you can serve his needs. If he's not interested, you can still ask for referrals. A tiny bit of ink, a few moments of your time, and two little words, "Thank you," can provide you with big opportunities.

Make sure you keep your questions in a conversational mode. If prospects appear somewhat skittish about the way the conversation is going, just back off and ask for their cards and permission to contact them later. Save your official prospecting with those people for a later time, which may be at a later date or just later in the evening. If people show legitimate interest, however, continue asking questions. After you determine that they have a need you can fulfill, pique their interest. If what you market requires a more formal sales presentation, start making preparations for one.

## Present your case

During the qualifying phase, your prospect may have mentioned a current situation relating to your product or service. You can push your product without seeming pushy by telling your prospect how you were able to help out someone else in a similar situation.

| You: | Is your company troubled more by maintenance or by over-the-road costs? |
|---|---|
| Them: | Well, we have a fine repair shop, but the cost of diesel fuel is just eating us up. |
| You: | XYZ Trucking had a similar challenge last year. We were able to show them how to get more power at a lower cost for fuel. |

You can present your case effectively without ever showing any of those fangs. Illustrating how you helped someone else is not very threatening and may even lead to one of those "Well, do you think you could do something like that for us" responses.

## Call for action

After making your informal presentation, don't waste a lot of time but do offer one of your business cards. Trading cards is such a ritual these days that you probably don't even have to ask for your prospects' cards. If your prospects don't have cards, ask them to write their names, addresses, and phone numbers on the back of your cards.

Don't allow the other person to say, "I'll get back in touch with you." You have to stay in the driver's seat. If people show real interest, volunteer to pull together some information or tell them that you will call later to set up appointments. End the conversation by saying thank you, and then move back into the crowd for some more serious mingling.

## Follow up

Send out thank-you notes to all of your new prospects by no later than the end of the next day. Don't put off this little chore. Your conversations may have really generated some interest in your product or service, and you want to keep that interest alive.

Remember that the lions with the big fangs may be stalking your prospects with lean and hungry looks. Keep your note short and sweet, but make sure you include a thank you. Mention the event at which you met (because some people attend an awful lot of meetings). Also, refer specifically to the individual, the company, or a situation you discussed, and tell him that you will call within the next week.

Practice these six steps of working a room, and you'll have half the people in the room talking about your skills at conversation. Meanwhile, the lions are all still circling the perimeter, licking their lips, and scaring off prospects.

# Tom's Nasty Words

Few things are as powerful as words. However, never forget that many words sound positive but create negative pictures or feelings in listeners' minds. Most salespeople use such words every day, completely unaware of their negative effects on prospects. I call these Tom's Nasty Words. I cover them in detail in _Selling For Dummies_ (IDG Books Worldwide, Inc.), but I believe a brief mention is appropriate here. Table 9-1 offers a handy, at-a-glance summary.

| Table 9-1 | Winning Words and Phrases | |
| --- | --- | --- |
| _Instead of..._ | _Say_ | _Comment_ |
| Sell or sold | Help, acquire, get involved | People don't want to be sold anything — instead, use the other words to make them feel like partners in the process. |
| Contract | Paperwork, agreement, form | Contract conjures up images of being obligated for a long, long time and legal battles to get out of it. |
| Cost or price | Investment, amount | When you say price and cost, prospects visualize their hard-earned money slipping through their fingers. An investment, however, is something that comes back to them. |

_(continued)_

## Table 9-1 *(continued)*

| Instead of . . . | Say | Comment |
|---|---|---|
| Down payment | Initial investment or amount | This is not the first of a long string of payments. It's the initial move toward a major life goal. |
| Monthly payment | Monthly investment or amount | Prospects won't visualize themselves paying bills. They'll see themselves in a more positive light, making a regular commitment. |
| Buy or pay | Own | Buy and pay just mean that prospects fork over some money, but ownership means that they actually acquire something of value. |
| Deal | Opportunity | Again, you want your prospects to get involved with your product or service. |
| Objection | Area of concern to be addressed | When prospects object, they are expressing concern. Champions address these concerns and move on. |
| Problem | Challenge | A problem is negative. It stops you in your tracks. A challenge is something you can overcome. |
| Pitch | Presentation, demonstration | Pitch sounds like "I want your money" or "I'm going to throw something at you." Contrast that with demonstration, which sounds like "I have something worthwhile to show you." |
| Commission | Fee for service | Respond like this: "Fortunately, the company has built a fee for service into our transaction. However, the service you receive will far outweigh any fee, and that's what you really want, isn't it?" |
| Sign | Approve, endorse, okay, authorize | The thought of signing on that dotted line raises all kinds of red flags, but authorizing or okaying something is merely a formality. |

| Appointment | Visit | *Appointment* sounds like too much of a commitment, especially for a consumer or in-home sale. |
| --- | --- | --- |
| Store | Location, display area | A *store* is a place to buy things; a *display area* is a place to learn. |
| Cheaper | More economical | *Cheaper* conveys lesser in quality. *More economical* conveys thrift. |
| Customer | Client, people you serve | Champion salespeople keep their attitude of servitude at the forefront of every client contact. |
| Just looking | Research | Ask about the *research* they are doing in order to make a wise purchasing decision. |
| Referral | Quality introduction | You don't want just the name of a warm body to talk with. You're asking for a personal introduction. They need to have confidence in you in order to want to do this. |

Carefully examine each word in your presentation and remove the negative ones, especially those nasty ones I just mentioned. Continually ask yourself whether what you will say is always to your prospects' benefit and whether they can understand what you mean by what you say.

Words are the tools of the sales professional's trade. These tools may seem simple, but they have great power for promoting good or for presenting challenges. True salespeople use words to show they really want to serve their clients, and it's awfully hard to do that when your own words keep getting in the way. Study these nasty words again, and then put the replacements to work for you because they make all the difference in the world.

## Color Your Word Pictures

You can use words to paint beautiful pictures. Ask any novelist or short-story writer. Instructors and how-to books encourage fiction writers to "remember the weather" in their writing, and it's also good advice for salespeople. Remember, weather and the overall environment affect people's attitudes. Just about everyone has five senses: sight, sound, touch, smell, and taste. A writer creating a good story (or a salesperson creating a good presentation) should involve as many of those senses as possible. The reader/listener gets a clear picture of the countryside, the hero, the villain, or your product or service.

## Jarring jargon

Every business or industry has its own terminology, words, symbols, and phrases, but don't get trapped into using them to impress your prospect. Jargon is technical and intimidating to the uninitiated. Using insider's language when making a presentation on mining to an engineer is one thing, but using computer jargon to interest someone at the retail level is something entirely different.

Before launching into your presentation, determine your prospect's level of understanding of the jargon and adjust accordingly. Determine a good test question for your industry. In other words, If they know what RAM is, you should also be able to talk about processor speeds and gigabytes of storage without having to explain all of that. If you have any doubt about their level of understanding, define each industry term the first time you use it. If they get it, you'll see the light of understanding in their eyes. If their eyes glaze over or they look confused, backtrack to a more elementary level of conversation. Talking over someone's head just gets in the way. Some people will become frustrated and give up trying to follow you. Others will struggle along trying to keep up, missing a lot of valuable sales points along the way. You can't sell if you're not speaking the same language.

Take a look at the following examples:

Mr. Smith, when you walk out on the construction site and see these modular units gently easing in place, I want you to feel how the joints mold together. Run your fingers across that smooth surface and then rap your knuckles against it. That solid, crisp tap is the sound of the finest structural wall for the dollar on the market today.

or

> Mrs. Doe, I want you to picture yourself at the very end of your manufacturing line placing your hand on the top fiberboard plank on the pallet. After we install our new system for you, those planks won't really feel any different. They'll still be solid, smooth, and with perfectly formed edges. Each one you touch, however, will have saved you 25 percent more than before the installation. Now picture reading that fact in the annual report to your stockholders.

No matter what your product or service, you can paint beautiful word pictures about how it can benefit your prospects. Be sure to do your homework before you start painting, though. An exquisite picture of less downtime on the job won't do you an awful lot of good if the buyer is mostly interested in increasing job safety. Remember that you create the mood of the sale with your own imagination and verbal skills, and like a true artist, you have to paint what your patron (prospect) most wants to see and purchase.

## Dead-End Questions Lead Directly to Dead Ends

You can ask two basic types of questions: open-ended and closed. I call the latter group dead-end questions because that's exactly where they lead. A dead-end question requires a simple, brief, and, sometimes, one-word answer. Closed questions don't help you prod prospects to talk about themselves so that you figure out how you can help them. Closed questions work against both you and your prospects.

Dead-end questions usually begin with two words that guarantee a short answer. Try to avoid the following openings whenever you need important information:

- ✔ Do you . . .
- ✔ Will you . . .
- ✔ How many . . .
- ✔ Are you . . .

Use closed-ended questions to get specific information about very specific areas, or use them to rein in a conversation that's drifting the wrong way.

| You: | I believe our line of trucks can help solve your fuel concerns. |
| --- | --- |
| Them: | Yeah, the cost is skyrocketing. Just like everything else. Have you priced bass boats lately? |
| You: | Outrageous. How many drivers do you have on the road on a given day? |
| Them: | A hundred. |
| You: | That's a lot of drivers and trucks. I bet you're always looking for ways to cut down on your fuel bills. |
| Them: | Oh, yeah. Say, what were you saying about getting more power at less cost for XYZ? |

Notice how the question about the number of drivers turned the conversation back in your favor. But be careful when you use dead-end questions, because they usually lead to dead ends.

# Asking Questions That Fly Instead of Die

Use as many open-ended questions as possible and for as long as you can to get important information from them. Open-ended questions keep your prospects talking. Not only are open-ended questions the best way to get information directly, they also make prospects feel important because they end up doing most of the talking. Never forget that you can't learn anything by dominating a conversation. That's one of the reasons why the quiet sales professionals are ahead of the backslappers at the end of the month.

This is a good time for you to play reporter. No, I don't mean that you should don a rumpled gray suit, a floppy fedora, and start hanging around the 13th Precinct. Reporters have designed their questioning techniques to get their subjects to open up and to tell their stories. Journalism schools teach students a few basic but powerful words that are virtually open-ended questions by themselves. Journalists call these power openers *the five Ws* (and they always toss in an *H* for free):

- Who?
- What?

✔ Where?

✔ When?

✔ Why?

✔ How?

Most people find it very difficult to answer those questions (or questions built around them) with short or one-word answers. Even if you get a one-word answer, you can keep digging for your story because it's practically impossible to answer every question with a short answer. Unless you run up against someone who shrugs and says, "I don't know" to everything you ask, you will hear something important from prospects sooner or later.

| | |
|---|---|
| You: | Who is in charge of truck purchases over at your place? |
| Them: | John Smith. |
| You: | What's his title? |
| Them: | Purchasing agent. |
| You: | Where is his office, near yours? |
| Them: | Right down the hall. |
| You: | When is the best time to see him? |
| Them: | Anytime. Just give him a call. No, wait, better call tomorrow. He's on vacation next week. He's big on deep-sea fishing, you know. |

By knowing and using the five Ws, this salesperson kept receiving information even when faced with a battery of extremely short answers. The salesperson also may have found a good conversation starter — deep-sea fishing — when he finally meets Mr. Smith.

Keep from sounding as though you're conducting an interrogation, or you may find the other person backing away from you, half expecting someone wearing a menacing uniform to stalk into the room and ask, "Your papers, please!" Keep the conversation as casual as circumstances permit. You may be tempted to respond to some of these questions by jumping in immediately with a feature or benefit of your product or service. Resist this temptation.

Except for those rare times when the opportunity presents itself, don't sell when prospecting. Instead, keep prospects talking by asking more open-ended questions like the following:

> Do you prefer a 16-foot craft or larger? I'd be interested to know why.

or

> How did you get involved in sailing?

or

> Where do you prefer to do most of your sailing?

Instead of cutting off your prospects, give them opportunities to help you fine-tune your approach. The more clients talk, the more you know how to select the right craft in the right price range that can perform best in their favorite sailing waters. By questioning prospects, you let them tell you exactly what they want.

## Approaching the Retail Customer

What is a customer's stock answer to the question, "May I help you?"

Simple. "No thanks, I'm just browsing."

"May I help you?" is a no-question. You don't want to use them.

The customer's answer of "no" effectively shuts down the conversation — unless the salesperson wants to run the risk of becoming a pest, which can squander any opportunity to make a sale. If only retail managers and staff added one little word to that sentence, they could change the course of retail history. "Come on now, Tom, change the course of retail history?" Yes, with one little word. The word is *how*. "How may I help you?" requires a real answer — an answer with some thought behind it. The answer to the question "How may I help you?" brings real interaction to the initial contact.

The previous section discussed the use of journalistic questions in prospecting. Asking questions beginning with one of those magic words is a much better and safer way to approach a retail customer. These questions do not threaten, yet they keep the lines of communication open. Following are some example questions of this type and the kind of information you can expect:

- ✔ **What are you shopping for today?** The answer to this question gives you cause to lead them to the appropriate item they are seeking, drumming up conversation along the way, making them like you and trust you.

- ✔ **When was the last time you were in our store?** If you've recently remodeled or reorganized, this answer could turn you into Mr. or Ms. Tour Guide, helping the prospect find items that have been moved or directing him to the new line of whatchamajigs that you're carrying now.

- ✔ **Where else have you been shopping today?** If they've visited the competition, you'll know they're doing price comparisons and you need to get your selling antenna up for decision-making time.

- ✔ **Why did you decide to come to our location today?** If you have a special sale going on, that's great. If not, there must be a particular reason they've come in. Perhaps a friend just bought an item at your location and they're coming in to check it out for themselves. In that case, they're practically sold already.

- ✔ **How did you find our business?** There's a difference between the person who wandered in because he was in the area and the person who drove 25 miles to get there because you carry a one-of-a-kind item.

## Don't be a space invader

In retail, first of all, be careful of your approach. Too many salespeople rush in like charging rhinos when they set eyes on someone stepping into their location. Right away you have intimidated most of the people you want to serve. No one likes to be charged by a rhino, especially when surrounded by glass display cases. Never walk directly toward a prospect when they enter your retail outlet. Do not rush, rather approach respectfully. Make contact without causing fear or concern. Just let them know that you are available to help them when necessary and then back off to give them some breathing space.

## All the right moves

Easing away from a customer is a marvelous way to put him at ease. For one thing, it's the last thing in the world he expects to happen. The sheer relief drives away a lot of tension.

You don't want to circle around like a hungry shark, but you do want to keep an eye on your customer. Usually he will make a beeline for the object of his interest the moment you leave. By watching his actions, you can soon figure out the reason for the visit and can begin formulating your plan of action to be of service.

When he begins examining the article, that's the time to ease back in his direction. Again, don't come charging in. Just make sure you're nearby to handle any questions about the purchase.

A friendly nod or a brief smile of acknowledgment is okay, but don't stare. It makes you look hungry.

## Respond to prospect signals

If a prospect spends any time at all examining a particular item or set of items, it is a clear sign that he wants to move from prospect to customer. That's the time to ease over and ask a service question. I recommend that you open with an open-ended question, something that can't be answered with a conversation-slowing "yes" or "no." Open-ended questions also provide you with information to help you move the sales process along to the desired conclusion.

If you're selling automobiles, for example, you may ask if the purchase is to be used as a work car or family car. The answer to this question

- ✔ Tells you that the individual is interested in making a purchase.
- ✔ Involves the prospect.
- ✔ Gives you specific information to help you get even more information to better match the buyer with the right automobile.

You can press on by asking how many people are in the family; how much travel will be involved; if the vehicle will be used primarily in town or also on a trip; whether the prospect is more interested in safety, fuel efficiency, or power; and so on. All of these questions, handled politely and respectfully, put and keep your prospect at ease while putting you ever closer to the sale.

# Chapter 10

# Getting an Appointment

*N*othing can be more true than the saying, "Nothing happens until somebody sells something." However, before you make the sale, you have to obtain an appointment to pitch your product. Consider some of the arrangements people have tried to make with you over the years. Think about what worked, what didn't, and what had you hanging up before the "thanks, we're not interested" had even cleared your throat. Chances are that what turns you off turns off someone else just as quickly. If any of those nasty little habits have crept into your own presentations, start weeding them out right now.

Over the years, I've observed many salespeople selling their products when they should be selling themselves. At the slightest opening, they push the features and benefits of their products when prospects aren't ready for such an abrupt and forceful presentation. The pushy, unthinking salesperson loses appointments, goodwill, and sales. When calling for an appointment, sell the benefit of meeting with you to the prospect, not the benefits of your product or service.

## *The Keys to Getting an Appointment*

You need to do three things when you want to set up an appointment:

✔ **Be courteous to a fault.** Prospects may be offended by your little bit of profanity or off-color humor.

✔ **Do whatever it takes to meet face-to-face.** At a face-to-face meeting you can determine the type of prospect you really have and how you can best serve her. You have to do that in person unless doing so is physically impossible.

When trying to get an appointment, remember that persistence pays off. Don't get frustrated with the layers of bureaucracy that you must wade through and just give up. Your interpersonal skills, specifically telephone skills, can help you get to the decision maker. (See the "Vital Telephone Skills" section later in this chapter.)

✔ **Reconfirm the details.** You may get the appointment, fail to reconfirm it, and lose an opportunity because the prospect forgets the time or date of the meeting.

That's it. The process is simple, but you must do all three all the time. You can't sit on a three-legged stool if one of the legs is missing. Too many people forget one or more of these vital three steps.

The very word *appointment* seems to scare some people. An appointment sounds formal, and some people may think it a bit threatening. Instead, I recommend that you use *visit* or, better still, tell the prospect that you just want to pop by. Someone just popping by for a visit is a downright relaxed and friendly thing to do!

See Chapter 9 for more words and phrases that I recommend you avoid.

## Vital Telephone Skills

The pathway to riches is that silver tongue and golden voice of yours, but one of your biggest assets is a little box — the telephone. Most appointments in the industrialized world are made over the telephone, and most of those calls are cold calls. (They're called *cold* because that's the kind of feeling salespeople get when making them.)

Champions master the fear of calling strangers, punch in the numbers, and speak with confidence even if their knees are rattling like castanets. Fear is just part of the job. The undisputed best way to sell anything is in a face-to-face environment, and the best way to set up face-to-face meetings starts with that phone in your sweaty little hand. If you really believe in your product, you shouldn't let your own fears keep you from being of benefit to someone else. Shame on you. Now punch in that telephone number. You can always put on a pair of mittens if your cold calling gets too cold. I find the ones with the cut-out fingertips work best.

Your calls need to contain the following steps:

✔ Greeting

✔ Introduction

✔ Gratitude

✔ Purpose

✔ Appointment

✔ Telephone thank you

✔ Letter thank you

The successful appointment call starts before you ever pick up the handset or flip-phone. The call starts in your mind. You have to know where you're headed with that call, and you must know your seven-step road map. Write down the steps on a notecard or piece of paper and use this handy reference until you're comfortable with them and can work from memory.

## Step 1: Greeting

| | |
|---|---|
| You: | Bob Smith? Oh, hi, Bob, gladda speak to ya. I'm Ralph with Monongahela Metal Ingots and, boy, do we have a special you're just gonna love and I mean l-u-v! |
| Them: | Click. |
| You: | Bob? Oh, Bob? Hmm. Disconnected. Must be a bad connection. |

Ralph, our metal ingot salesman, certainly didn't show a lot of courtesy, did he? He didn't get the chance to meet Bob Smith, and he certainly didn't get to reconfirm the details of a meeting either. Old Ralph tried to bull his way into a sale instead of an appointment and received nothing except dead air for his efforts. He tried to sell the prospect his product instead of himself and therefore failed at both.

The greeting sets the tone for the entire telephone call and often for the appointment that follows. Courtesy is key. Always use the person's name right up front:

Good morning, Mr. Smith.

or

> *I'm calling for Bob Smith.*

Using those greetings isn't being too formal; they show proper respect. You should say good morning, afternoon, or evening because it's friendly and professional without being time consuming, and it sets you apart from the crowd of impatient competitors who just say hello.

Our old buddy Ralph made a major mistake by calling his prospect by his first name before getting permission. Some people don't mind this, but others are offended by it.

Be formal at first. Wait until your prospect gives you an okay, such as "Why don't you call me Bob?" You run into all types, from folks who prefer to go on a first-name basis during the call to those who want the Mr., Mrs., Miss, or Ms. formality years after they've become your best customer. It's their decision. Let them make it. The customer really does know best, especially his or her own name.

## Step 2: Introduction

Unless you work for the Monongahela Metal Ingots Company, or another company whose name includes its product, you need to mention what you sell right away, but do it creatively.

> We're an international firm that specializes in helping businesses like yours produce a higher quality metal thingamabob with the most economical use of raw materials.

The real key here, as always, is to state things in terms that benefit your prospect. Of course Bob Smith is interested in higher quality. Of course he wants to reduce his cost for raw materials. You certainly haven't sold him by this point. He doesn't even know exactly what you sell. Your product could be ingots. It could be something tangible, such as office equipment, furniture, homes, or cars. It could be something intangible, such as insurance, pool service, house cleaning, or business consultation. The prospect doesn't know what you sell, and you have to get him interested very quickly so you can move on to your research.

Remember the overeager or high-pressure salesperson who called you and pushed for a sale right then and there? You know, the one who started hitting you with product features about half-way through your "hello." Yeah, that one. That's what I call *in-your-face selling,* and I don't believe the technique actually generates many sales. When you're on the phone, you're searching for knowledge, not closing a sale. You want prospects to give you enough information so that you can interest them in a face-to-face meeting. Never lose sight of that goal, or you may just lose your opportunity.

All this happens within the first couple of seconds of the conversation. Keep things moving along until your prospect provides you with some information. (See the section "Keep moving forward on piggyback" in this chapter.) Then you can go immediately to the next step.

## Step 3: Gratitude

Always thank your prospect for allowing you time in his busy schedule on a busy day, even when you hear in the background "Bob, we tee off in half an hour." Express sincere gratitude for the time and tell your prospect that he won't be wasting a second of it. Simple and brief is best. You want to move on to other things.

I want to thank you for visiting with me this morning, Mr. Smith. I promise to be brief.

Be very cautious at this point. Keep the mood conversational, and don't sound like you'll be rushing through anything.

Keep this conversation professional and avoid fawning or flattery. Something like the following makes all the points without gumming up the works with "flattorial goo."

Thank you for getting together with me. I'll only be a moment so you can get back to your schedule.

Try not to say "I'll only *take* a moment." The last thing you want to do is implant an image of you or your company taking anything. Words carry meaning, and sometimes that means what you say isn't exactly what the prospect hears.

## Step 4: Purpose

This step is where you tell the person on the other end of the phone why you're calling. Instead of just jumping into a description of your metal ingot line, try to get the prospects talking about their situations. Remember, you're not selling here. You're on a hunt for information.

Get to your purpose with a question such as the following.

If we can show you a way to improve the quality of your product at a lower cost, would you be interested?

Of course he's interested. He may not show it, but he's very interested. That doesn't necessarily mean he's interested in your product, however. Our prospect, Bob, will most likely say "yes" without hesitation. Who wouldn't want a better product at a lower cost?

After he agrees, move on to a couple more brief questions. Remember, the prospect may have an unstated, more pressing reason to buy something from you.

A lot of champions use the survey approach. They tell prospects that they are conducting a survey to gather information.

The company I represent has given me an assignment to conduct a brief, two-question survey of managers in the metal ingot industry. We would appreciate your opinion. Could you help me by answering these two questions?

Asking for a professional or expert opinion from people justifiably boosts their egos without making you seem as though you're flattering them just to get in the door. Most people say "yes, of course."

For more tips on questions to ask prospects and how to pose them, see "Techniques, Tips, and Telephone Tales" later in this chapter.

## Step 5: Appointment

This is the moment you've been waiting for — time to arrange the appointment. Know how much time you need and realize how other people value their own time. Twenty minutes or less seems to be the magic time slot. Don't panic. You may surprise yourself at how well you can do your job in that amount of time. A short meeting keeps you focused on what's really important, so don't be intimidated. Besides, you're very unlikely to get an hour or even half an hour. The shorter the time, the better your chances of getting in.

Use the following technique to reinforce your commitment to respecting your prospects' time. (The technique is another way to set yourself apart from the crowd.) Offer a choice of times for the appointment, and make those choices in off-hour increments of time.

> Would 1:40 Wednesday or 9:20 Thursday be best for you, Mr. Smith?

Phrasing the question this way gives him a choice, while still keeping you in control of the situation. You don't want the prospect to check his schedule and "get back to you." Too many things can get in the way of getting back.

Asking for an off-hour time gets you noticed. Also there's just something about setting a meeting at an off hour that says you're a salesperson who will be punctual and respect your prospect's time. Try it.

## Step 6: Telephone thank you

Thank Bob Smith for his time. Reconfirm the time, date, and location of the appointment.

Get directions, either from Bob or his assistant. Do you have any idea how many places 101 Center Street can be? Make sure you know the city in which the prospect is located. If you're totally unfamiliar with the area and if the potential sale justifies it, drive by the location a day or so in advance of the meeting. Take note of real or potential traffic challenges and plan alternate routes in case of construction or traffic delays.

Showing up late because you couldn't find the address speaks volumes about your attention to detail, your ability to plan ahead, and your commitment to customer service. Tardiness is not the best way to start a business relationship. Rescheduling is awkward and sometimes practically impossible. "I'll have my secretary call you when I return from Singapore," Bob says.

## Step 7: Letter thank you

If the long-hoped-for, hard-won interview is scheduled more than two days out, follow up the phone call immediately with a brief, professional thank-you note. Express your gratitude for the prospect's time on the phone and for the upcoming opportunity. Mention the time, date, and location of the meeting.

> *Thank you for talking with me on the telephone. In today's business world, time is precious. You can rest assured that I will always be respectful of the time you invest as we discuss the possibility of a mutually beneficial business opportunity. I'll do my best to provide you with valuable information when I pop by your office on Tuesday, September 23 at 1:40 p.m.*

This letter isn't only basic business courtesy, it's basic good business. The letter makes the get together "real" in the prospect's mind, a commitment. You'd be surprised how "unreal" an appointment can get if an old golf buddy or sorority sister calls your prospect for lunch or coffee or just to visit during your scheduled time. Also, it's just possible you've gotten a time or date wrong after all; the letter may save you from missing the appointment. The prospect or her secretary can call and straighten things out.

If appropriate for your business, use quality letterhead with your professionally taken photograph on it. This is an especially good idea for independent contractors, real-estate agents, and freelance professionals. The photo increases the prospect's comfort factor if he has an idea of what you look like before the meeting. A poorly produced, cheap-looking (even if it cost a bundle) letterhead makes a bad impression and can start you off at a disadvantage before you even knock on the door.

You should include one of your business cards which, as with the letterhead, should be neat, professional, and reflective of your business. Remember, you don't need your entire life story on a card. Stick to the basics: logo, company name and slogan, your name and title, photo (if appropriate), address, phone, fax, and e-mail.

# Techniques, Tips, and Telephone Tales

As with any skill set, a whole bunch of "little things" can make a big difference in the degree of success you achieve with those skills. Foremost, you must be comfortable with what you're doing. Otherwise, you'll come across as fake. No one wants to get involved with a faker. Then, you have to pay attention so you pick up on every opportunity to move your potential client from being a prospect to becoming a soon-to-be-satisfied client who has just committed to meeting you face to face.

## There's only one you — be you

Every person is different, thank goodness. We all have different strengths and weaknesses, abilities and skills, interests and needs. Some of us are masters at retail selling, while others shine in big-ticket items. One person is attracted to high-tech industrial work in the field, and another develops remarkable skills at telemarketing. For every salesperson who wants to stick close to home, another one wants to travel the roads.

No one is a master of every skill and ability. You find those areas in which you perform best and hone those skills to perfection. You have to be you. This book is full of lists of techniques used in prospecting. Try them all until you find the ones that work best with your personality. Struggling to be something you're not is foolish when you can be perfect at what you are.

When phoning a prospect, use only the techniques that you feel are right for you. Develop a pace and a delivery that is truly your own. Don't try to be a "real hard charger" if you're a more laid-back individual. The person on the other end of the line may sense that you're ill at ease. That feeling can zip across the wires like an e-mail message.

Your prospect may be across town, across the country, or across the sea, but you're still personally connected by the telephone. That call may just be your one shot at getting to the appointment. Do you really want to trust your first, best, and maybe last chance to someone else? Be yourself, and you'll be fine.

## Keep moving forward on piggyback

Forward momentum is important in an initial call. You have to keep things moving along without awkward lulls or pauses in the conversation. Otherwise, the conversation dies — along with your opportunity.

I teach a simple technique called *piggybacking* to help sales-people keep things moving along.

All you do is ask a question and then follow it with a second question based on the information learned from the first. Try this approach, and you'll see how easy it is to master and perfect.

CHAMPION STRATEGY #1

| You: | What are your biggest headaches in manufacturing? |
| --- | --- |
| Them: | Quality control, plain and simple. |
| You: | In what areas of quality control do you have concerns? |
| Them: | Mainly in our quality control lab. |
| You: | Would that be an equipment or personnel challenge? |

Keep piggybacking question on top of question until you get the information you need. Is her quality control problem related to raw materials? Outdated analysis equipment? Inept analysts? When you receive your answers, you will know what kind of prospect you have at hand.

Don't forget that you ask the questions to gather information and to control the call — not to have a conversation for the sake of conversation. Don't pepper the prospect with a barrage of questions just because you can.

When prospecting, sometimes the fastest way for two people to arrive at a single destination is to piggyback.

## Questions for qualifying

You need to find answers to specific questions to determine whether a full presentation is justified on your first visit. Naturally, you must customize the questions to the specific product or service you offer, but you need to know the following information:

- ✔ What the prospect has now
- ✔ What the prospect enjoys most about it
- ✔ What the prospect would change about its current product or service
- ✔ Who the decision maker is for purchasing this product or service
- ✔ When you can make a presentation about a solution to the problem

Customizing your questions to the prospect's business is important. For example, if you sell raw-materials analysis equipment, you can ask

Is your equipment state-of-the-art or a few years old?

or

Are you experiencing challenges with the equipment or with the personnel running the equipment?

or

Do you have computerized digital doohickeys?

If you find out that the prospect is equally concerned about both equipment and personnel, you can open the door to a full-blown presentation with the following question:

If we could show you a cost-effective way to acquire the latest in spectrographic technology plus complete training on its use at no additional investment, would you be interested?

How can the prospect possibly say no?

## Listening to your prospect

Asking all the right questions will do you no good if you don't really hear the answers. Listening is a skill bordering on being an art. If you don't master it, your piggybacking and follow-up questions aren't going to get you very far.

Real listening involves four basic steps, which I cover in greater detail in Chapter 4:

- ✓ Hearing
- ✓ Interpreting
- ✓ Evaluating
- ✓ Responding

Using the four steps to develop your listening abilities is a bit like digging for gold. You have to keep probing for those golden nuggets hidden in all that dirt. Gently, politely ask questions, getting more and more specific all the time. Sometimes the small bits of information lead to the big finds. The more you know about your prospect, the more effectively you can respond and the more control you have over the phone call.

## *"No" can get you to "yes"*

> You: **Is your quality control testing equipment state-of-the-art, Mr. Prospect?**
>
> Them: **No.**

When you hear the answer "no" to a question like that, you have been given a clear, definite indication that you can be a real benefit to your prospect and his company. The prospect needs what you have to offer! At this moment, a salesperson has an obligation to get that appointment so the prospect can be helped. After all, as a champion you're in the business of bringing benefits to people.

At this point in your conversation, use what you've learned from their responses to make the connection between your product and the prospect's needs. All you need is the opportunity to prove it. That opportunity is called an appointment.

## *"No" can mean "no (for now)"*

Sometimes the prospect really doesn't need your product, or you may have caught the prospect on a bad day when he just says "no" to everything. Don't get discouraged. Just say thank you and ask if you can send some information for future reference. People rarely refuse to accept such material. Instead of having the door slammed in your face, you have just kept your foot carefully placed in front of it. True, you might just have a slightly bruised big toe, but the door is still open.

Send the material and then make a note to make a follow-up call at the proper time during the itch cycle for your product or service. (For more details about the itch cycle, see Chapter 5.) Contact the prospect again and try to arrange a visit. Time changes all things. The information may have stimulated some thought. The prospect's present supplier may have just fouled up a major order, or the prospect may be in a frame of mind to hear some fresh ideas. That toe just kicked the door wide open.

## *Enthusiasm with courtesy and respect*

Have you ever heard of a salesperson calling for and getting an appointment and then responding to the prospect's "yes" with his own "@#%$@, that's great!"

The enthusiasm is great, but the use of profanity, even mild profanity, shows a lack of courtesy and respect for the prospect. He may be a preacher, Sunday school teacher, or just someone with a fine appreciation for polite conversation.

You must at all times show total respect for your prospects' feelings. Here are several techniques that can help you maintain the highest level of professionalism without throwing water on the fires of your enthusiasm.

✔ **Ease into the conversation at the same rate that your prospect does.** If the prospect remains formal throughout, you remain formal throughout. If the prospect starts relaxing, you can relax, but always follow the prospect's lead. Never lead the prospect.

✔ **Never discuss religion or politics.** Bringing your personal matters — any personal matters — into the conversation just isn't a good idea. Don't discuss your health, your kids, or your challenges unless your prospect brings up the subjects. Because you call busy people, proper respect dictates that you respect their time.

✔ **Don't knock the competition.** Don't criticize competitors even if your competition knocks you or if your prospect knocks your competition. You may score a few points by firing a few shots at a competitor, but some of those shots may ricochet and hit you. By this, I mean that knocking the competition is unprofessional. It's like slinging mud in politics. Some of it is bound to get on the one doing the tossing. As a professional, you are above the need to do this. You can beat the competition with facts, figures, and through outperformance. Who needs mud for that?

✔ **Monitor your speech for poor grammar and speech habits.** "Yeah" or "Uh-huh" are obvious no-nos. Other phrases that are perfectly all right can become distracting irritants when overused. "I see" or "yes" can be very useful, but they don't add anything to the conversation when used every minute or so. Constantly check the way you talk and weed out all inappropriate and possibly irritating language, such as "ya know."

## *Be a straight shooter*

Honesty really is the best policy, and your personal integrity can open or slam shut many doors. A reputation takes years to build, but it can be destroyed in a second by a single word or sentence.

If a prospect asks you a tough question, answer honestly. Suppose Bob Smith, the prospect with quality control problems with his company's metal ingots, is really interested in your raw-materials testing equipment, but the factor that really hooked him is the no-cost training program. He says he'll buy if you can start within 30 days. You know that your training staff is booked for 45 days. If you bluff, hoping to tapdance your way into the sale, he'll eventually find out. You'll lose all respect and probably any chances at future business. Face it: When he finally hears the tap-tap-tap sound of your shoes, he knows he can't trust you. What's wrong with being honest?

> Mr. Smith, I'd love to promise you installation and training even faster than that time frame, but our staff is booked solid through the middle of next month.

Have you lost the sale? Maybe, but through no fault of your own. But you have not blown your credibility or that of your company. Bob may just be in a hurry to get moving, and another two-week delay isn't really a "deal breaker" after all.

I highly recommend that you work up a list of possible hard questions before you make a prospecting call. Try to think of anything that could possibly come up and then formulate your honest answer. Then you won't have to stumble, mumble, and fumble for the right words when you get hit between the eyes. Preparation will get you over the rough spots. Be a straight shooter, but have your ammunition ready so that you don't have to shoot from the hip.

# *Finding the Hard-to-Find Prospects*

Suppose Bob Smith is so busy managing metal ingot production that he believes he has very limited time for many meetings. In fact, he's set up a group of people, like destroyers around an aircraft carrier, to screen all his calls. Fine — all champions love a challenge. You get to do some fancy flying.

## *Assistants can be your best friend*

Contact the receptionist and tell her you want the name of the person with decision-making responsibility for your product. Her responsibility is to know this information and her job is to provide it. Receptionists tend to be very helpful and respond well to a friendly, professional voice.

CHAMPION STRATEGY #1

| | |
|---|---|
| Them: | Good morning. Thank you for calling Tom Hopkins International. How may I direct your call? |
| You: | Good morning. My name is Madeline Kelly and I am in business in the community. I'm calling regarding your staffing needs. Who in your company is responsible for that? By the way, who am I speaking with, please? |
| Them: | My name is Sharon. |
| You: | Thank you, Sharon. I really need your help. Who in your company is responsible for interviewing and hiring the staff members? |
| Them: | That would be Bob Smith. |
| You: | Thank you for your help. Can you get me in touch with Mr. Smith? |
| Them: | One moment, please, and I'll connect you. |

If you only connect with Bob Smith's voice mail, you'll probably want Sharon's help again to find out the best time to reach him directly. It never hurts to develop someone on the inside as an ally.

If a receptionist has been particularly helpful, send a short thank-you note with your business card. This bit of professional courtesy isn't only the right thing to do; it may also pay off with big dividends in the future.

Bob Smith may have an assistant. If so, the receptionist should direct you there. Again, get the name and spelling correct. This assistant has her finger on a "kill" switch that can wipe out any chance of a face-to-face meeting with the decision maker. Treat the assistant with the same respect and courtesy that you would extend the boss. The assistant isn't an obstacle blocking your path. You may be able to gather some information from the assistant and perhaps even qualify the company with greater precision. Ask for the assistant's help and explain that you provide a product that can enhance the company's product or service.

| | |
|---|---|
| Them: | Mr. Smith's office. This is Janice. |
| You: | Janice, my name is Madeline Kelly. I'm in business in the community and I could use your help. I understand that Mr. Smith is responsible for the staffing needs at Tom Hopkins International, is that correct? |
| Them: | Yes, that's correct. |
| You: | That's great. Can you please put me through to him? |
| Them: | He's unavailable this morning. Perhaps I can answer any questions you might have. |
| You: | Great. I so appreciate your help, Janice. I need to determine the best time to talk with Mr. Smith. I need only five minutes of his time. Can you tell me when's the best time to call back? |
| Them: | Early in the morning is usually best. |
| You: | That's a great help. Then, if I call you at 8:15 a.m. tomorrow, you'll be able to put me through? |
| Them: | If he's not on the line, yes, that should work. |
| You: | Wonderful! Thank you again for your help, Janice. I'll talk with you in the morning. |

Assistants are always looking for ways to help their bosses and to enhance their own reputations. If bringing your product to the attention of Bob can make her a hero, the assistant may want to do so as quickly as possible.

One other area that receptionists and assistants can help is spelling. Bob Smith is a pretty common name, but suppose he spells it Smythe? Ask for correct spelling and pronunciation and write it down. A misspelled name on a letter can follow you like an albatross around your neck, bringing bad luck every time you try to sail into the harbor. "Oh, yeah, that's the guy that can't even get my name right. Tell him I'll call him back. Ha ha."

## Show 'n' tell

Salespeople often make presentations to decision makers who work in the lower rungs of large corporations. Realize that these people have careers and they want and need to advance. They want to do good jobs, of course, but they don't want to make decisions that could cost them promotions or even their positions. You can easily address this legitimate concern. While showing how the features and benefits of your product will benefit their companies, tell prospects that they can only enhance their value in the eyes of upper-level management by selecting your product.

Tread lightly here. You shouldn't pander to people's egos just to make a sale; besides they'll spot you a mile away if you do.

## *Follow procedure — if you can*

Some companies have formal structures for setting up presentations. Asking for the proper procedure shows that you respect the company's way of doing business and that you won't try an end run around the assistant or the system. Try to work through that system.

If asking for the procedure doesn't work, or if your time frame doesn't permit it, then you may have to try that end run after all. This is an opportunity to get creative. Here are some suggestions:

- ✔ **Offer to meet before or after business hours.** This approach works well with a lot of busy people who feel that they don't have enough time during the regular workday.

  I know a young executive who was trying to get through to the president of a very large New York advertising agency but was blocked by a very effective series of receptionists, secretaries, and assistants. He called one evening about an hour after the official closing time, and the night receptionist connected him directly to the president who liked to work when everyone else had gone home.

- ✔ **Send a good old telegram.** It goes directly to the prospect and it is virtually guaranteed to be read. Would you toss a telegram in the round file? Neither would I.

✔ **You can send gifts, as long as you don't overdo it.** Make sure that the prospect is worth the time and expense. Don't spend too much, either. People may think you're trying to buy your way in. Also make sure that the gift is appropriate. A bedroom garment for a female executive is out of place, as is a free evening at Exotic Girls 4-U Gentlemen's Club for a man who just may be a prominent leader in his local church. Be aware that some companies set limits on the value of gifts that employees may accept. Don't put your prospect in the position where she'll have to go to the time and expense of returning your gift.

Cookies or candy, items that the prospect can share with the entire staff, are good choices. Also consider an attractive calendar, but not the company calendar or one with your name across the bottom. Discover an interest and find a good-quality calendar that matches. Other gifts can include note paper, pens, magnets, small plaques, or framed motivational phrases.

I know a businessman from Louisiana who was blocked from arranging a telephone call with a New York businesswoman by a very protective secretary. This incident occurred during winter. He finally got through to the businesswoman after he sent the secretary a beautiful, but inexpensive, ceramic magnolia blossom and a note hoping "this bit of the sunny South will help warm your days."

✔ **If a face-to-face meeting really is impossible, try to set up a telephone presentation.** This isn't the best of all possible worlds, but it is certainly better than no presentation at all. Revise your presentation to account for the requirements of the telephone. If visual aids are necessary, you can send or deliver them in time for the meeting. You can even fax charts or other printed matter so that you and the prospect can refer to the same materials during the telephone meeting. For more tips on how to prospect from a distance, see Chapter 6.

Prospecting is, at times, an art, and art requires a creative mind. As a champion, you were born with one.

# Once You Get the Appointment, Don't Get Your Hopes Up

I don't want to discourage you, but there is a chance, a real one, that when you show up for your appointment, your prospect will, as they say, be among those not present. That's just part of the game. Emergencies come up. Old friends drop by. People forget to write things down; and some people just aren't committed to their commitments. When it happens, accept it, reschedule the appointment at your earliest convenience, and move on to the next prospect.

Your chances for an actual face-to-face meeting are significantly better when the appointment is scheduled at the prospect's place of business or home. When scheduled at your place of business, you can pretty well count on four out of five turning into no-shows. That's right; only about 20 percent ever actually show up, according to informal studies.

# Chapter 11

# Putting Others at Ease

*A*ny sales call or presentation generates a certain amount of tension — in both you and the potential client. Certainly, the tension varies according to the salesperson, the prospect, the weather, events around the world, and the situation at the moment of the call. If, in the background of your telephone call, you hear sirens, gunfire, and "We ain't comin' out, copper!" you may not be able to reduce your prospect's level of tension significantly at the moment. Bide your time and wait 'em out. In most other situations, you can do a lot.

To put your prospect at ease, you need to be fluent in three areas.

✔ You really need to know your product or service and how it can benefit your prospect. You can't build much confidence if she asks a question and then has to wait while you frantically flip through brochures trying clever stalls such as "Wait . . . ," "Lemme see here . . . ," or the ever-popular "Uh. . . ."

✔ You must know correct business etiquette and use it appropriately.

✔ You need to have the skills and abilities necessary to handle a prospecting call. Until you have a handle on those three things, you will be uneasy in putting people at ease.

After you master the techniques in this chapter, you'll notice that people who are relaxed make better prospects. Relaxed, your prospects think more clearly, recognize the logic of your statements faster, and make wiser buying decisions. A big part of your job on every call is to help your prospect or customer find that quiet place within where she is comfortable enough to go ahead and agree to a visit, commit to a presentation, or purchase your product. You do that by being a *professional*. As a professional, you present the image that you're someone the prospect wants to be with — someone the prospect likes, trusts, and wants to listen to.

# You Know You're a Professional When . . .

Now seems an excellent time to briefly examine the attributes of a real champion. Take a look at the following eight ways to recognize a real professional salesperson. Evaluate yourself honestly as to how well you stack up and as to what areas require a bit more work on your part. People make fast judgments about other people. Statistics tell us that a definite opinion is formed within the first ten seconds of a meeting.

You have ten seconds to make a professional impression on your prospect. After those first ten seconds, you may either be too late or you may find yourself trying to overcome a bad impression, even as you continue to make a bad impression. Your early, heck, your immediate goal is to show that you are a true professional and that the prospect's best interest lies in investing time with you. Here's how you start doing that.

✔ **You develop a professional's attitude.** Your work is not just a job, it is a profession deserving respect and your best efforts. You honor your commitments, take excellent care of your customer, and you're constantly seeking ways to improve your service. This attitude comes across in your demeanor. Don't for a moment think you can fake it.

## Dressed for success or stress?

Before you head out to prospect in the morning, take time to give yourself a visual once-over. Ask yourself "Am I dressed in a way that encourages people to like and trust me?" If the answer is "no," then you're not dressed for success. You're dressed for stress!

You don't have to be a fashion plate to be dressed for success. In fact, if your apparel is too trendy or too flashy, your appearance may distract your prospect and actually work against you. Play it safe by dressing the way your prospects dress. If your prospects wear expensive, hand-tailored suits, however, that doesn't mean you don't have to rush out and buy a $1,000 three-piece suit with diamond buttons and a solid gold lining. You can't be a very effective salesperson if you're worried about wearing this month's mortgage payment. If your prospects wear suits, you wear a suit. That's all.

Another good rule is to dress like the people your prospects turn to for advice. For example, a small-businessman who wears slacks and a short-sleeved shirt should feel comfortable around someone dressed like his lawyer, accountant, or loan officer. Put yourself in the mind of your prospects and think about what puts them in an open frame of mind. Find their comfort zone.

Some other tips:

✔ Men should wear a minimum of jewelry — nothing beyond a watch and a college or wedding ring unless, of course, you're a retired football player fortunate enough to have a Super Bowl ring. Women can certainly wear jewelry, but they should stay with the conservative approach. Prospects have difficulty staying focused while dodging blistering blasts of sun rays off your 4-inch gold earrings.

✔ Men should not wear makeup unless they are to be interviewed on television, in which case they should pray that they have competent help. Women can wear makeup as long as they stay with the conservative approach. Not wearing makeup used to be a fashion statement for women, but wearing no makeup is as distracting as wearing too much.

✔ In briefcases, thin is still in. If you carry a large, bulky case, people may think that perhaps you're carrying around the week's laundry to drop off at the cleaners on the way home from work. Keep your briefcase neat, clean, and without noticeable cracks, dents, or tears. Brown is still the preferred color for most men and women.

✔ Always carry a quality pen and pencil set. You don't want to hand over a cheap, leaky pen to someone that's about to sign the agreement that will put your kids through college.

Every once in a while you'll have a bad day and walk into an office dressed nothing like your prospect. This is when you have to come up with something fast. Generally this problem happens when a well-dressed salesperson pops in on a prospect who is dressed very casually. The best thing for men to do is to ask whether you can get a bit more comfortable, and then remove your coat. Pretty quickly loosen your tie just a bit, and then roll up your sleeves. Don't be too obvious about it; just do it. Doing all this tends to shorten the gulf of fashion between you and your prospect.

Women, of course, must come up with a different tactic. When women unbutton and loosen up, they send entirely different, inappropriate messages.

✔ **You look and dress like a professional.** You can read more about this in the related sidebar, "Dressed for success or stress?"

✔ **You make your business look professional.** Periodically reviewing how your business is presented to the public is a good idea. Just like scuffed shoes or a badly wrinkled suit, worn carpet or a dirty office sends a clear message to anyone who bothers to look. Your prospects and customers will most certainly look and take note.

✔ **You are neat and organized.** The information and materials you need are always readily at hand so you can answer a customer's question as quickly and honestly as possible. If you don't have the information, you know where to get it. You respond honestly that you do not have the answer, but that you will get it and you set a time limit for getting back with your customer. You always set deadlines that you know you can meet with time to spare.

✔ **You use the language of a professional.** You always plan the call or presentation from the perspective of the individual you are calling. There is no place for slang, vulgarity, poor grammar, or technical jargon in your speech. You ask intelligent questions and provide concise, clear answers that people can actually understand.

Jargon is one of my pet peeves. It doesn't make the salesperson look any smarter. It just makes potential clients resentful because they don't understand what is being said. The real smart people speak plain and concise English, a most elegant and intelligent way of communicating and the language of business throughout the world.

✔ **You keep up with your profession.** Professionals know what is going on inside the business or industry, and they devote a significant amount of time every week to make certain of it. Your confidence in your business or industry knowledge shows up in your overall demeanor and acts positively in putting others at ease with you. Those who don't keep up get left behind.

✔ **You do the hard work of selling.** You knock on the doors. You make the phone calls. You canvass the neighborhoods, go out on cold calls, set up appointments, and make presentations. You know that you can be of real benefit by bringing others your product or service and you do your absolute best to bring that to as many people as possible. You are working daily on overcoming what you fear most, which gives you the power to control your fear.

> ✔ **You maintain the highest possible ethical standards.**
> Honesty and integrity are an integral part of the fabric of
> your life. They are not merely conveniences to be dropped
> and picked up according to the situation. You don't practice
> "situational ethics."

Okay, you have a pretty good idea of what you need to bring to a
potential selling situation. Now I want to get specific about how
you use that foundation of professionalism to put your prospects
at ease so you can better serve their needs.

# Being on the Prospect's Side

A prospect is not an enemy to be battered into submission. She is
actually your partner in success. You're both on the same side
and it is part of your responsibility to make sure the other party
knows it. You have an awful lot in common. One area of common
ground is the fact that you are both consumers who meet with
salespeople all the time. The only difference at the moment is
that you are an expert in the area in which the prospect most
needs an expert.

Sometimes making this point directly is very helpful. Eventually
you will come up with the ideal phrase for your personality. Until
this happens, I want you to use the following phrase:

CHAMPION STRATEGY #1

> Ms. Prospect, when I'm not helping people get involved
> with my product, I'm a consumer, just like you, looking for
> quality products at the best price. What I hope for when
> I'm shopping is to find someone who can help me under-
> stand all the facts about the item I'm interested in so I
> can make a wise decision. Today, I'd like to earn your
> confidence in me as an expert on (insert your product or
> service). So feel free to ask any questions you might have.

Use it just as written here. Practice it so that it sounds natural
and present it with genuine sincerity in your voice and in your
heart. It has worked for salespeople all over the world.

Believe me, this is a great way to show that you are on common
ground with your prospect. You can't just repeat the words,
however. You have to mean them. It really explains your relative
positions well and removes some of the adversarial aspects a
prospect can bring to a prospecting call.

The key to the situation is to always put your prospect's needs before your own. Show that you are genuinely interested in serving their real needs and that you are committed to superior customer service. When your prospects realize your level of commitment, they are already taking giant strides down the pathway to a relaxed presentation. They are well on their way to liking you and trusting you.

## Caring for Your Body Suit

The way you carry yourself, the way you sit, cross your legs, hold your hands, make eye contact and a hundred other body actions "speak" as loudly as your voice and your wardrobe. Realize that we all communicate with much more than the words that flow out of our mouths. Often your body language speaks loudest of all. A champion learns this sign language not to control people, but to communicate effectively, to increase understanding of the prospect's position, and to help put her at ease. Keep these points in mind:

✔ **Consider your posture.** People are too often unaware of their body positioning throughout the day. Your stance is important. Your posture sends a message about your level of energy and enthusiasm for what you are doing. Women standing with their feet very far apart present an ominous image. Yet, assuming the fashion model pose of having one foot slightly angled and in front of the other can be seen as too feminine and delicate — not the image you want if your product is anything more heavy duty than lingerie or perfumes. Carrying your shoulders properly indicates confidence, whereas a slouch, even a slight one, shows the lack of it.

My dear friend and fellow speaker Ron Fronk conducts seminars that teach seven gentle exercises he calls Master Motions that give you an energy boost during the day. He begins each set with what he calls Power Breathing. "Energy, attitude, and posture are interdependent," Ron says. "When you stand tall for a few moments and breathe deeply, you give yourself what many call a second wind." Too often we ignore our breathing patterns. With daily stresses most people tend to take short breaths, not taking in as much oxygen as the body truly needs to perform at its peak. Eventually, it shows in your posture, in that knot in your shoulder, stiffness in your neck, and afternoon desire for a nap. Stand tall! Breathe deeply and you'll present a more powerful image.

✔ **Consider your stride.** If you walk purposefully, people get the feeling that you have purpose and determination in your life. Dragging your heels, walking too slowly, walking with your head down (as if you were watching every step), or taking large steps can make a negative impression on your prospect.

✔ **Consider your body size.** If you're tall, be sure to stand back slightly when you meet someone who is shorter than you. It's uncomfortable for them, putting them in a subservient position to have to look up at you. If you're shorter than the people you're meeting, you need to be extra careful about your posture and gestures. Don't do things in minuscule unless your products are microscopic or require delicate handling.

   Body size is especially important in male-female contacts. Many men hold the belief, whether it's a conscious belief or not, that men should be taller than women. If you're a tall woman, you need to consider how to work at putting men who are shorter than you at ease. It may be wise to sit down as soon as appropriate after meeting someone of an extreme height difference to get things on a more level playing field, so to speak. This strategy is applied very successfully by the best teachers of youngsters. They get themselves on the child's eye level as quickly as possible to build trust.

Remember that initial impressions, firm ones, are formed within the first ten seconds of a contact. Most salespeople are off to a running start or are already lagging behind as the first "hellos" are exchanged. Your job is to be well ahead of the game after the vital first ten seconds.

Your goal is always to be a person others like and trust. Your body language is what usually gets this complex process moving or grinding to a slow halt. You can find any number of books on the subject that go into considerable depth and I recommend that you do some serious study in this area. For now, I think it is important that you master the following three areas of speaking through body language:

✔ Smile

✔ Make eye contact

✔ Shake hands firmly

## *Smile, and the whole world smiles with you*

Try this little experiment sometime. When you're feeling a bit out of sorts, just smile. If you're like most people, your disposition will change. You'll actually begin to feel better and maybe even realize that whatever is bothering you isn't worth bothering with at all. That's the power of a smile, and it's a power you can and should share.

A good smile comes naturally to some, while others have to work at it. A good smile is a *genuine* smile. Have you ever noticed the "smiles" in beauty pageants? These poses are learned techniques that supposedly present a smile without creating wrinkles. I don't know if the tradeoff is worth it, though, because this type of interchangeable expression lacks credibility, personality, and warmth. If you were to walk into a prospect's office with such an insincere expression, you'd probably be shown the way out rather quickly. A fake smile in sales is worse than no smile at all.

This may sound silly, but a simple smile can pay off for you in big ways. If you do not have a good, open smile then practice until you get one. That's right, stand or sit in front of a mirror until you develop a smile that reveals your genuine interest in the prospect. Your smile should warm the heart of a prospect like the golden rays of the sun. An open smile affects your whole face — your lips part, your eyes light up, and your brow relaxes. Check and recheck yourself every time you visit the restroom, your rearview mirror, or a plate glass window. Don't feel foolish. There are much more embarrassing things you could get caught doing in front of a mirror.

The power of the smile can be felt over the telephone. In some instances, a telephone connection can diminish the intensity of your voice or enthusiasm, so for my telemarketing students, I always recommend that they project a little more intensity over the phone lines than they do in person.

You can feel the happiness and enthusiasm for a smile in the words of a letter, in brochure copy, even in books. Can you tell I'm smiling now? I am because this is fun for me.

There's just something in the way humans communicate that lets the other party know that we're feeling good about the conversation. That really helps put them at ease.

## *The eyes have it*

Okay, that's a bad pun, but it's also good sense. There's a reason "shifty-eyed" people are not trusted. If you're constantly looking down or away from your prospect, even if you're just nervous meeting people, she will think you are trying to hide something. I don't mean for you to get bogged down into a meeting-busting staring contest. Just make friendly eye contact, glancing away now and then so you don't intimidate your prospect. Remember to smile with your eyes, too.

My students often ask me what's too much or too little eye contact. We'd have to conduct a scientific study to answer that in a strict manner. In my personal experience, I have found that eye contact when I present facts is essential so I can read in their eyes whether or not they're believing me. Eye contact when you ask for the final approval is critical. You want to know they understand that you're asking them to make a decision.

If you prospect with people of different cultural backgrounds than yours, invest a little of your time in understanding how eye contact is used there. In some Asian cultures heavy eye contact is seen as being aggressive and rude. You need to learn the meaning of their definition of "heavy" and adapt your presentation to their needs.

## Shake hands and come out selling

I once heard of a young salesperson who was instructed by a business owner on the "proper way to shake hands." The young man was to grip the other person's hand very firmly, look him in the eye, and lean into the grip with a broad smile. This particular young man happened to be over 6 feet tall and weighed nearly 280 pounds. When he met a prospect, such as your basic little old man weighing a frail 150 pounds at best, the young man towered over the old man, and with all teeth flashing and, in a booming voice, said, "Hi, let's do business." What kind of impact do you think he made on the prospect? Does the word "intimidating" come to mind?

The proper way to shake hands is to take the other person's entire hand and give a brief, firm shake or two and then let go. That is the same rule for men and women. A woman with a too-strong handshake is as unprofessional as a man with a dead-fish handshake. No one likes a weak handshake, and it makes a bad impression with virtually everyone. On the other hand you don't want to crush anyone's fingers, either. Certainly don't keep pumping away like you're trying to get water from an old-fashioned well. I've seen people practically have to start a tug of war just to get their hand back from someone who refused to stop "being friendly."

If you're meeting with a husband and wife and you shake one hand, shake the other as well. If the sale involves children and they are present, it is certainly okay to shake those little hands too, unless you get a signal otherwise. Kids generally take to this "grown-up" activity and it never hurts to get them on your side if they can influence the meeting or the sale.

Watch for subtle, and sometimes not so subtle, signs or body language that indicates a handshake would not be appropriate. Some people suffer with arthritis and this simple gesture may be a constant source of pain. Other people may be suffering from a cold and they're trying not to spread it around. Some folks just don't like to be touched by other folks. Whatever the reason, if you get the signal, avoid the shake. No matter what your intentions, no matter how friendly the act, if the other party doesn't want to shake hands and you force the situation, you will put him in an uncomfortable position. You're probably doing the same thing to yourself at the same time.

## Greeting Someone

The initial greeting is very important and can set the tone for a positive or negative meeting. The outcome is generally up to you. Popular ways of saying "hello" range from the formal to the not so formal:

- Good morning/afternoon/evening or good day
- Thank you for coming in
- Thank you for seeing me
- Hello
- How are you?
- How are you doing?
- Hi
- Howdy

Which one of these greetings you use depends upon a number of factors. If you have a good relationship with the prospect, a simple "hi" is appropriate. Of course, if you are greeting the same individual in a formal meeting or for the first time, you would want to say more. When in doubt, you can hardly go wrong by sticking with the formal approach. Remember your body language and smile.

## Building a Relationship from the Common Ground Up

After the introductions and after you've established a nonthreatening position with your body language, you move into the next phase: establishing the common ground. The easiest way to do that is to just look around you for conversation starters. Your goal here isn't to enter into a long-term discussion of lighthearted topics, you merely want to break the ice with a few moments of small talk. This allows your prospect to ease away from a natural fear of a sales encounter into realizing that you are an open individual with whom he or she can comfortably do business.

For example, Mr. X may have a number of model airplanes decorating his office. This is a natural for warming up a meeting. You can ask if he is a model builder, if he flew those planes in the service, or any of a number of questions. People love to talk about their interests and it's a great way to reduce the tension in the first moments of a meeting.

Ms. Y may have a series of golf trophies on her wall or golf-oriented items decorating her desk. If you play golf, you already have something in common. You can discuss techniques, professional athletes you admire, or favorite courses you both play. If you don't play, you can come up with a question or two about one of the items to get her talking and seeing your genuine interest in her interests.

## How to put a prospect at ease

✔ Feel and act with confidence and authority

✔ Shake hands quickly and firmly if the signals are clear

✔ Smile with genuine sincerity

✔ Make pleasant, nonthreatening eye contact

✔ Involve the prospect in the process. Ask questions.

✔ Listen to what's really being said

✔ Pause thoughtfully

✔ Answer questions openly and honestly

✔ Keep your focus completely on your prospect

✔ Discover your prospects' real needs and empathize with them

The absolute best way to put your prospect at ease is to place her best interests before your own. She'll sense your consideration and respond in kind.

When you meet Mr. and Mrs. Z in their home, you will be surrounded with conversation starters. These include family photos, family mementos, interesting crafts or artwork decorating the home, kids, obvious hobbies, and even the wonderful smell of Mrs. Z's delicious cake and coffee. Anything that looks handmade is a natural: Ask if they made it and you'll get them going on about their interest in handicraft. Even if they didn't make it, they may start relating a story of the quaint little shop in Missouri, Maine, or Morocco where they made its delightful discovery. Look around and you'll find what you, and they, need to get the conversation started.

## *Avoid awkward beginnings*

If you come across a rare home or office where you just can't see anything to get the prospect talking, don't get anxious. You don't want to create an awkward situation by looking like you're struggling to come up with a subject, any subject, to talk about.

Don't try something as obvious as talking about the weather unless a very specific, unusual weather phenomenon has occurred and is a legitimate subject for conversation. Instead, pick a safe, noncontroversial topic from the local news that is of general interest and follow the lead of your prospect's reaction to it. Ask about the neighborhood, good local restaurants, mention the landscaping or kids' bikes in the front yard, something, anything that may be personal and dear to their hearts.

If you meet someone in an elevator, a simple, nonthreatening comment or question about a piece of clothing or an item she's carrying, or the question, "What brings you to this building?" can generate enough of an opening for you to exchange cards before the elevator reaches her floor. I call this "floor-to-floor" prospecting.

Waiting in any line — grocery, fast food, theater, soccer sign-ups, or waiting for your driver's license — gives you an opportunity to meet the people standing in front of you or behind you. If you're pleasant, they shouldn't treat you like you have the plague. Who knows, it could be Bill Gates's kid in line ahead of you at McDonald's someday and, boy oh boy, do you have a great idea for her dad. You never know who may open the next door of opportunity for you.

Paying someone a sincere compliment can be a great conversation starter providing that the compliment is legitimate and that you state it sincerely. I want to stress that most people have built-in radar for detecting when you're buttering them up.

## Watch out for a setup

The owner and top salesman for a motion picture company specializing in corporate and business education were making a presentation to an upper-level manager (with the power to say "yes") in a large educational institution. The woman executive brought the subject around to two other local filmmakers who specialized in producing very low-budget features of varying quality. The salesman, wary of a trap, stated that he believed the filmmakers had earned a definite niche in the market and that they were serving that niche very well. This proved to be a wise answer when the manager revealed that one of the film producers was her husband and the other her son. The scientific term to describe that episode is "dodging a bullet."

Prospects will sometimes set you up just to see how you react. Do your best to keep from falling into any such trap. If you have to answer a question about a controversial subject, keep your answer as noncontroversial as possible and try to ease the conversation back to the more important matter at hand — providing service to your prospect.

Insincere flattery works against you in every situation. For a prospect, you instantly go from that nice salesperson to the greedy guy or gal who just wants to take her hard-earned money and run.

A famous Hollywood story tells of the actor who discovered the secret of acting. "It's all about sincerity," he said. "Once I learned how to fake that, I knew I had it made!" Maybe you can fake sincerity on the big screen where you have take after take in production to get it right and where you keep only the best shot and discard the bad ones. In sales, you get only one take. If you blow that one, you're not likely to get another shot at getting it right.

## *Steer clear of controversial subjects*

Avoid discussing any controversial subject — it's a good policy. Religion, politics, and sex are the top three on the no-no list. Your community also may have special subjects at the local level that can set off prospects. People store up amazing amounts of energy in regard to controversial subjects and you never know what may set off the powder keg. You're better off avoiding an explosion by never causing a spark anywhere near a prospect.

An excellent technique for avoiding controversy is to toss the hot potato back to the prospect. For example, if the prospect brings up a politically sensitive issue, you may respond something like this: "Actually, Ms. Prospect, I'm so busy serving my clients that I've haven't kept up with that subject. What do you think about it?"

Steering the controversial topic back to your prospect lets you keep the discussion rolling without taking a position that could build a wall between the two of you. When the prospect responds, you learn her position without exposing your own. If you can see that this topic may come up again, you have at least bought yourself a little time to get up to speed on the subject and come up with an answer that, hopefully, keeps you out of hot water.

## *Now What Do I Do?*

Now you do what you came to do in the first place. You know your product or service, your persuasive techniques, and you have placed your prospect's needs before your own. You have worked hard to make sure the individual likes and trusts you and you are prepared to do what is in her very best interests.

Now you help your prospect reach the right decision for her company or herself — to purchase your product or service because that really is the right thing to do.

# Chapter 12

# Can You Really Help These People?

*A*n account executive in a midsize metropolitan market I'll call No Name City made a cold call on the president of a large, stable manufacturing firm in that area. The firm and the service company represented by the account executive should have been an ideal match. Each company could have provided something needed and wanted by the other. Unfortunately, things didn't work out that way, and this story lacks what should have been a happy ending.

"I am sorry you've wasted your time," said the president of the manufacturing firm. "If I had known your company was from around here, I never would have let you in my office. Don't take this personally, but I will never, ever work with any company in your industry from No Name City!"

Apparently, the president had worked with two or three local companies and suffered unethical treatment from each. He and his company were treated so badly that he vowed to work only with service providers from a different market.

We all pay when someone in our business acts without ethics. Unethical salespeople not only do a disservice to their customers, they also make life more difficult for all of us in sales. High standards of honesty and integrity should be as much a part of your career as education, training, ambition, and punctuality.

Because you can't count on everybody having such high standards, you, as wise prospectors, must be prepared to face prejudices that you had no hand in creating. Researching a large company you want to work with could reveal such prejudices. Talking with some of the employees before attempting to reach Mr. Decision Maker is a wise idea here.

A champion's heart has no room for unethical behavior.

# Help People By Helping Them Make Decisions

One theme comes up a lot during question-and-answer sessions at my lectures and seminars: Using certain champion techniques is unfair. Some people are concerned that they will talk someone into buying something that she really doesn't want.

I give you many techniques and tricks of the trade in this book, but not every one of you can use each. Some recommendations will work better with your particular personality, the personality of the prospect, and the selling situation. The only way any of these techniques can ever be unethical is if someone uses it for an unethical purpose. As with any tool, you can use these tips and techniques for good purposes or for causing damage.

If you take the time to properly qualify your prospect, then you know if your product or service can benefit them. When you know those needs, your duty is to make the benefits of that product or service available as quickly as possible. Part of that duty requires you to help the prospect make decisions.

Remember, a prospect wouldn't be spending valuable time with you if there weren't some legitimate interest. The world is just moving too quickly these days to waste a minute of the day on unnecessary purchases. Despite the occasional stories about the Brooklyn Bridge or swampland in Florida, most people don't buy something they don't want, especially when you get into big-ticket items. Even if the prospect knows that she needs the product or service, even if she really wants it, you still face an uphill struggle to get her to make the decision to make the purchase.

You've qualified your prospect properly, and now it's time to provide the superior service she deserves. That service includes telling the truth, answering all her questions, and helping her get to the word *yes*. If you really have put her interests before your money, then you're truly doing the right thing and there is no reason in the world to think yourself unfair or unethical.

If you know the needs of your prospect, then not allowing her the benefits of your product or service would be unfair.

# Greed is a costly expense

This story I heard recently is an example of how expensive greed can be.

An advertising/marketing firm was having trouble with one of its major accounts. Miscommunication, questions about billing procedures, and challenges with making deadlines were creating a major rift between client and agency. The account was not only very profitable, it was also one of those prestigious, high-visibility types. The agency president decided to save the situation. He invited the president of the account to lunch at an upscale restaurant to discuss and resolve the situation.

The presidents met at the appointed time. The agency owner brought the account executive and the art director to help emphasize the importance of the company's business to the agency. The executives resolved the problems amicably, and the meeting broke up with the agency head grabbing the check and heading back to the office.

At the end of the month, the client was shocked to see that the agency had billed him for the entire lunch. Worse, the agency had billed him for the hourly rate of the art director and the account executive on top of everything else.

The agency had saved a bad situation only to make it worse by letting greed rear its ugly head. The client fired the agency the next day.

We, as professionals, have a duty to uphold the highest standards when dealing with customers, but I think we have another duty. We have a duty to the profession of selling. I have tried throughout all my selling days to create an honest, positive impression of people in the industry, partly because that's just the way I am. I sincerely want to be of genuine service to my clients. Additionally, I want to be a good representative for my industry. I don't want to create any challenges for all the other salespeople in No Name City.

The key to success in sales is to make people like and trust you, and that is surprisingly easy. If you ever have doubts about what you're doing, just ask yourself if the action really puts your prospect first. The truthful answer tells you all you need to know.

# Honesty — the Vital Ingredient

You can't become a champion unless you're honest. You can't lie, cheat, beat, or steal in any degree. I include "little white lies" in that list too. Such little lies have a way of growing into big problems. When you start out on a dishonest path, even if you're taking baby steps, you're walking on shaky ground. I've seen it happen before when a salesperson tells just one little white lie. Of course another lie follows, and then another, until a pattern becomes established. Eventually, and that person loses far more than a sale or two. The lack of honesty costs the salesperson his credibility.

No matter what your product or service, if you don't have credibility, you don't have anything to sell. That's why, when it comes to sales, a champion always

- ✔ Delivers on promises
- ✔ Upholds a personal set of standards
- ✔ Keeps client confidences

That list isn't too hard to remember, is it? Putting these principles into practice isn't too hard either. The daily act of ethical behavior should feel totally natural and bring on a feeling of well-being. It's when those other, ugly little thoughts surface that we begin to feel upset, awkward, ashamed, embarrassed, and just a little bit sick to our stomachs.

## Be a delivery person

Every contact you make with a prospect involves some kind of promise: a call back, an appointment, delivery of information, and so on. Always deliver, no matter how small or how large the challenge.

Delivering on your promises builds long-lasting relationships and good reputations. I've always found that the people who make smaller promises, but who keep all of them, have a much better track record in sales than those who promise the moon but who don't always deliver. A prospect may never remember the fact that you have returned all his calls, but the one call not returned will live forever. Clients never remember the 101 things you do right and that's okay. If you promise a call within two days, be sure you make it. If you promise to drop by the prospect's office with promotional literature, make sure you or someone pops in with the goods. If you say you'll call back at 2 p.m., don't leave a prospect sitting at a desk, drumming her fingers and looking at the clock.

## Selling yourself boosts credibility

Should you tell your prospects subtly about that quality award you received? Should you put the fact that you were named to your company's Executive Achievers Club on your business card? Absolutely. As long as you don't brag about your service or your achievements with your prospects, keeping them informed about the high level of service you perform is very important to building and maintaining your credibility.

People are naturally going to pay attention to the way you conduct yourself, but in the skeptical times in which we live, look for simple ways to reinforce your position. You can do all of this in casual conversation in a way that informs without boasting.

You're doing a good job. Make sure customers know just how good.

The goal is to build a feeling of trust so that no matter what you promise, the customer knows you will deliver. The client also begins to realize that if you don't promise something, it probably can't be done.

That conduct puts you head and shoulders above all those salespeople hawking real estate up there on cloud nine.

If you mistakenly state a falsehood or discover you can't deliver on a promise, don't wait for your prospect to find out the hard way. Pick up the telephone or pop in and explain the situation as soon as possible. The more time that passes between your call and the time your prospect makes the discovery, the more it sticks in her memory. You also have to work longer to win back your credibility . . . if you can.

## Be a standard-bearer

An ethical salesperson never violates his personal code of behavior, no matter what the temptation. You might think about it, and that, too, is okay. You can't control your random thoughts. You can, however, control your actions, and that clearly marks the difference between a true professional and all the wannabes.

In spite of what you may see in the movies, on television, or in tabloid headlines, most people respect a person of integrity and want to trade with that type of person. People look up to those who have a code of behavior and who live it. Compromising on your standards only lowers your image in the eyes of anyone and everyone who sees it happen. Even people who try to get you to compromise will admire your strength of will and commitment. If, in those rare occurrences when you actually lose a temporary advantage, an appointment, or a sale, for example, compromising your standards would be far more costly to you in the long run.

In a very real way, living up to your own high standards is delivering on a promise to yourself.

### Protect proprietary information

Salespeople often encounter valuable information about a company, how its product is made, how the service is performed, and plans for expansion. In-depth research is a natural and necessary part of how you provide the best service possible. In some cases you may even need to sign a nondisclosure agreement to protect valuable company information. Even if you never sign such an agreement, always respect the confidentiality of your prospect or customer. The information you come across or that is shared with you is not meant to be shared with others, certainly not with any competitors you may also serve. This is not as easy as you may think. A seemingly unimportant bit of news or information may have no significance to you, but in the wrong hands it can prove costly to your prospect and, eventually, you.

People in business can generally discover the source of an information leak. Even if you made your disclosure casually without realizing the seriousness of your remarks, the damage is the same. Even if you were totally unaware of the significance of speaking out of turn, your prospect will know that you cannot be trusted with important information. Talking about your prospect's business just isn't good business.

During World War II, a popular slogan warned against talking out of turn: "Loose lips sink ships." When it comes to client confidentiality, loose lips can sink your future with that company and probably many others too.

## Ethics and the Law

Today, no one expects a salesperson to know every law and regulation regarding his business or industry. Yet we work in a very regulated society. An ethical approach to all sales situations helps keep you on firm ground and out of trouble.

✔ Thoroughly educating your prospects about your product or service before closing the sale is important. Don't leave any surprises for them down the road. Surprises have a nasty tendency to turn into land mines that can blow a relationship to smithereens.

✔ If you have the authority to negotiate or set prices, don't hesitate to do so. If you don't have authority but you state a price anyway, your company most likely has to live with your quoted price. That agreement may not be one that bodes well for your future with the company. Avoid even the appearance of setting a price if you don't have the authority to do so.

✔ Be very careful about exaggerating your product's capabilities, and make sure that you know what you're talking about before opening your mouth. Always make certain that any claims made about your product, service, or company are up-to-date and accurate. Be sure you can back up your claims with survey results, statistics, or other methods of proof. Quoting a specification from last year's brochure may get you into more trouble than quoting an inaccurate price.

Laws and regulations change constantly, but you must make an effort to know and understand those that pertain to your performance in the marketing of your product or service. You may not need to know the legal weight for shipping in interstate commerce, but you'd better be up to speed on warranty and guarantee regulations.

## Ethics 101 — the Final Exam

A sales professional lives by a code of personal standards, but sometimes a situation comes up that is just too puzzling for a fast judgment call. A time may come when you're really confused about the ethics of a decision. Run through the following checklist, and you should develop a good idea of the proper direction to take.

✔ Would I want someone to do this to me?

✔ What would I do if someone did this to me?

✔ Can anyone get hurt if I do this? Who and to what degree?

✔ Can I look Mom and Dad/the preacher/my mentor in the eyes when describing this action?

✔ Would I be proud to see this on tonight's news program?

✔ How would I feel if my kids/wife/best friend knew about this?

Most of the time, you'll have a clear idea of right from wrong, even if it's only a "gut feeling." When in doubt, don't panic or think you're in a crisis situation. Just take a moment to ask yourself these questions, assess your feelings, and then trust them.

You'll do the right thing because that's what a champion does.

## Taking Care of People Takes Care of Business

I often think a lot of our ethical problems come up because we sometimes forget how to take care of our prospects and customers. We let the pressures of the job, the excitement of the moment, or just our natural drive to succeed get in the way of doing what a champion does best — putting the other person first. We must never forget that we're building long-term relationships with our prospects.

Following is an eight-step blueprint to help keep your building program on schedule.

1. **Aim to win at your profession.** You play sales like a game, a serious one, that can help an enormous number of people throughout the years. If you're truly committed to outstanding service you will play to win. That's the way to build a win-win relationship every time.

2. **Associate with the people you admire and respect.** An old saying goes, "If you lie down with dogs, you'll get up with fleas." Human beings tend to adopt the ethical codes of the people around them. Hang out with the kind of people you want to become.

3. **Deliver on every promise to a prospect or customer.** Make sure that they receive full value for every dollar they've invested, and then some. Earn and maintain a reputation as someone who keeps his or her word, even if that means making fewer promises and smaller promises.

4. **As people have helped you up the ladder of success, remember it's part of your responsibility to help others make the same climb.** The who and the how is your choice: coworkers, customers, or even people down on their luck who need a hand.

5. **Prospects and customers are not the enemy.** They are your partners in success.

6. **The competition is not the enemy.** Running down a competitor is one of the fastest ways to run down yourself and a sure-fire way to turn off your prospect. Even if your competitor exhibits this poor behavior, don't get drawn into playing that game. It's a sucker bet, for sure.

7. **Always be on the lookout for new business.** Obviously, this applies to your own efforts, but keep a sharp eye out for ways to promote business for your prospect, customer, coworker, and, in some cases, your competitor.

8. **Look for ways to improve your product or service.** Fight to see that good ideas get a fair hearing and a fair trial. This step is more than good business, it's excellent customer service.

   Come to think of it, always looking for improvement really is good business after all.

You have faced and will continue to face challenges to your integrity. The opportunities for taking unfair advantage of a situation are everywhere. You'll run into opportunities to commit sins of omission of important details, and times when stretching the truth might just gain you an appointment or sale. A champion not only faces these challenges, he faces them head on.

# Part IV

## What's a Few Referrals Among Friends?

The 5th Wave    By Rich Tennant

"I met my husband when I sold him an air
purifier. That's him over there with some of
my referral-in-laws."

# In this part . . .

*T*his section is where you begin to build your
business. I cover how to nicely and professionally ask for and get referrals from every
prospect. You don't get referrals just once. Your
solid clients should be sending you referrals on
a continuing basis. Discover how to keep yourself — and the benefits of your product — in the
forefront of your clients' minds so that they, in
essence, become agents for your product.

# Chapter 13

# Getting Your Next Prospect from Your Last Prospect

*In This Chapter*

▶ Working smarter

▶ Understanding when and where to get referrals

▶ Obtaining referrals

▶ Following the seven steps to better referrals

▶ Arranging referral visits

*A* "sure thing" doesn't exist in this world of ours, but I often think that the closest thing to a sure thing is a referral sale. People in sales know referrals are significantly easier to meet with, talk to, follow up, and get an agreement from than any person contacted through a cold call. Many people don't realize just how much the math works in favor of referrals.

Studies show that the closing ratio with nonqualified prospects is only 10 percent. However, the closing rate with qualified referrals is 60 percent! As they say down at the track, "How's about *them* odds?"

Working with referral calls doesn't mean you work any easier. You get a considerably higher return for the same effort. It's as if you've found a couple of extra workdays in every week.

Yet for some reason that I just don't understand, even experienced salespeople often shy away from asking for referrals. They seem to think that their prospects or customers will volunteer names of people who may be interested in their product or service. That's about as silly as expecting people to say, "Great, we'll take three of whatever you have," reaching for their checkbooks and saying, "I'll just sign it, you can fill in the amount later." Like sales, referrals are something you have to make happen. This chapter shows you how.

## Don't Get Caught Out in the Cold

I don't suggest that you abandon cold calling. Far from it, cold calling is and always will be a big part of most everybody's sales programs. I do suggest that you beef up your lagging referral business. Look at it this way: Somebody is going to get all those referral sales, so why shouldn't it be you?

A referral isn't a sale; a referral is someone favorably inclined to speak with you, and that's about it. Champions treat referrals with the same respect and courtesy they treat any other person. Their energy level and enthusiasm is high. They are prepared, and they are excited about sharing the benefits of their products. They take nothing and no one for granted.

Why, then, don't more salespeople get referrals? All the excuses, all the dissembling, all the "good" reasons for not getting referrals really boil down to just two:

- ✔ The request for referrals is inadequate.
- ✔ The request is never made.

Some salespeople feel that it's impolite to ask for anything further once a sale has been closed. Some salespeople fear they may offend clients if they ask for referrals. Some may suffer from cowardice or laziness.

People, this is serious business. If you're self-employed, you punish only yourself. If you work for someone else, you have an obligation to do the job right. If someone provides you with the very real opportunity of making money, building a career, earning a living, and supporting your dreams, don't you think you owe it to him to finish the job?

---

### Treat referrals carefully!

A word of warning before I go further. I've seen salespeople develop the attitude that referrals really are sure things. They waltz to calls or appointments with referrals believing that the sales are done-deals. This attitude isn't professional, and it does a real disservice to the people who make referrals. When salespeople take referrals for granted and do not treat them with the respect they treat other prospects, they make those who make referrals look bad for referring someone so ill-prepared, out of touch, and overconfident. *You* are the real loser if you have this attitude.

---

# Call Off the Hounds

Where do you get referrals? Take off your Sherlock Holmes deerstalker cap, put away the oversized magnifying glass, and put the bloodhounds back in the kennel. There's no need to go looking for the trail of the referrals. They're all around you, everywhere, every day. Think not? Then take a look around.

## Family and friends

These people are probably the easiest, most accessible source of referrals you have, yet they may be the ones you resist asking the most. That just doesn't make sense. If your product is good and if you're personally dedicated to superior customer service, why should you deny those things to people who need them? The excuse is generally something along the lines of "I just don't want to bother them." What bother?

Do your competitors have a superior product? Will they provide the kind of personal, dedicated service that you will! Will the competing sales force jump through hoops for their customer if a problem arises? By not calling on your friends and family members, you leave them and their friends and associates to be served by the competition. Ask yourself: Is this the act of a friend?

## Networking

Most professional, business, and civic groups have regular meetings for handshaking, backslapping, and wolfing down chicken 'n peas. Smart salespeople use these meetings for networking to obtain referrals. Volunteer to work on committees and special projects that can put you in touch with a different group from your "regular crowd" and provide even more opportunities.

You can use any kind of gathering to interact with even more people: concerts, religious or school functions, recreation, sports, hobby clubs, and similar group meetings or get-togethers to interact with even more people. Even Saturday's game of golf, the fishing trip, and the annual Girl Scout planning session can provide you with a wealth of contacts and opportunities for referrals.

You can get people around you to talk business by expressing your own excitement over your triumphs of the day or week. As long as you don't boast or brag, you will find that people are attracted to energy and excitement. Become a magnet by being enthusiastic. People around you will always ask why you're so "up." When they ask this question, they have asked you about your business. Tell them about your business and during the course of the conversation ask for referrals.

## Satisfied customers

What do most people want to do the moment they buy something? That's right. They want to talk about it. This applies to the homemaker who's just found a new kitchen gadget, to the owner of a new car, and to the manager of a mill with a brand new, multimillion-dollar boiler system. People want to talk about their "new stuff," whatever it may be.

Can there ever be a better time to get referrals than when excited buyers show their new whatchamacallits to anyone and everyone within earshot? They are going to talk about their purchases, so shouldn't you benefit from all your hard work in making those purchases possible? There's bound to be at least one or two people among their contacts who will also get excited about the whatchamacallit and want one of their very own. Because you're the responsible party for all of this excitement, your name is bound to be passed around. That's why I always recommend a 7-to-10-day follow-up with a new client and a 30-day follow-up. Take advantage of the height of your client's excitement in showing off his new prized possession. Your job on the day of the sale is to ask who he'll be showing off to right away and get those referred names now!

If you leave a customer's place of business without referrals, you haven't done your job to the best of your abilities. It's a bit like having a great meal at a fine restaurant, but walking out before the dessert tray rolls by. You've had a good experience, but look at all the goodies you've let pass you by.

Satisfied customers can't give you solid gold referrals unless you continue to provide them with solid gold service.

People talk, especially in business. If you don't take care of your customers, or if you're unethical in your business practices, word spreads. Satisfied customers may tell only three people about their positive experiences with you. Dissatisfied customers go out of their way to tell 11 people about their unpleasant experiences!

The numbers (or the odds, if you will) are always on serving your customers.

You have to earn your referrals, and if you continually provide superior service you will earn your fair share.

# No sale? Ask for a referral anyway!

I had one client with whom I had invested several of my weekends in showing properties. For some reason, I just wasn't hitting the mark in locating the right property for him. During a follow-up phone call, he told me he found an ad in the paper that sounded good, went, looked at the property, and bought it — without my assistance. Bye-bye fee. I was, however, happy that he found what he wanted. We had struck up a rather companionable relationship during our time together so I decided to at least get the referrals. I handled it something like this:

Tom: Jack, I'm so happy that you've found the home you wanted. I am sorry that it wasn't one that I helped you with, though. I'm constantly trying to improve the level of service I provide my clients. Let me ask you, do you believe I did a good job for you?

Jack: Of course, you did, Tom. You worked hard in locating all those potential properties. I appreciate your efforts.

Tom: If you truly believe I did a good job, then you wouldn't mind referring me to three of your friends or relatives, would you?

Jack: Of course not, Tom. The service you provided was great.

Tom: I'm glad you feel that way, Jack. Tell you what I'm going to do. I'll send you three of my business cards. All I ask is that you give them to three of your friends or relatives and ask them to contact me for their real estate needs.

Jack: Sure, Tom. I'd be happy to.

Tom: Great. I'll check with you every now and then so I can get those names from you.

I have to tell you that every now and then some manhandled, dog-eared card of mine came into my office attached to the hand of a new client who was saying, "Jack told me to ask you to help us find a home."

## *Other salespeople*

I've never believed in the theory that the competition is the enemy. Throughout my sales career, I've seen some of the strongest competition among strong friends. Champions are always looking for other champions, even if they're in competing businesses. The reason is simple: Professional salespeople are always in a position to refer business to others, and they want to refer people to fellow professionals. They also know that other professionals will someday, somehow, return the favor. That's how this game is played.

Suppose your company has inquired about providing industrial tree-trimming equipment to a pipeline construction company. While doing research, you learn that the company needs units that reach heights of 50 feet. Your units, however, can reach only 42 feet. Your company can't handle the job. You can let the prospect walk out the door to look for someone else, or you can recommend a fellow salesperson who works for a competitor that can handle the job. That's a win-win-win situation. The prospect gets quality service, the competitor gets business, and because of your professionalism, you will receive a favor somewhere down the road.

Think of your competitors as friends rather than enemies.

## *Speaking engagements*

If you get a reputation as being very good at something, such as sales, people want to hear what you have to say. Business and civic clubs, seminars, and schools all are looking for experts to impart valuable knowledge. If you can handle yourself in front of a crowd, you can look at these speaking engagements as fine ways to bring in referrals. Anyone who becomes a speaker automatically becomes an expert.

Prepare your speech or program carefully, as you would with a sales presentation. Expert status can melt away like snow in mountain sunshine if you fumble more than a couple of questions. Make your style appropriate to the subject matter. Usually the occasion requires a light to moderately serious approach. Be wary of believing that you have achieved celebrity status and keep your mind on the speech . . . and on the job of getting a handful of referrals.

# Give As Well As You Get

In boxing, you often hear the phrase, "Well, he gave as well as he got." That means for every punch a particular fighter took, he delivered one of equal intensity. Providing referrals is a lot like that except that you trade opportunities instead of body blows. You should recognize the value of referrals by providing referrals to other sales professionals.

Even if referrals are not and cannot be a part of your business, you should help other salespeople by providing them with referrals for two reasons:

✔ It's the right thing to do. You want to help friends and associates, even those who are good competitors, and you want to see them succeed. You also want the prospects that you refer to be taken care of by ethical, hard-working professionals.

✔ Referrals provide you with considerable public relations value. Call it racking up brownie points or building IOUs, but the point is that you'll be helping people who at some point will be in a position to help you.

# Seven Steps to Referrals

Getting a referral is like climbing a ladder. You step up to the top one rung at a time. The referral ladder has seven rungs, seven steps to success. Naturally, you don't climb a ladder just for the exercise. You use the ladder to get from one place to another. I recommend that you have a destination in mind before taking the first step. Set a personal goal to get a certain number of referrals from every contact. Ease into the process by getting just one referral per call or visit. Then increase the number to at least three.

Here's the ladder — start climbing! (Details on how to do each step follow this list.)

1. **Isolate the referrals' faces for your prospects.**

2. **Write the referrals' names on cards.**

3. **Qualify the referrals.**

4. **Ask for referrals' addresses.**

5. **If customers don't know the addresses, look for them in the phone book.**

6. **Ask your customers to set up an appointment with referrals.**

7. **Ask to use the customers' names when you call the referrals.**

This system will work for you, but you have to use it, and you have to use it every time you make contact with prospects and customers. Learn it, practice it, and have faith in it. After all, seven is a lucky number.

## Step 1: Isolate the referrals' faces for your prospects

> **Them:** Well, the city is just delighted with your cable puller, and we couldn't be happier with the way you've taken care of us.
>
> **You:** Just doing my job, Mr. Mayor. Say, uh, you don't know anybody else that needs cable-pulling equipment, do you?
>
> **Them:** Can't say that I do, offhand.
>
> **You:** Okay.

This salesperson has blown an opportunity. The absolute prime time to ask for referrals is when your customers are delighted with your product and the way you have served their needs, but this is the one moment when so many salespeople freeze up.

This prime-time freeze results from two powerful factors:

- ✔ The salesperson has closed the sale and is reluctant to ask for more.

- ✔ The customer is excited about the purchase and isn't really focused on anything other than the euphoria of the moment.

You need to bring your customer and yourself back into focus so that you may bring this feeling of euphoria to others who need your product.

If you ask outright for the names of referrals, your unfocused customers will probably draw blanks. You have to channel their thoughts into specifics — the people who they realize need your product or service. Here's an example of how you can refocus the prospect:

| | |
|---|---|
| You: | I can see that you're really excited about owning our cable puller. |
| Them: | Well, in less than a year all those wires will be underground. That's a better view for the tourists and a lot less hassle for our utilities department. |
| You: | I take it that you're happy with our service? |
| Them: | Delighted would be a better word. |
| You: | Thank you. I guess you'll be talking about this to a few fellow city managers and mayors. |
| Them: | Count on it. We have an association, you know. |
| You: | I bet they'll be interested in your innovations here. Is there anyone in your trade association who may be considering moving their overhead wires underground? |

Do you see how that happened, how the customer wasn't forced into running through his entire memory for possible names? Instead, the salesperson channeled the customer's mind into familiar territory where he could focus on specific names of individuals who may need cable-pulling equipment. The technique works just as well for used cars, real estate, high-tech equipment, and retail articles behind the counter.

## Step 2: Write the referrals' names on cards

Write down the information about a referral immediately on index cards. Don't trust your memory. Facts, figures, names, and dates have a way of slipping away from the brightest of minds. Make sure that you get the correct spellings and pronunciations of all names.

## Step 3: Qualify the referrals

Ask simple questions, such as, "What made Mr. Jackson of ABC Company come to your mind?" Your prospect may reply, "We talked at the last association meeting. I told him what we were considering, and he said it was a project on his list, too."

You must get all the information you can about the needs of the referral so that you can provide real service rather than what you think the referral may need.

## Step 4: Ask for addresses and phone numbers

If your referral is named John Smith, you may have a rather difficult time working your way through the phone book tracking him down. Always ask for addresses and phone numbers and write it down on the index card. If your prospects don't know, get as much information as you can, such as the referrals' streets or neighborhoods. Get any kind of information that will help you locate the referrals. People usually refer others whom they know well enough to also know how to reach them. I don't think you'll get too many referrals like this: "Oh, yeah, I was talking to a guy at the gas station last week and he mentioned he was looking for a better Whatzit. He drives a blue Pontiac. I'm sure you could talk to him if you can find him." Unless you're really hard up and need gas, you shouldn't invest much of your time hanging around that particular gas station waiting for your blue-Pontiac-driving lead to come in again.

## Step 5: Look in the phone book if your prospects don't know the addresses

If your prospects are willing to give you addresses but don't know them, just get the telephone book and ask your prospects to help you find the right names and addresses.

## Step 6: Ask your customers to call and set up appointments

I know what you're thinking: But, I just can't ask somebody to make an appointment for me.

Yes, you can, and all you have to do is ask. Nothing can be more simple.

Mr. Mayor, I appreciate the referral, I really do. Why don't we call him/her right now so you can share your excitement over what our company has done for your city. You wouldn't mind calling to make the introduction so we can arrange a convenient time for me to visit, would you?

If your prospects don't mind doing that, proceed immediately. However, if they are the least bit hesitant, back off and relieve the pressure.

## Step 7: If customers won't make calls, ask for permission to use their names

People may not be willing to make calls for a number of reasons. They may not know the other individuals very well. They may just be shy or even afraid of making a sales-related call. Asking for permission to use their names when you call referrals "takes them off the hook," so to speak. Few people will be willing to call, but most will be more than willing to allow you to use their names.

You won't always get referrals, but don't worry about it.

A referral isn't a relationship, and some referrals just aren't going to work out. That's no reason to stop asking for them. Keep in mind that, even if referrals don't purchase your product or service, they still can refer you to others who do need that product or service.

Ask. Make asking for referrals an automatic part of your day, like breathing. When you do not ask for referrals, you do not just deprive yourself of sales, you deprive consumers the right to enjoy the benefits of the product or service you represent.

## Chapter 14

# Keep Yourself and Your Product in the Prospect's Mind

***E***verybody is a prospect. Referrals are prospects; so are the people you've already contacted and who have said "no"; and so are your existing customers. However, after an initial contact and a follow-up or two, many salespeople allow this field of potential sales to lie fallow or, worse, allow the competition to develop and harvest the sales. Many salespeople just don't know how to keep themselves in a comfortable, positive place in their prospects' minds.

You need to stay in touch with your contacts, referrals, and existing customers to develop a flow of new prospects. In this chapter, I show you how to do just that with two strategies:

✔ **Follow-up.** A phone call, a note or letter, or a visit keeps you and your business well-entrenched in your customers' and prospects' minds. A follow-up is also a way to get more appointments for more presentations for more sales and more referrals. This is not something to do in a haphazard way or only on slow days. A champion develops a systematic, regular, almost scientific program and consistently follows through on follow-up.

✔ **Customer service.** Anyone who has known me over the years must have heard me say hundreds of times in print or on tape that we are in the service business. The service we give reflects the income we earn. I sometimes ask people to take the word Service and make the S a $ sign. If you really want to increase your income, find creative ways to give more service.

If these strategies are so simple and obvious, why do so many salespeople lose so many valuable prospects? Because providing customer service and following up on prospects is easy to not do. This stage of the sales process, however, is effective and helps you pave a wide, clear path to increased sales — and that's the path of the champion.

# *Prioritizing Your Follow-ups*

All prospects are important, so you should follow up on all of them. However, you need to prioritize your follow-up calls to help you allocate your time and resources appropriately. Recheck your priorities all the time, too. A freezing-cold prospect may suddenly become blazing hot when you hear that it just snatched a big contract that may require your product or service.

Break down your prospects into these basic categories:

- ✔ **Referrals.** Your have a much better chance of giving a presentation to a referral than to someone who has no idea who you are. A referral means you are no longer a complete stranger and you bring with you a significant comfort factor. You're almost a friend of the family.

- ✔ **Existing customers.** Thanking someone who has helped build your business is always appropriate. These folks are among the best prospects you will ever find. Ask how things are going and whether you can help with any challenges. And be sure to tell them you're committed to continued superior personal service.

- ✔ **People who didn't buy from you.** Just because a prospect didn't make a purchase doesn't mean he never will. Something I have stressed in other chapters is that everyone is a prospect or knows someone who is. His situation or needs may have changed or he may have encountered someone since your meeting who needs just what you're offering.

- ✔ **Hard-to-reach prospects.** Call these people last, but still call. Just because some prospects may be real challenges doesn't mean that you should give up on meeting them face-to-face. Sometimes these people just want to work with people who have the tenacity to pursue them. They're looking for the real professionals.

Only you know which prospect you should call right now. And who you choose to call should change as people and businesses shift in and out of the categories, as their business cycles (and yours) fluctuate, and as you receive information. Just remember to look at your list of prospects regularly and make those calls now.

# Three Sure-Fire Ways to Follow Up

 Your attitude toward following up with clients determines how successful you are. Many salespeople regard it as a chore, something they have to but don't want to do, a dreaded part of the selling cycle they would like to avoid. In sales, as in life, you get back whatever you send out. If you send out disinterest and a lack of enthusiasm, that's exactly what your prospects send back.

Smart salespeople realize the tremendous value (literally riches) to be found in a well-planned and executed follow-up program. These folks, full of enthusiasm, don't want to just call up to say, "Hi, how are things going?" They realize that they increase their chances of closing a transaction when they follow up on clients in a pleasant and memorable manner.

I emphasize the word *pleasant*. A client probably would never forget your arriving in the lobby in shining armor atop a great, white steed. He definitely would never forget the horse's unexpected contribution to the show either, especially the cleaning bill, the new shoes for the receptionist, or little old lady who fainted into the fish tank.

This is not what they mean by "the sweet smell of success."

You want to use your enthusiasm and your creative mind to make prospects want your product or service. You need to take these methods, adapt them to your own personality and your prospect's personality, and use them to make a moment that will be as rewarding for your customer as it eventually is for you.

You can follow up in three basic ways:

- ✔ By phone or voice mail
- ✔ In print by e-mail, snail mail, or fax
- ✔ In person

## Following up on the phone

The telephone is the most common way people try to get in touch with other people, the least expensive, and the easiest to use. Plus, you can practically guarantee that you can reach the organization you want to contact.

The phone is also one of the most frustrating business tools. Working the phone gives you a real workout. Why? Because people can easily dodge you. Sure, you can call any company, but can you speak to the decision maker? Today's busy executive has a vast

array of legitimate ways to avoid taking your call. The receptionist can become a brick wall, an impenetrable barrier to communication. Beyond that lurks the personal or executive secretary. See
Chapter 10 for more tips on effectively using the phone.

When you (at last!) reach the inner sanctum of the boss's office
you get . . . voice mail. You can't afford to fumble around with an
incoherent and embarrassing message guaranteed to end all
possibility of a return call, a message like this one:

> You: Hello, Mr. Prospect . . . uh . . . my name is . . . uh . . .
> Joan Doe of the Joan Doe Canoe . . . uh . . .
> company and I'd like to talk . . . meet with you
> and talk, show you some of our can . . . .
>
> Them: Beeeeeeep!

Use your professional creativity to stand out from the "please
return my call at your earliest convenience" crowd. Prepare a
message for voice mail. Come up with something brief that will
create a real yearning to hear more about what you have to offer.
How? Well, ask yourself what motivates most people in business.
Right! They want a better product at a lower investment. That's
universal. Use it to open the door.

> I'm sorry you missed my call, Mr. Prospect, but you may
> still have an opportunity to find out how to increase
> customer safety, reduce your repair expenses, and
> increase profitability in every one of your river excursions.
> Look for a packet of information that will be sent to you
> August 10 and expect a call back from me, Joan Doe, to
> discuss how your company can benefit from our product
> line. If you would like information immediately, call me
> tomorrow between 8:30 and noon at 555-5555.
> Thank you.

That simple message does a lot for you. First, it shows you're not
scared to death of voice mail or . . . uh . . . answering machines.
Second, it shows that you were prepared to handle any type of
situation when you made the call, which separates you from the
pack. It promises information about the possibility of a better
product at a more economical investment, something everyone

wants. The message also implies that the prospect will become a hero within the company because he or she will be the one who "found" this remarkable new canoe manufacturing company. Subtle maybe, but Mr. or Ms. Prospect will get the point.

Don't be so prepared to get voice mail that you're caught off guard when Mr. or Ms. Decision Maker does answer the phone. Smart prospectors are mentally prepared for either situation before they dial the phone.

By sending the information packet and promising a follow-up call, you also show that you provide personal service, that you're not merely a temporary go-between who will be out of the picture after the sale is consummated.

Perhaps one of the biggest advantages of this format is that it eliminates that awful game called telephone tag. You have, or should I say Joan has, provided a wide window of opportunity for the prospect to make the connection. If the prospect cannot call you during that time period, he or she can have someone else call and arrange a time when you both can talk.

This format for answering voice mail should dramatically increase your percentage of return calls, even from difficult prospects. The reason is simple. You've taken the time and initiative to put the customer's needs and concerns first. You've taken the time to be a professional.

## Following up directly by mail

Anyone can make a call and then drop a brochure or form letter in the mail — anyone except the person who wants to make a presentation. Only the truly successful people know how to make direct mail an extraordinary service. Think about your prospect and personalize your follow-up.

You can show you're thinking about your prospect by sending FYIs (for your information materials). An FYI can be virtually anything that interests the prospect. Send a newspaper article, a magazine feature, or some bit of information that relates to the prospect's business by mail, e-mail, or fax. Add in a short note and your business card. If you're sending a fax, be sure it has your company heading on it and that your name appears in plain sight. Use the FYI to show your clients that they are important to you.

You should be informal with your FYIs. A short letter or handwritten note is much more personal and believable than a long letter written and typed by a secretary. A lot of salespeople write their notes right on the FYI material. Such notes may be little more than "thought you'd like to read this" or "well done."

You also may offer a premium, a small benefit to the prospect when he responds to your mailing. A premium could be a special promotional package designed specifically for prospects, a price-break offer on goods or services offered in your promotional package, or any number of creative promotional ideas that attract prospects.

Some companies send mailings that include only the premiums as a method of building goodwill with customers. Mailing also provides additional opportunities for contact with that prospect. The company lets the prospect know that someone will call within a few days for feedback on the promotion. The follow-up call is another opening of the door that just might lead to a presentation.

Naturally, when your company prints a new brochure, you can send it to your prospects. But you should strive for a much more targeted, individualized, customized, and personalized direct-mail effort.

## Following up in writing

I stress the importance of saying "thank you" in all of my books and in every one of my seminars. That's because I believe so strongly in the power of the words. The basic thank-you note is one of the most effective forms of saying thank you. I write notes to taxi cabdrivers, hotel personnel, flight attendants, travel agents, the people organizing the details of a speech or seminar, anyone and everyone who has been of service to me. Do you know what is really interesting about this small effort on my part? Whenever I return to a place that I have been, people remember me for just being nice.

If you're not doing this right now, then start immediately. Take a look at the following standard set of thank-you notes for all kinds of occasions. Use them to keep you and your product on your prospects' minds. After you have a bit of experience, put your own personality into them.

✔ **Telephone contact.**

Thank you for talking with me on the telephone. I know that time is precious, and you can be sure that I will always respect the time you invest as we discuss the possibility of a mutually beneficial business opportunity.

✔ **In-person contact.**

Thank you for taking time to meet with me. It was a pleasure to meet you, and I appreciate the time we shared. I have been fortunate to serve many happy clients, and I hope someday to be able to serve you. If you have any questions, please don't hesitate to call.

🖊 **Presentation or demonstration.**

Thank you for giving me the opportunity to discuss with you our potential association for the mutual benefit of our firms. We believe that quality, blended with excellent service, is the foundation for successful business.

🖊 **After a purchase.**

Thank you for giving me the opportunity to offer you our finest service. We are confident that you will be happy with this investment toward future growth. My goal now is to offer excellent follow-up service so that you will have no reservation about referring to me others who have needs similar to yours.

🖊 **For a referral.**

Thank you for your kind referral. You can rest assured that anyone you refer to me will receive the highest degree of professional service possible.

🖊 **After a refusal (yes, say thank you in these situations, too).**

Thank you for taking time to consider letting me serve you. It is with sincere regret that your immediate plans do not include making the investment at this time. However, if you need further information or have any questions, please feel free to call. I will keep you posted on new developments and changes that may benefit you.

🖊 **After a prospect buys from someone else.**

Thank you for taking your time to analyze my services. I regret being unable at this time to help you appreciate the benefits we can provide you. We keep constantly informed of new developments and changes in our industry, so I will keep in touch in hopes that we can do business in the future.

🖊 **After a prospect buys from someone else but offers you referrals.**

Thank you for your gracious offer to give me referrals. As we discussed, I'm enclosing three of my business cards, and I thank you in advance for placing them in the hands of three of your friends, acquaintances, or

*(continued)*

*(continued)*

relatives whom I may serve. I will keep in touch and be willing to render my services as needed.

✔ **To anyone who gives you service.**

Thank you for your continued and professional service. It is gratifying to meet someone dedicated to doing a good job. I sincerely appreciate your efforts. If my company or I can serve you in any way, please do not hesitate to call.

✔ **On an anniversary.**

With warm regards, I send this note to say hello and, again, thanks for your patronage. We are continually changing and improving our products and service. If you would like an update on our latest advancements, please give me a call.

I'm sure you can think of more than a few examples from your recent experiences in which you could have sent thank-you notes. Those who extend courtesy and respect get it back in return. Think about it. If a receptionist is particularly helpful in contacting a decision maker, send one of these little notes. How many of your competitors do you think take the trouble? Who is going to get that juicy tidbit of information, the direct-line phone number, or the way to really contact Mr. Prospect? Who gets positive word of mouth within the company, you or your competitor who never makes eye contact and can't even remember the receptionist's name?

Get yourself organized to take advantage of the power of thank-you notes right now! Put "choose appropriate thank-you notes" on your to-do list for today. Then put a large self-stick note on today's page of your planner with the following heading on it: People I Will Thank Today. Seeing this every time you look at your planner will help you remember to watch for people you can thank and begin building your business by leaving them with a positive impression of you.

Sometimes a small gift is appropriate as a thank you. If you're unsure whether a particular item really is appropriate check with etiquette books by Dear Abby, Miss Manners, Emily Post, and the like. Some gifts are tax deductible, but check everything with an accountant or a tax attorney just to be certain. Look at all the benefits you'll rack up: recognition, awareness, strengthened relationships, and tax deductions just for being nice.

## *Following up in person*

You may want to deliver a gift in person. A representative from a printing company pops by my company just before break time every now and then with a fresh loaf of cinnamon bread or a bag of bagels for the office staff. Only one or two people in my company may work with him, but everyone knows him and is always happy to see him. When someone asks us about our printers, whose name will come to our minds first?

# Get together to stay together

Businesses have annual meetings, so why shouldn't you and your customers have them? Use the meetings to let your customers know that you're still interested in serving them and to prospect to find out how you can be of further service. The frequency depends on your business and your customers' needs. You can conduct some or all of these meetings by telephone; do whatever you must to ensure that you do meet. You may want to keep things informal and say, "Hey, why don't we get together," or you can give the meeting a formal atmosphere by calling it a performance review.

This is an important meeting and should be treated as such. Schedule it and make sure that your customer sets aside enough time to adequately discuss his situation. Make sure that you have available all information you need to review the previous month/quarter/year. Have notes or materials to back up any statements you make about the industry, product trends, or the way things are going.

Organize your end of the meeting. Prepare a list of questions. You want to know if your customer is satisfied with the product or service, if he has any additional needs, if he expects changes, where he sees the industry heading, and so on. Don't fear ranging far and wide. Your customers may be planning changes that you should know about. At the appropriate moment, you can introduce a new product or service and ask when you can pop by for a presentation.

If you plan to meet face to face, try to have the meeting over breakfast or lunch. Having the meeting with a meal makes the atmosphere a bit more relaxed and reduces the chances of being interrupted. Make sure you select a relatively quiet place with large tables and plenty of light. You may want to let your client recommend a location.

At the conclusion of the meetings, express your sincere appreciation for your customers' business and tell them that you're committed to serve their needs. Reconfirm any appointments you have set. What am I leaving out? Right! Ask for referrals.

Even if you're not bearing gifts, you should pop in on your clients every now and then. Even if the decision maker is out of the office or too busy to see you, your presence shows you care. Who knows, he may just be finishing a phone call with someone who needs the products or services you represent, and you may be walking into a whole batch of new prospects.

## Good Service = More Sales

I know a successful automobile dealership that has a service department whose service speed is consistently ranked, well, I'll just say somewhere well below good. However, the same customers always rank the department as excellent, and give the department a lot of business even after their warranties run out. A contradiction? Not really. You see, the people who receive not-so-fast automobile service are delighted with the amount of personal service they receive. Technicians take time with the customers, explain problems, make follow-up phone calls, and bring customers cups of coffee as they wait two hours longer than promised.

If you have good customer service, you retain customers and make them want to send other business your way. Statistics bear this out. According to one study, if you have good customer service, five out of six customers who have complaints will keep coming back, even if you don't promptly solve their problems.

Prospecting and acquiring a new customer takes five to ten times more effort than keeping a present customer or getting a new one from an old one. A *Wall Street Journal*/NBC News poll asked more than 1,500 consumers how often they made purchases from businesses that have excellent service but charge higher prices. Seventy-five percent replied either sometimes, most of the time, or all of the time!

Clearly, one of the best ways to keep customers aware of you is to provide superior service. You may not know how to fix a radiator leak or rewire a generator, but you do know how to pour a cup of coffee, provide a sympathetic ear, look into a situation, and prove that you're committed to your customers' needs.

## Meeting Customer Needs Builds Loyalty

There is no such thing as an ex-customer. You should not let someone who just purchased a product or service from you walk out of your sales life. That person is going to need another product sometime in the future. You need your customers' loyalty, and you can prove your loyalty by sticking by your customers when they have a problem (or, as I prefer to call it, a *challenge* or *dilemma*). The customer will remember you as the person who abandoned him at a time of trouble or as the white knight who came to his rescue. Even if there never is a real rescue, he is still going to remember you as the hero who at least made a valiant effort on his behalf.

To be a champion, you must provide excellent customer service. Here's how you go about it.

✔ **Take care of the customers and then correct the problems.** Assure them that you'll look into the situation, whatever it is, but first listen to what they have to say. In many cases you won't have any choice in the matter. When customers have something go wrong, they hit other challenges such as missed deadlines, recalled orders, and extra costs. Let these people express their frustrations in whatever form they choose: anger, tears, threats to go to the Better Business Bureau, or merely angry silence. Show that you're concerned about their personal welfare. Say you're sorry. Make a personal apology directly from your heart, not the public relations department. This simple step often goes an awful long way toward taking the sting out of the customers' predicaments. The simple fact that there's actually somebody on their side has been known to dry many a tear and uncurl many an angry fist. Fix it. Assure them that you're going to take care of the matter personally. Get the customer involved in the process by asking questions.

| You: | Good afternoon, Mr. Customer. I got here as quickly as I could. What type of challenges are you having with the system today? |
| --- | --- |
| Them(icily): | I don't know. It keeps giving us error messages, and my entire staff is frustrated to no end. This is the third time we've had to call you in two weeks. How long will it be *this time* before we can get back to work? |
| You: | I'm confident I can have an answer for you shortly. |
| Them: | I certainly hope so. We can't do business this way. Part of the reason we went with this system is because of its reliability. It's |

*(continued)*

*(continued)*

| | |
|---|---|
| | costing us a lot of money not to be able to use it. |
| You: | I understand how frustrating the initial challenges with a new system can be. I know your major concern is to get everyone back online. Is it more important to get one particular person back online first? |
| Them: | I really need the figures that Susan is working on first so we can, hopefully, land another account. Then I need everyone else online so we can get the job done and keep the account. |
| You: | Okay, then, I'll start with Susan and continue from there. Would you like me to report back to you periodically so you'll know how things are progressing? |
| Them: | That would be great so I can figure a way out of this mess we're in. |
| You: | I understand, Mr. Customer. I'll get on it right away. |
| Them: | Look, I'm sorry I blew up at you. This situation is just really frustrating. I know once all the bugs are worked out everything will be fine. Just keep me posted on what you find. |
| You: | It's all right, Mr. Customer. We'll get through this, and I'm confident you'll be happy with the results. |

Never assume that people somewhere else down the line, in another office or across the country, are doing their jobs. Make it your personal responsibility to see that what needs to be done is done. This take-charge attitude is so rare in many companies that you may literally amaze your customers. I have heard people express loyalty out of similar situations. "Oh, sure, I can get a better deal across town, but after what Jane Doe did for us last year I wouldn't even consider going anyplace else." It happens. Do whatever you have to do to make sure it happens to you.

## Think while they're shouting

You should be thinking about the customer's dilemma; you should focus 100 percent on what your customer says, shouts, or weeps. However, during those breaks when you're running to the service department, or the coffee machine, or for more tissues, think about the appropriate response to your customer's situation.

Consider the following questions:

✔ What the heck can we do?

✔ Can we really do that?

✔ How much will that cost the company? Cost me?

✔ How much will it cost if we don't do it?

✔ Can I handle this situation to my customer's satisfaction? If I can't, who can I get to help?

✔ What kind of gift matches my customer's personality if that becomes necessary?

✔ Why didn't I go into med school like Mom wanted?

Thinking about how to solve the problem before you commit to solving it should keep you and your company from making a rash promise in the heat of a bad situation. Rash decisions can only serve to give you a rash.

---

✔ **Give the offended party a gift.** Such a gift isn't a bribe, just another way of saying "I'm sorry." The amount of the gift should depend on the situation, so you and management need to select an appropriate gift in advance. (You don't think your spouse is management? Think again.) Spend some time thinking about the gift. Customize it to your prospect's personality. A pen and pencil set or a four-color calendar with the company logo probably won't cut it. Use your imagination. If the prospect is a stamp collector, find an appropriate book on the history of stamps. Make sure the gift is something that will be used rather quickly. That four-color calendar on the wall may turn out to be a daily reminder of a bad day that has your name plastered all over it. Make certain you present the gift right away. The longer you wait, the less value it will have and the less effectively it will smooth rough waters.

✔ **Follow up with your prospect.** This is an essential step because you sincerely want to make sure the problem is solved or is at least on schedule toward being solved. Make sure the customer is satisfied and that everything is okay between the two of you. You also can use the opportunity to prospect your customer. Perhaps you and your company can meet some of the customer's other needs.

Salespeople lose sales opportunities every day for the simple reason that they have not firmly planted themselves or their product or service in the minds of potential clients. Develop a fanatical zeal for customer service and follow-up and dedicate yourself to extraordinary service. You will discover extraordinary success.

# Part V
# It's a Numbers Game

The 5th Wave    By Rich Tennant

"I don't take 'no' for an answer. Nor do I take 'whatever,' 'as if,' or 'duh.'"

## In this part . . .

*F*ace the facts: You won't always win. You won't get an appointment every time. You won't make a sale every time. You won't get referred leads every time. When disappointment comes along, however, you will know how to deal with it after reading this part. You'll also know how to maximize your planning strategies for success.

## Chapter 15

# How to Handle Failure and Rejection

*In This Chapter*

▶ Understanding what motivates you

▶ Avoiding the "Three Stooges of Fear"

▶ Changing your attitudes about failure

### The Champion's Creed

*I am not judged by the number of times I fail,*
*but by the number of times I succeed.*
*And the number of times I succeed*
*is in direct proportion to the number of times*
*I can fail and keep trying!*

Make no mistake, you will make mistakes and be rejected. Most people consider mistakes and rejection to be failures. That's why I started this chapter with The Champion's Creed. I want you to understand the important link between failure and success.

I like to ask people the question, "Have you failed enough to succeed?" I just love to see the confused looks cross their faces. A sales champion knows that no one can achieve success without experiencing some failure. It comes with the territory. The degree to which you successfully handle failure and rejection in a large part determines your degree of success in prospecting.

Robert Townsend turned a small rental car company called Avis into the "We Try Harder" people. In his book, *Up The Organization* (Fawcett Books), Townsend writes that his decision-making batting average was only one out of three. Think about that for a second. Two out of every three of his decisions were mistakes, failures. Yet he and his team took a middle-of-the-pack company and made it into a force that successfully challenged the entrenched giant in the rental-car field, Hertz. Clearly, there's more to failure than just failure.

# *Have I Mentioned that Attitude Is Everything?*

Hmm, well, maybe I have mentioned that a time or two in this book, but it still bears repeating. I want you to make a dramatic change in your attitude, this time about making a mistake or failing.

Your attitude is your best weapon against rejection. Failure and rejection inevitably bring on feelings of inadequacy. "I didn't do it — I can't do it — I'll never do it." Well, you have a powerful weapon in your arsenal; it's *enthusiasm*. Those ten simple letters can make the difference between hiding behind your desk, desperately hoping the day will end without another horrible mistake, and rushing out excited about meeting and beating the prospecting challenges of the day. Enthusiasm is the difference between a real professional and a failure.

Franklin Delano Roosevelt had it 100 percent, absolutely, positively right when he said, "The only thing we have to fear is fear itself." Keep that enthusiastic outlook as you face prospecting.

# *Understanding Your Motivators*

Everybody does everything for a reason: love, hate, greed, self-sacrifice, or even for "well, what the heck, let's do it." What motivates us to do things has been the subject of intense debate for as long as people have been debating. As we move from the migrating camps of the caveman into the new camps in the stars, that inquiry into why we do what we do will migrate with us. I have come up with a list of five primary motivators that work within each of us. Just one of these motivators may be your primary driver, but each motivator touches you. Know which is your most powerful motivator and use it to get yourself up and going again when you experience the inevitable rejection in sales.

## *Wealth*

Money or valuable assets are worthy goals. Don't think for a second that the quest for those goals is somehow tainted. Admitting that you need and desire money and all the things it will provide for you and your family is okay. I know a lot of salespeople who state openly and (too frequently) loudly that their sole motivation is to improve the lot of mankind through their specific product or service. Perhaps, but I bet there's a bit of "it sure would be nice to spend a couple of weeks in Europe" in there, too.

The quest for money for money's sake is a doomed enterprise. Think of the many times you've read about the "Joe Average" who hit it big in the lottery only to be flat broke in a year or so. If money alone were the solution to all problems, you wouldn't hear about such stories.

Wealth, whatever that term means to you, can be one of your motivators or even your primary motivator. Anything can motivate you, provided you remember and practice the basic rule of success in sales:

The money you earn is in direct proportion to the amount of service you provide. Look around at the most successful, wealthiest salespeople in your business or industry, those who are head and shoulders above everyone else in prospecting skills. I bet that they are more concerned with providing excellent service than totaling up the day's receipts.

Wealth is great. Championship performance for your prospect is how you attain it.

## Security

Sorry folks, you can never be completely safe and sound.

You can be rolling along without the slightest challenge. Money and power can be pouring in, but life can still deal you a body blow that can put you down for the count. You have no guarantee of freedom from danger, fear, want, or the common cold. No matter how hard you try, no matter how much you want it, life does not come with a security clause.

We humans are only as secure as our ability to handle life's insecurities. Fear and want play a big part in every successful person's life. Fear of not being safe and sound is a tremendous motivator. Lack of security drives many of us on to higher and higher levels of success.

But if you can't be safe and sound, why bother? Because nothing is inevitable. Because life is wonderful and grand. Because you want to contribute to society, provide for your family, make a name for yourself, tour the ruins in Central America, write that novel, go back home to see old Aunt Bessie one more time, or do something you've never done before.

You get what you want by giving up some of what you have and leaving behind unrealistic needs for security. Taking chances is what success is all about. And to take a chance, you must realize that nothing is safe and sound. That's not a negative statement, but freedom in a very real and practical sense. Think about where we would be if someone bowed to the pressure of safety and security and never "sailed the ocean blue in 1400 and 92." If courageous people had not been willing to risk all, to give up all they had in order to get what they wanted, then wagon trains would never have rolled west, and mankind would never have flown or started our journey to the stars. As for you, you'd be selling crude spear points, bone rattles, and magic feathers to cave-dwelling prospects with a lean and hungry look in their eyes. Talk about lack of security!

Take a hard, assessing look at yourself. If you aren't willing to give up something to get what you want, then maybe you should consider another line of work. Keep in mind, however, that the least secure job in the world is probably a "secure job."

I'm reminded of a community that took justifiable pride in its one, large industry. The rule for security was "grow up, graduate high school, get married, and get a job for life down at the plant." That plan of action worked well for generations of families who woke up every day wrapped in that warm security blanket of a "lifelong job down at the plant."

The community forgot one thing — life changes. Through no fault of the community, through no fault of the company that ran the plant, the plant lost thousands and thousands of "secure" jobs, and a lot of people woke up in the unemployment line instead of in that comforting security blanket.

That's why I love sales. As a salesperson, you are the master of your own destiny and achievement. Should the "secure" job disappear, the champion salesperson has skills and abilities that are valuable to a phenomenally wide range of organizations. When the gates on the old plant are locked, the salesperson can just move on to the next, great opportunity.

A real achiever can lose everything again and again, yet still bounce back. Select a successful self-made person, take away all her wealth, power, and connections, drop her into the middle of any city in America with nothing more than the clothes on her back, and she will rise to the top wealthier, more powerful, and better connected than ever before in a matter of a few years or less. She will take whatever risks she has to, give whatever she has to, and will come out a winner. I guarantee it.

## *Recognition*

People like to see themselves in the newspaper, on television, in an article in a trade journal, on the wall above the plaque that reads Sales Representative of the Month, or just in the reflections of friends, family members, and coworkers. People want recognition for their achievements. Sales professionals get "the bug" as kids and never really outgrow it. Admit it, you get as big a charge out of that clipping in the newspaper as you did turning somersaults for your relatives when you were 10. (Note that I didn't bring up the time you got that peanut stuck up your nose in front of Aunt Bessie.)

If you receive an award, accept it with grace, but don't let it go to your head or start believing everything people say about you. We all have a need to be recognized, and that's healthy just as long as you earn it by having a commitment to benefit your clients and prospects.

The real honor and recognition comes in the form of a respectful sparkle in the eye or a lilt of friendship and trust in the voice of your prospect.

## *Acceptance*

The more you achieve and the higher you climb in an organization, the lonelier you will become. This is an undeniable truth that you had better get used to. If you seek to win acceptance from other people, be aware that you are stepping onto dangerous ground.

The Cajuns down in Louisiana call this the "crab bucket" mentality. Old men and women crabbing on the bayou point out the big old bucket in which they toss the day's catch. "Watch 'em close," they say. In a short time, the latest catch tries to climb its way out of the bucket. As it nears the top, the other crabs at the bottom of the bucket reach up and pull it back down. "People are the same way," say the wise old Cajuns. There is a lot of truth in that story.

When trying to improve yourself, to expand your business, or bring in a bigger paycheck, ask yourself how many times you have received negative feedback from associates, coworkers, or even friends and family members:

Sure do hate to see you take on all that overhead.

or

> Pretty bad time of the year to start off something new, don't you think?

or

> That might work out West/East/North/South, but it won't fly around these parts.

or

> You dang fool.

People who say such things are negative influences, and you should never underestimate the power of negativity. It can drain your energy like an old battery on a cold winter's day. Again, consider the source. Does the "advice" come from happy, successful achievers or from malcontents who blame others for their own failures?

 The best way to counter the crab bucket mentality is to surround yourself with people who are positive, upbeat, excited, and enthused, and who take real pleasure in the successes and achievements of their peers.

## Self-acceptance

The acceptance of others whom you respect and admire is a genuine pleasure, but also make room for self-acceptance. If you don't love yourself, you won't perform at your peak. Performing your work with excellence is key to self-acceptance. Your income will rise according to the level of service you give to others. Your feelings of security in an insecure world will be strengthened. You will achieve success and be recognized for your legitimate and worthy accomplishments. You will find and fit into a group of peers who are almost as giddy over your successes as you are. Last, but not at all least, self-acceptance will arrive and with it a new world of freedom, a realization that we lucky few live in a world of choice.

Our paths through this world are ones we carve out for ourselves. They are not dictated by the ups and downs of international commerce, the negative words and actions of underachievers, or our economic conditions at the moment, but by our own actions.

# Overcoming S.O.P.

"S.O.P." probably isn't a common saying around your office, yet you run across S.O.P. situations every day. And until you recognize and manage these situations, you can be a victim of S.O.P.

So what does S.O.P. stand for? Well, I have three definitions:

✔ *Scared of progress*

✔ *Scared of prospecting*

✔ *Signs of panic*

Let me share some thoughts with you about each category.

## S.O.P. — the original

Think about how many good ideas have never even been given a chance.

> This way was good enough in 1957, and it's darn sure good enough now!

or

> This is just the way we do things around here.

or

> S.O.P., kid, Standard Operating Procedure.

or

> Give up, they'll never buy a new idea.

People who say these things aren't really stuck in the past. They're really just scared of progress. That's what S.O.P. really means to them.

Change, of any kind, is their big fear, and that is truly sad. Change usually brings with it some discomfort and some pain. But the benefits of change often outweigh the perceived benefits of the old "tried and true." If you stop and think, look at the history of the world, and examine your own life, you may learn to not only accept change, but also to rush out and greet it with open arms.

## Son of S.O.P. — the sequel

Like a movie, S.O.P. can return. You may be *scared of prospecting*. All my experience, all my seminars and lectures, all my conferences and meetings with people all over the world, have shown me that most salespeople don't like to prospect. This undertaking is the hardest thing in the business world for them to do. It's as if salespeople were little kids who believe they won't have to have the flu shot if they hold their breath, close their eyes, and wish real hard. Well, life doesn't work that way.

You are a professional, and you need to pick up the phone and call those prospects; dash out of the office with a bounce of excitement in your steps; and meet lots of people who can benefit from what you offer. What you would least like to do should probably be your first priority. Get moving and charge into taking charge of your life.

## S.O.P. meets the Three Stooges

S.O.P also can mean *signs of panic,* which can appear in three basic situations:

- ✔ When you lose security
- ✔ When you doubt yourself
- ✔ When you fear failing

Prospectors tend to panic when they feel a loss of control. Losing control happens when you begin to doubt yourself; when you allow your fears regarding failure to rise to the surface. Next thing you know, you're worried about not having enough security. Rather than getting stalled by panic, use your fears as motivation for success. You also should recognize that these fears can keep you from succeeding. I call these three fears the "Three Stooges" because they create havoc and confusion whenever they show up; only these guys really aren't funny.

You should fear the loss of your security. Remember though, champions have to be willing, have to be excited, to give up something to get what they want. The budget-busting expense of night school is not a loss of income. It is a golden opportunity. Taking out a loan to finance a small business isn't really a frightening risk. It's an open door to a successful future. Leaving a "cushy" job to carve out your own place in the world isn't performing without a net. It's stepping out and becoming the best at what you do and living up to your full potential.

Self-doubt is a nagging, energy-draining, enthusiasm-killing fact of life. A career in sales, built on the solid foundation of successful prospecting, is one of the few avenues where men and women can truly take charge of their destinies.

Self-doubt is fueled by the natural tendency to focus on the negative side of everything you do. "Darn it, I never should have [fill in the blank]". You must realize that making mistakes is simply the best way in the world to learn what not to do. Champions always learn from mistakes but never dwell on them. They celebrate what they do right and they learn from what they do wrong. They take note, get over the pain and embarrassment, vow to never do that (whatever it was) again, and then move back out into the world of prospects better prepared and more motivated than ever before.

Fear of failure is so powerful in some people that they actually stop, say "to heck with this," forget their dreams, and go back to driving the turnip truck.

I believe in the rule that says you control your life by doing what you fear the most. In sales this is close to the concept of doing what you want to do least first. If you are afraid of the telephone, sit down and call some people. Scared of cold calling? Start pounding the pavement and knocking on doors. Never take counsel of your fears. Instead, face them one at a time; take them on and conquer them. Victory may not come within a day or a week or a month, but it will come if you apply yourself and begin working on your fears. In fact, your fear will someday seem practically silly in perspective.

Don't get me wrong here. I grew up loving Moe, Larry, Curly, and Shemp. I just don't want their prospecting namesakes working on my team.

# What on Earth Makes You Think No Means No?

An associate told me about a super salesperson who was extraordinarily successful in prospecting by telephone. This individual, a young woman just out of college, seemed to have a real knack for it. The company's other sales personnel had targeted a list of high-profile prospects and had been calling repeatedly month after month without success. Then the young woman was hired and started working her way through the same list. Almost immediately the company began to get appointments to make serious presentations to the real "powers that be." It seemed the woman had the ability to get through a company's bureaucratic layers and into the decision maker's office. When asked about the real key to her success, her employer said, "She just doesn't hear the word 'no.' "

This woman offers a good lesson: *No doesn't always mean no.* In fact, it often means something entirely different. As you meet more and more prospects and as you improve your skills, you should find yourself not hearing no when you hear no. You should no longer timidly back out of the door, apologizing all the way for interrupting your prospect's busy day with your unworthy intrusion. You should respond with courage and conviction, press on, and extol the benefits of your product or service that the prospect so richly deserves.

You need to understand what is really being said between those two little letters that have you so intimidated — *N* and *O.*

*No* may mean

> Slow down, you're going too fast for me to absorb all of this wonderful and fascinating information. Take it easy. I want to get all of this.

or

> Wait, go over that part again. I'm really interested, but I'm a detail sort of person.

or

> That's all well and good, but what's in it for me? You really haven't shown me anything about the features and benefits that I am most concerned with.

or

> You're doing all right, but you are really not keying in on my personal likes and dislikes.

or

> I need to hear more about the value of this investment.

You must realize that occasionally, no really does mean no, but those times are actually very rare. Tucked in there between *N* and *O* is a wealth of hidden information. As you progress and enhance your skills you begin to develop your ability to read between the lines . . . ah . . . between the letters.

For more tips on how to handle no, head over to Chapter 11.

# Strategies for Overcoming Failure

Nobody closes a deal with every prospect every time. But as your skills and abilities improve, so do your closing ratios. To get to the championship level, you need to face failure, sometimes on a daily basis. Your attitude toward those lost sales to a surprisingly large degree determines how long your journey to professionalism takes, how rapidly you will advance, and how high you will climb.

## Strategy 1: See failure as a learning experience

I never see failure as failure, but only as a learning experience. What many salespeople call failure, champions celebrate as an opportunity to learn. When a presentation goes sour, a "done deal" becomes undone, or you get a serious no without any hidden meaning, you can do two things:

> ✔ **Plan A.** Get angry and frustrated, slam doors, throw things, kick your tires (and ruin a good pair of shoes) and run up a substantial bill at podiatrist's office; or

> ✔ **Plan B.** Figure out what went wrong.

I'd go with Plan B if I were you. Not only is it easier on the feet, medical bills, and tires, this approach is also a tried-and-true way to keep from making the same mistake twice. Never let a temporary setback get you down; just keep plugging away. There are hundreds of true stories about men and women who achieved success because they never gave up on their dreams in spite of being turned down time and time again.

The comic book character Superman built the international empire that is DC Comics. Yet back in the 1930s, every major comic features syndicate turned down the strip! One even wrote, "We are in the market only for strips that are likely to have the most extraordinary appeal, and we do not feel Superman gets into that category." One of the most popular comic book characters of all time sat on the shelf for six years.

The two young cartoonists refused to give up. They learned from their experiences and just kept on prospecting their dream until they came out on top. Great Caesar's ghost — what a concept!

## Strategy 2: Use negative feedback to help you improve

Never see failure as failure, but only the need to change course in your direction. That's all. Use a prospect's negative comments as guidelines to steer yourself toward a successful meeting. You may be frustrated after you make a presentation to a prospect who agrees with everything you say yet ends up handing you a *no*. You may not have a clue as to which direction to go.

How you deal with negative feedback is all in how you look at things — in your attitude. Negative feedback is information. You can choose to take it personally, take your anger and frustration out on your coworkers, take the covers and pull them over your head, or you can take the ball (information) and run with it.

## Strategy 3: Find the humor in failure

Never see failure as failure, but only as an opportunity to develop your sense of humor! You have to learn to laugh at yourself. Some of the most serious salespeople I know also have some of the best senses of humor. They find something funny even in the worst botched presentation. In fact, the worse the incident, the funnier the story and the more the salesperson enjoys telling it.

Don't underestimate the ability to find the humor in terrible situations and relate it to others. That ability takes some of the sting out of the failure, takes your mind off the negative side of the event, and helps you get back to work all that much sooner. I believe you should take your work and your obligations very seriously. But, admit it, you pull some really funny stunts, don't you? Share the wealth. We all can use a good story now and then.

## Strategy 4: Look at failure as a golden opportunity to perfect skills, techniques, and abilities

Here's that word *attitude* coming up again. Imagine you've been prospecting with a particularly tough individual. He's thrown back everything you've tossed his way, and you have gotten nowhere. As you leave with your pleasant "thank you for your time," be sincere and know that you may meet the prospect again.

You need to continually practice your prospecting skills. Consider that unsuccessful transaction as practice. Think about it as on-the-job training and realize that after the presentation you are better than you were ten minutes before the meeting.

## Strategy 5: View failure as a game that you play to win

Failure isn't failure, it's a game and you're playing to win! Prospecting is serious business, but it helps to think about the process as a game. Whether the game is golf, tennis, checkers, or the game of life, most of the folks I know play to win. Champions know that prospecting is a numbers game. The more calls you make, the more rejections and failures you get. However, the more sales you make makes all the effort worthwhile.

Master these five strategies for handling failure, and you can really change your attitude about failure and start to see improvements in your prospecting skills, in your self-confidence, and in the returns on your prospecting investments.

It's not how many times you fail that matters, it's the number of times that you succeed. If you don't believe me, just ask Superman.

I end this chapter in the way I began it, with The Champion's Creed, because repetition helps you learn this valuable lesson.

*I am not judged by the number of times I fail,*
*but by the number of times I succeed.*
*And the number of times I succeed*
*is in direct proportion to the number of times*
*I can fail and keep trying!*

## Chapter 16

# Goal Setting Keeps You Focused

*In This Chapter*

▶ The difference between wishes and goals

▶ Turning wishes into goals

▶ Short-, mid-, and long-term goals

▶ Commitment and vision

▶ What to do when you reach your goals

*T*he salesperson who has nothing for a goal surely gets it. Real success just doesn't come to you. As the old TV ads declared, "We made our money the old-fashioned way — we earned it." Real success is something you must earn. Success does not and cannot just happen. Success can come to us, but not on its own.

Whoa! Slow down. I can almost hear a chorus of "but wait a second," and I know you're thinking about those news stories about the poor couple on vacation who places a dollar bet down at the casino, winning a huge fortune. I've read and heard and seen those same stories. What you very rarely hear about, however, is the status of that couple a year or so later. Chances are that they've already lost the fortune and are back to being a poor couple again.

 Sure, you've heard this adage before, but it bears repeating: Unearned wealth has no real value to people because they didn't have to sweat blood and tears to get it. The money has no meaning, and because it has no meaning the people don't invest or protect it, and usually it is gone within a remarkably short period of time. Certainly, people do hit the jackpot in any number of ways, but you never hear about the tens of thousands who don't hit that jackpot. Besides, consider the odds. What are your and my chances of winning a fortune by pure luck? We all know that the odds are always with the house.

Wouldn't you really rather stake your future on your own talent, ability, and drive?

Setting goals helps you earn your success, and because you achieve that success through hard work, it has real value and meaning. You fight to protect and increase it. You don't want to squander your success, but instead you build on its firm foundation. It's true that anyone can reach a certain level of success without going through the process, but no one can reach their full potential without setting goals.

This approach is especially true for salespeople. Without goals we can easily become distracted from real success. We can become dispirited and frustrated. We don't know when to celebrate our victories because we have no clear definition of victory. We slip, trip, stumble, and fall. We lose focus.

You can't reach the top unless you stretch, and setting goals makes us stretch.

## Wishes Aren't Goals

Deep within, each person possesses a tremendous well of untapped power. How many times have you heard that we use only 10 percent of our total brain power?

> ✔ Are you working at peak performance levels right now?
>
> ✔ Have you reached your potential as a salesperson, as a human being?

I don't believe anyone can say yes to those questions because there is so much unused power within every human mind and spirit. Setting goals, achieving them, and then setting and achieving even higher goals helps us penetrate a vast reservoir of energy and inspiration.

Wishes are general:

> ✔ "I wish I had a lot of money."
>
> ✔ "I wish I had a good car."
>
> ✔ "I wish I had more for the kids' education."

In stark contrast, goals are very specific:

> ✔ "Within three years my annual income will exceed $100,000."
>
> ✔ "By the end of next year I will own, debt free, a Cadillac/ Jeep/motor home."
>
> ✔ "I will set aside $3,000 per year in a college fund starting this calendar year."

See the difference?

In addition to these goals, you encounter a number of smaller goals all leading directly to the achievement of the big one. For the college-fund goal, for example, the smaller goals can be: "I will set aside $250 this month come hell or high water for the college fund . . . I will make ten prospecting calls the first thing every morning . . . I will attend that optional product marketing lecture tonight. . . ."

A wish allows you to get away with being lazy, with underachieving, with procrastination.

Hey, old Mr. Gottbucks walked into the showroom today, and I sold him a brand new Whatchamacallit! Wow! I made more money than last week, so I'm really getting somewhere. Think I'll take another coffee break and celebrate. Those "orphan" prospecting calls can wait till tomorrow.

See where wishes lead?

That's right — nowhere.

You can turn your wishes into goals. Anybody can. All you have to do is take that fuzzy, indefinite wish and make it a reality. You do this by creating a goal that

✔ Is specific

✔ Is attainable

✔ Is measurable

✔ Requires organization

✔ Energizes you

I want to go into a bit of detail on these subjects, but first . . .

## Set Aside Time to Set Goals

Get away from all your distractions. Find a quiet time and place to seriously think about your goals. Take pen and paper and don't be afraid to scribble lots of notes that you'll end up tearing into little pieces and tossing away. This is your time to think . . . and to dream. Go ahead and write down that wish of finding lost treasure and love deep in some forgotten, romantic jungle. That's probably one you'll tear up. Then again, some people do like to travel, a worthy goal. If you're married, be sure you include your spouse in your goal-setting plans.

You've had some imprecise thoughts (wishes) about success. Now is the time for preparation to get specific, to turn wishes into goals, but first you have a lot of soul-searching to do. Think carefully about what you want to do, to earn, to achieve, to set aside for your future. Do you really want to write "the great American cookbook?" Well, books take time, research, writing, rewriting, finding agents and publishers, learning and handling the business end of writing, and then trying to remember what town you're in on all those early morning TV shows. All of these activities require an incredible investment in time, and somebody has to pay for all that time.

That somebody is you. How ya going to do it?

Set goals, that's how.

At your brainstorming session (or sessions), you may find yourself intimidated. You can easily find yourself pacing the floor in circles thinking, "This is crazy, I'll never be able to do that!" Some people just can't picture themselves escaping a bandit gang by swinging across the alligator-infested river on a flimsy vine, one arm full of treasure and the other wrapped around a new romantic interest. Hmm, this is getting better all the time. Others become afraid of success when actually setting out on a plan to achieve it. Some even get stalled because they fear setting the wrong goals.

Fear kills success.

If you have a dream, don't let anyone persuade you that the dream is "crazy." Your dream should generate courage rather than fear. Take that prospective cookbook writer, for example. He's worked out a schedule for researching, cooking, testing, and writing, but is suddenly intimidated by the huge task of actually selling the darn thing. The budding author can easily throw in the kitchen towel and give up the fat-free dream.

Instead of giving up, why not combine a knowledge of prospecting with setting some goals?

- ✔ I know nothing of agents, therefore I will visit my local library today.

- ✔ I know nothing of the profession, therefore I will read all the back issues of *The Writer* and/or *Writer's Digest* that I can get my hands on this month.

- ✔ I know nothing about agents or publishers, so I'll also take pen and paper and go through all the back issues of *Publisher's Weekly* in the library.

- ✔ I will write and mail 100 inquiry letters this week.

All of a sudden this dream becomes a task that you can do, an achievable goal in spite of the intimidating lack of knowledge about publishing. Fear and thoughts of being "crazy" get replaced with activity that has a purpose, and little goals drive away big worries.

Suppose the writer discovers halfway through that he doesn't want to write a cookbook after all. Does this realization mean that the initial goal was wrong and that, perhaps the book idea actually was "crazy" after all? I don't think so. Remember, the title of this chapter is "Goal Setting Keeps You Focused."

Sometimes your focus changes. Perhaps the writer may just want to start a simple newsletter about favorite recipes and cooking tips. Maybe he will get a great idea for a novel about a chef who gets embroiled (sorry) in all kinds of mysteries. Perhaps all the cooking research could turn the writer into a chef and a new career in a the restaurant industry is in the future. The whole point is, *setting goals gets you from point A to point B*. Hey, if you end up with a wonderful new career at point C instead, remember that you would never have gotten there without that unexpected zigzag near B. Changing a goal down the road is far better than never setting one at all.

## What Goals Should Be

To borrow a phrase from the '60s, goals have to "turn you on." You set goals for things that excite you — things that make you feel great when you envision yourself being, having, or doing them. If a goal doesn't turn you on, then it's just a "to-do" item on your life's list. You'll keep moving the goal from today to tomorrow and never dedicate any time to progressing toward it. Think about what turns you on, and then use the following steps to achieve it.

- ✔ **A goal must be specific.** This old saying may be trite, but it's true: To be terrific, you must first be specific. This first, important step is where an awful lot of people trip up. If you set a specific goal, you then have something to live up to. Negativity can creep in easily at this stage with thoughts like: "I'd better not be too specific here. What if I don't make it?" Too many folks try to play it safe by hedging on the details. You can't just cross your fingers and think, "I'll make a lot more money next year." It just won't happen.

- ✔ **Don't be intimidated.** The other steps in the process can help keep you in focus. Think about your current position, what you can reasonably expect to do with hard work, and then step on out. "I will earn $75,000 annually within three years." That statement is specific, and that makes it a goal.

✔ **A goal must be attainable.** A wish to earn $1 million by the end of the current quarter is very specific, but if you're the new salesperson on the used-car lot, you may want to lower your sights. I pause to note that I'm not saying you can't become a millionaire selling used cars. You could end up owning a chain of used-car lots throughout the country, but I still don't think it'll all happen within 90 days.

✔ **Attainable doesn't mean that you should set a goal that is easy.** On the contrary, I believe that a goal must be better than your best, but one that is believable. If your goal isn't believable, you won't have faith that you can attain it, and you probably won't get where you want to go.

✔ **A goal must be measurable.** I encourage you to measure the attainment of your goals in terms of activity rather than production. Instead of concentrating so hard on making X amount per day or week or month, concentrate on X number of prospect calls per day and week and month. Set your short-term goals in terms of contacts with prospects. Production follows activity. Do your job right, and the money will not only follow, it'll flow!

✔ **A goal must require organization.** "I want a nice car some-day" doesn't require any organization and barely any thought. A goal requires serious organization of your thinking, your work schedule, of how you handle your business, and of how you live your life.

## Avoid negativity

Beware of the influence that negative people can have. The tiniest amount of negativity can plant a small seed of doubt (buried, but ready to germinate and grow), no matter how confident you are. Some of us are much more likely to buy into negativity than others, but we all have to watch out for its dangers. Again, that's where your goals can help keep you focused and on target. Set a believable goal, stay with your program, and you will attain it.

✔ **Put your goal in writing!** Writing makes it real — makes your goal a commitment. Write down a specific plan, too. Read your goal and your plan often. Your mind begins taking off on its own, working out all kinds of ways to make things happen for you. If you don't believe this now, show a little faith and just do it. You will be amazed at what your own subconscious can do for you if you just let it.

✔ **A goal must energize you to take action.** No one will go the extra mile, make the personal sacrifices, take the chances, or work the long hours if all she can see at the end of the road is a bunch of ho-hum. A key element of goal setting is the excitement it generates. A goal should be so real that you leap out of bed every morning filled with the drive, the necessity to get one day closer to it. You want to go to work,

## Share the sacrifice

All right, face facts. If you're really committed to your loved ones' financial security, there will be times when you just can't make the Scout meeting, the concert, or the important event. You've chosen to make that sacrifice, but it's one that everyone in your family or circle of friends shares, and they probably didn't have much of a say in the matter when you set all those lofty goals.

That hit home, didn't it?

Because the people you love will share the sacrifice, I encourage you to share the reason for that sacrifice. Explain to them what you are doing, what it requires of everyone, and how everyone benefits. That explanation probably won't take the disappointment out of missing the big event, but it should remove the sting. Share your sales victories that you achieve at the office, on the job, or on the road with them too. Make them a part of your victory celebrations. They've earned a share.

Another benefit of sharing the reason for personal sacrifice is that you build a support group and internal motivation where you need it most. For example, it's Saturday morning and you'd like to sleep in, but your spouse knows you need to attend that important prospecting seminar down at the civic center. Suddenly, you need support and motivation, and an understanding spouse can make all the difference in the world.

That wonderful smell of hot coffee and your favorite breakfast floating into your dreams is a terrific encouragement to get up, out of bed, and on your feet. A quick jab in the ribs doesn't hurt either.

more than that, you need to achieve. Your goal becomes a real passion, one that not only creates power, but that creates a better life for you, your family and close friends, and your community.

✔ **A goal must be personal.** Speaking of those kids, or the spouse, or close friends, setting some personal goals is very important. Having a life outside your business is important, as is making time for your family and friends, your spiritual growth, your education, and your health. Make room in your goal-setting program for all of that, too. What good is that million bucks going to do the young car salesperson if it all goes to medical bills because of the ruined health getting it? What is the value of a college fund if the kids think of you as "that person we get to see for a little while on holidays?"

## Timing Is Everything

As with the junior used-car salesperson mentioned in the section "What Goals Should Be" (the one who wanted to make a million bucks in three months), timing, not dollars, was the problem. Proper time planning is a big part of any goal-setting program. Unrealistic schedules are just as disheartening, just as frustrating, and just as harmful as unrealistic monetary goals.

Timing falls into three distinct categories (are you sitting down and ready for the revelation?):

✔ Long range
✔ Medium range
✔ Short term

Ta-dah!

Okay, I suppose that list really wasn't much of a surprise, but you may be alarmed at the number of salespeople who limit themselves to only one or two of the three. All the categories are important, and each has its own areas that require your attention.

### Long-range goals

Never put the cart before the horse. Always set your long-range goals first. I recommend 20 years out as a good starting point. Take a look at the following example:

> I want someday to live worry free in a grand house on the beach.

That statement is not a goal, it's a wish.

Here's how to make that wish a goal:

> In 20 years I will own a $250,000 home (current market value) on the Florida Gulf Coast. I will be debt free and have $1 million in the back.

See the difference? (Actually *back* was a typo for *bank,* but who am I to tell you where to put your money?)

## Medium-range goals

These goals may be the least clear in your head at the moment. After all, you know where you want to go (the Gulf Coast mansion) and you have a pretty good idea when and where to start — at work the first thing in the morning. That middle is the part that's just a bit out of focus.

Start by cutting your 20 years into two 10-year periods. Ask yourself what you have to do in those periods to keep your plans on schedule. Then break down the ten-year periods into five-year blocks and then repeat the process until you're down to a series of one-year segments.

Because the medium goals are admittedly a little vague, these are the ones you will probably change and adjust the most. That's okay because that's why you are creating your plans in the first place. Goal setting keeps you in focus and sometimes focus changes, remember?

## Short-term goals

Set short-term goals by months, weeks, and days. I recommend that you go no further into the future than 90 days at a time. Longer than that seems to give most folks a lack of urgency, a false sense that there's really more time available than there really is.

Set your goal and immediately do something to make it real. Don't hesitate for a second to get into action. If one of your goals is to have the kids' college bills paid before they graduate high school, open that college fund down at the bank today. Put your goal-stated amount of money for that month or quarter in it. Now, if all of a sudden you realize that this particular amount means you can't pay the house note, then maybe a little adjustment is in order. The main thing is to do something immediately to make the goal real, to create that all-important sense of urgency.

If you find yourself backing off for any reason other than the normal human "hey, wait a minute," trait, then something is wrong. You don't really believe that your goal is attainable. If it were, you would be really excited about making the immediate move to make it real. Don't panic or feel that you have betrayed the kids' future. After all, making the house mortgage and keeping a roof over their heads goes a real long way toward keeping their grades up. Just take some personal, quiet time and re-evaluate your program, get things in focus and move on ahead.

And don't wait to open that college fund either. You have pocket change plus all that money lost under the cushions in your couch. Hey, it's a start and that's just what you need.

## Commitment — a Vision Thing

The higher you set your (attainable) goals, the harder you have to work to reach them. That's just the way things are. Of course, the harder you work for them, the sweeter the taste when you savor your success. If you're not doing very much reaching and stretching, then you probably haven't set your goals high enough. By not continuing to challenge yourself, you can fall victim to complacency. You can stagnate as a professional and never attain the status of champion.

Sticking with a program, especially one that calls for sacrifice and hard work, requires a deep commitment. When times get tough, when the inevitable setbacks occur, when things get so crazy you don't know whether you're coming or going, you have to hold on to the commitment to your goals. Never allow yourself to be seduced by the easy way of the underachiever. Stick with it no matter what others may say or do to discourage you.

You may have a natural tendency to accept a bit of success, part of a goal, and to be satisfied with that small achievement and to look away from your mid- and long-range goals. After all, you've worked hard for it right? Don't give in, not for a second. Don't ever settle for less than your absolute best.

One of the best techniques I know to help keep your goals in focus is visualization. You have to make your goals real. You have to see them, and I really mean see them in your mind's eye. Smell that new-car smell of your new Cadillac or Jeep or the 8-cylinder Whatever. Feel the leather seats or the bumpy mountain road up to a pristine campsite in the clear mountain air. Smell that air, too. Listen to the roar of the engine and the praise of your neighbors. See it! Feel it! Taste it! Make it real!

If you have trouble visualizing, then use pictures. If you want to earn a new car, go down to the dealership and pick up a couple of brochures or cut a picture from an ad in a magazine. Keep the image close to you and whenever you feel that commitment level start to slide, take out the image to help you visualize earning it.

This tactic may sound silly to some of you, but it's not. I'll bet you have more friends and acquaintances than you know carrying pictures of motorcycles, luxury homes, expensive furs, jewelry, and other goodies in their wallets and purses. Some people even create an entire collage of their goals and why not? Instead of just a picture of the new car, how about that picture pasted in front of the luxury vacation hotel you want to visit?

How about a picture of a graduation at that college you want for your kid, a new bass boat on a smooth fishing lake, an elegant wardrobe in an extra-large walk-in closet, or a quickly taken snapshot of your supervisor's office with your own photo pasted in that big, leather chair? (Well, you do want that job, don't you?)

Visualization works. Visualization makes your dream real, and that's what makes the dream come true.

# I Have a Good Idea of What I Want — Can't I Just . . .

No!

If you want to become a champion prospector, sales professional, and a champion human being, you cannot escape setting goals as specified in this chapter. If you try to get along without goals, you're just fooling yourself and, worse, denying yourself the ability to reach your goals and to realize your full potential.

Setting and reviewing goals keep you moving when every inclination is to take a break, stop for a rest, or just give it up for the day. You will find that having a set of clearly defined, well-visualized goals inspires you to new heights of effort and achievement. You discover new motivation, more excitement than you thought possible, and levels of energy that you never suspected. You don't even consider taking an unnecessary or unearned pause, break, or halt in your plan because that can keep you from your goal. The concept of an unproductive moment just to kill some time becomes unthinkable.

Okay, you might think about it, but you don't do it. Achieving your goals is just too much fun!

# All Right, Now That I've Achieved Those Goals, What's Next?

What's next? More goals!

Believe me on this. As soon as you start setting and achieving goals, you won't be able to stop. The process can become a positive addiction. Your doctor will even approve.

(Remember, you've dedicated part of your goal-setting process to your health.) As you reach one goal, you look forward to setting and getting another and another and another, each higher and more exciting than the one before.

Achieving a goal is like climbing a mountain or struggling up a tough hill. When you're on top and the great, big wonderful world is spread out before you and you're drinking in the clean, crisp air, the long hours getting there fade away. The struggle doesn't seem much of a struggle when compared to the view and the pride of accomplishment.

Soon the process becomes its own reward. "Oh, I just reached this goal. Good. Great. Swell. Now what can I do?" The question isn't one of desperation, but one of genuine excitement at the prospect of the next challenge. Pun intended.

# The Next Three Steps

When you do attain a really big goal, I want you to do three things.

### 1. Celebrate.

You owe yourself a celebration because you've earned it. I don't mean that you should rush out and buy that bass boat or diamond bracelet just because you made your goal of ten prospect calls a day for 90 days. That reward is out of proportion to the achievement. Still, a celebration and reward is due, so go ahead and buy that book, new pair of shoes, go out for the evening with a

loved one, or whatever is appropriate. Don't worry —
the boat or bracelet is on its way the moment you really
earn it, that and a lot more.

### 2. Get ready for depression.

People in live theater or motion pictures call the syn-
drome "post-production letdown," and that's an excellent
description of what occurs. The letdown happens
because the cast and crew have been running at 110
percent capacity for an extended period of time — just
like you as you're striving for your goals. All of a sudden
the show is over and, for the moment, there's nothing to
do — but everyone's still churning at 110 percent!

A depression sets in because everybody has been so
productive for so long and suddenly they feel that
they're wasting their time. "Shouldn't we be doing
something?!" The thing to do is realize that this feeling
is quite natural and that the depression will pass. Take
a day or weekend off to let your engines cool down
without strain. Somewhere during that time you realize
that your work is really your hobby and that it's time to
get back to it. The depression just goes away, replaced
by new and exciting activities because of the third thing
I want you to remember. . . .

### 3. Set new goals.

After your short period of post-production letdown
passes, get busy setting an entire new series of goals.
Stretch a little further than you did before. Reach a little
higher. Keep on growing. That's where the real success
in prospecting and sales comes from. If you don't keep
setting higher goals, complacency comes back into play,
you get bored and disinterested, and without warning
your hobby has become a job again.

The process of achieving a goal becomes its own reward. Extend-
ing your reach keeps the process stimulating and smart salespeople on their toes.

In fact, I like to start setting those new goals sometime shortly
before attaining the immediate ones. I love the challenge, and I
know most salespeople feel the same way. Having a new set of
goals, or at least a couple of thoughts on them written down, also
helps fight off post-production letdown.

New goals! Higher goals! New challenges, always!

# Chapter 17

# Time Planning Moves You Forward

*T*hink about it: All you are given in this world is time. As a salesperson, time is really all you have to work with, all you have for planning, and, in a very real sense, all you have to offer. As champions you should realize the sobering fact that none of you knows how much time you have left in inventory.

Start thinking of time in very hard-nosed terms. You don't know how much time you have, so maximize what you know you have, today. You can apply the adage "It doesn't matter how long you live, but how well you live" to your sales and prospecting efforts. How much time you put in on the job doesn't really matter; rather, how much job you put into your time is the key.

You may think the business leaders of the western world are aware of the value of time, that they are practicing masters of time planning and management, but you're wrong.

The book *In Search of Excellence,* by Thomas J. Peters and Robert H. Waterman, Jr., (Warner Books) reveals an astounding fact: According to a university study, most managers do not regularly invest large blocks of time for planning and organizing. Worse, the time they use is fragmented into tiny segments of activity. According to the study, the average time allotted to any particular aspect of their business was only nine minutes!

The respondents in the study are highly skilled people in responsible positions who are supposedly well-trained in management. Nine minutes! Folks, you can't even eat a good candy bar in nine minutes.

Everywhere I go I hear a universal complaint: "If only I had more time, I'd. . . ." Ask people what they'd like to have more of and you get a lot of different answers: money, vacations, family time, hobbies, education, and so on. Ask the same people what would make their lives easier and you get a more unified answer. "I need more time!"

# If You Need To Get Something Done . . .

. . . ask a busy person to do it. I know you've heard that saying before and it's true, but have you ever considered why it is true? Logic, faulty logic that is, seems to say that a busy person has no more time for a project and that someone not busy at all should be tasked with responsibility for the job at hand. I disagree because I know the productivity levels of busy people. I know what they can do and I know how they do it.

I'm referring to people who are truly busy and not to people who buzz around doing "busywork," but not really getting anything done at all. You know the busywork type: They always seem, well, busy. They have enormous piles of papers falling off their desks. They dash about frantically from one "important" meeting to another, and they may complain about the unfair weight of their workload.

An interesting illustration of this type of individual involves a midlevel manager at the U.S. headquarters of an international manufacturer. I'll call him Mr. Dash N. Fidgette. The name is fictional, but the story is real. Dash had to create a joint presentation with an outside vendor, from whom I got this tale of "whoa."

One day Dash called his associate, frantically saying that he needed to rewrite the final draft of their proposal. He drove across town, an hourlong trip, for the get-together. The important meeting lasted approximately an hour. Rather than the major rewrite that was promised, Dash made very minor changes to only his part of the presentation. He spent thoughtful minute after minute debating whether the product was "lovely" or "pretty," "soft" or merely "not hard," and whether it was "multicolored" or was "available in many colors." Dash's vendor spent the hour smiling, nodding, and agreeing. What else could he do? After the meeting Dash drove back across town and probably complained all afternoon about not having enough time to handle his workload.

Dash N. Fidgette isn't a busy person. He's a manager foolishly wasting his time and, worse, his company's time and his vendor's. What Dash could have done was revise the document and fax or e-mail it to his associate for a quick review. I've noticed over the years that the people who really get things done, who amaze others with their productivity, work pretty much the same hours as those who never seem to get anything done. People like Dash may never learn what the truly busy person has learned: Time is not something you spend, it's something you invest.

## Spending Versus Investing Your Time

*Spend* is one of my "nasty words." I just don't like the connotation of that word. When you spend money for a new suit, that's money flowing out of your bank account, out of your pocket, and out of your life forever. When you *invest* in a new suit, you develop an entirely different attitude. That money's not a loss at all. The new wardrobe gives you a better appearance and more confidence in your prospecting presentations. The clothing is an investment, something that's actually going to bring money back into your life, pocket, and bank account by helping you present yourself in a more professional manner.

Spending versus investing — see the difference that a slight change in thinking can create? And you want to invest your time, not spend it.

Changing your approach toward time requires thinking about how you value your time. Start by putting a realistic dollar figure to your time. Just divide your gross income by your total annual working hours to arrive at your hourly rate.

Gross income ÷ Total annual working hours = Hourly rate

For example, if gross income is $30,000 per year and you work 2,080 hours annually (or 40 hours a week), then your hourly rate is $14.42 an hour.

Suppose you work straight-commission sales. Spending just one hour per business day on unproductive activity means that by the end of the year you have spent — *spent*, mind you — $3,763.62 (261 hours x $14.42/hour) on absolutely nothing. But worse, you've wasted your own time and that of your employer. You've deprived yourself of all the referrals and future business you could have generated within that time had you used it productively.

Salespeople, who earn fees for the service they give, are so fortunate — you get to set your own hourly rates and can change them at any time. When I hear someone in sales say, "I need more money," my response is, "Go out and make some."

I hope you appreciate the power and freedom that is at your command as a salesperson. No corporation, no union, no trade association, no one can dictate your hourly rate.

Many people prefer the comfort of knowing that at the end of the week, they will get paid a regular, hourly rate. Some of you, however, are cut from a different cloth. You know there is really nothing secure about a "secure job" and that payday may actually be weeks or even months down the road and that you have to deal with that. Those of you in real estate know exactly what I mean. How long is it from that moment when you first knock on that prospect's door until you market, haggle about the roof, repaint the back porch, sell, close the sale, and get your check?

Time planning helps keep you from getting discouraged during these stretches. Losing sight of your goals is easy, but don't worry. That happens to all of us. Just keep your focus on the job at hand, knocking on those doors, making those phone calls, dropping in for cold calls, and prospecting every chance you get.

Don't allow yourself to get involved in busywork. Instead, become someone who is truly busy, happily, actively, aggressively raising that hourly rate to new heights every day.

## The $86,400 Question

Have you ever thought or said that you're just too busy to get anything done? If you're having challenges managing time, then in reality you are having challenges managing yourself.

Suppose I sent you an agreement stating that I would give you $86,400 for you to spend any way you want with only three simple stipulations: (1) the money is yours for a specified period of time, say one day; (2) you must invest only in products or services that yield long-term benefits — no cars, fancy clothes, jewelry, and so on, and (3) at the end of the time period, you have to return any sums not invested. I bet you'd be off and running in no time, frantically seeking out the best way to invest your newfound wealth.

Instead of that agreement, I'll give you something better: awareness. You wake up every day with 86,400 brand new, crisp, clean seconds fully at your disposal, available to invest as you wish. That's the number of seconds in a 24-hour day. Will you spend those seconds, or invest them?

A champion invests each of those seconds, even the idle moments. If you have to do a lot of driving in your business, you can listen to music on the radio, whistle a happy tune, or grouse about other drivers. A more productive way is to invest the time in a series of good, educational, motivational, or inspirational cassette tapes or CDs. I know people who, when setting out on long trips, have a list of things to check before turning the car key:

❑ Gas

❑ Oil

❑ Battery

❑ Tire pressure

❑ Brakes

❑ Audiotapes/CDs

You have the time on the road, the car, and the audio player already, why not invest that time wisely rather than raising your blood pressure over all those annoying drivers?

Some folks spend a lot of time going to meetings, and they spend more time going back and forth on the road than they do face-to-face. Champions do their best to plan meetings so the meetings fall into the same geographical area within the same time frame. This strategy is just a matter of planning, of controlling the use of time rather than letting time be in control. Instead of jumping into the car and heading out, champions plan for traffic, know the side and back streets for rush hour, and check the traffic and weather reports so they don't get stalled or stranded by events.

# Plan Your Work, Work Your Plan

I know you've heard that phrase before, but it's a good way to handle your day-to-day business. An excellent technique that I heartily recommend is to formulate a daily work plan. You can find a number of preprinted plans at any office supply store or office supply section of a major retail outlet, or you can build your own. Following are seven elements I think you should include in your daily plan:

### 1. Getting out of the office or home.

Where are most of your customers (or, in many businesses, *all* of your customers)? The answer is out there. Think of all the prospects that have gone to the competition because a salesperson didn't leave the office at the right time. How many prospects and sales has that famous second cup of coffee in the lunchroom cost? The number must run into the millions.

Think about the theme line of the television show *The X-Files* and remember: "The prospect is out there."

### 2. Appointments.

Folks, it is so, so easy to forget an appointment, even an important one, and the prospect or client really doesn't care why. All she knows is that important time was set aside for a no-show. Missing an appointment sticks a big, bright red flag on the top of your head. When the client hears your name in the future, one of two things then occurs: That red flag waving in her face means you'll be completely ignored or, worse, the client will shout *toro* and charge! Neither action is conducive to successful prospecting. And you can count on the jilted client telling all of her counterparts about the bad impression you made.

People, write down your appointments and carry them with you.

### 3. Homework.

The one true constant in our world is change. You not only have to be aware of changes in the marketplace, in your industry, in your product line, and in marketing strategies, you also have to study and know them so you can use them. There are few things worse than being flattened by a prospect who's more up to speed on your industry than you.

### 4. Your family.

Sometimes you can get so caught up in taking care of your family that you don't take care of your family! The character Don Corleone from *The Godfather* tells his sons that a man who doesn't spend time with his family can never really be a man. A more contemporary approach applies to all workers and their families. The point is the same, man or woman, the sentiment is right on target.

Tu salud, Don Corleone!

### 5. Exercise.

Yes you can! Champions take care of themselves because they perform better when they feel better. Good physical conditioning makes for good presentations. I don't care what your job is, you can find time to take care of your health. The world is filled with health clubs that are open before, during, and after working hours. Many office buildings offer gym facilities to tenants. Exercise programs, tapes, and equipment seem to be stocking the shelves of half the stores in America, including my grocery store. You can even find a wealth of information on how to exercise on the job.

Hey, nobody says you have to take the elevator.

### 6. Yourself.

When laboring under your own stick, it's important to remember to give yourself the carrot, too. You have to allow yourself rewards for achievement. The big ones I'm not worried about. They're foremost in your mind already. Remember that it's important to give yourself small rewards along the way. That's one of the motivations that helps keep us going.

Rewards are, and should be, very personal, so I'm not going to run off an entire checklist of happy-toys. Think about what gives you joy and reward yourself with a little of it now and then. If you're an avid reader, then go ahead and get that big book you've been wanting. If you're a fitness nut, go ahead and get the new jogging shoes or that close-fitting exercise outfit. If you enjoy community service, grant yourself some extra time for some volunteer work down at the club, or church or cleaning up the playground. If you really just want to sit out in the backyard and go "duh" for an afternoon, that's okay too.

I recommend making some time to put something back into your community. You accomplish something important, you earn a pride of achievement, and you get to meet a great group of people.

### 7. Prospecting.

Hey, that's what this book is all about. Make time for prospecting every day.

I don't have to tell you that the least popular part of selling is prospecting, and that's usually the first thing a salesperson finds excuses not to do. Ask yourself what is the one thing about your job that you want to do last and that's probably the one thing you need to do first. Nine times out of ten, I'll bet that's prospecting.

# Analyzing Your Day

The next step on your adventure is to break down your day into its various parts. Time planning sometimes trips up people. The phrase "time planning" sounds so official, so replace it with "productivity." Now, does that make more sense to you? Time planning is planning your daily productivity so you can pack as much of the stuff into your day as possible.

## Be productive

If I had to give you only one rule about time planning, I would say to you with all the force in my being and all the conviction in my heart:

*Do the most productive thing possible at every given moment.*

That rule stands for time planning, prospecting, selling, and everything else in your life. It's as simple as can be, but it seems to be one of the most-ignored best rules ever. Wherever you are, whatever you're doing, constantly ask yourself, "Is this the most productive thing I can do at this time?"

Three actions help you with that rule:

- ✔ Keep a list of your important activities.
- ✔ Keep a list of your appointments and carry it with you.
- ✔ Know what your time is worth.

Be wary of the organizational trap. A lot of salespeople fall into it, spending hour after hour carefully preparing, plotting strategy, getting things in proper order for their prospecting activities, but never actually going out there. These people sometimes buy the most expensive, most complex day planners on the market. They devote tremendous amounts of time to their computer files or collection of index cards. They analyze customer wants and needs, individualize their presentations, and practice their approach. All of these tasks are important, but the problem is these people never put all that hard work into practice.

Maybe such people have a fear of failure or rejection. Certainly it's not laziness, but whatever the reason, organization becomes the goal rather than the reason for all that organizing in the first place. Getting ready becomes an end in itself.

Organization is important, but there comes a time when planning is no longer productive. That's why it is so important to constantly ask yourself if what you're doing is the best use of your time at that moment.

Time planning starts with goal setting, because that's the only way you really can tell what is most important at any given moment. You need to set goals for five areas of your life: family, health, finances, spiritual growth, and hobbies or education.

## Stay balanced

Balance among the goals in all of these areas is important. Becoming a human dynamo in sales is all well and good, but not at the price of your health or your family. If you force all of your energy all of the time into one single aspect of your life, burnout is inevitable. Personal relationships suffer. You eventually become dispirited and even disgruntled, and at some point your favorite hobby (sales) becomes just a job again.

Is that what you're working so hard for?

Think carefully about what really is the most productive thing you can do right now. The activity may actually be spending half an hour with those index cards, but it can just as easily be attending your kid's piano recital, buying your loved one a surprise gift, getting that flu shot, or just getting out of the office for a few minutes to clear your head.

## Plan your day at night

After you establish your goals precisely and in writing, you're ready to begin time planning. Set aside time at night right before you go to bed to plan for the next day. Make this a ritual and don't break it. The routine can become one of the most important parts of your day . . . and the day after.

Write down your priorities for the next day: calls to make, people to see, tasks to perform, and so on that are business-related. Add to the list any priorities that fall under the other five categories in your life. This process should take no more than 10 or 15 minutes. When you finish, fold up the list, forget about it, and grab a good night's sleep.

The next morning your most productive activity can be a jog around the block, helping to get the kids ready for school, breakfast, or another run at those index cards or the computer files. You'll be making similar decisions all day long.

Just keep asking yourself if what you are doing is the most productive thing at the moment. I repeat this a lot because that's exactly what you have to do. Train your mind to bring it up all day long. Write down the activity on a card and keep it in your pocket if you have to — whatever it takes to make this thought a habit.

Working in sales is a liberating experience, but it's not a career for everyone. You have to practice strict discipline. I've met too many salespeople who enter the profession with dreams of luxuries gained at little or no investment. You know the type — people who say they were tired of "9-to-5." A career in sales provides incredible opportunities for professional and personal growth, and there really is no limit to what you can achieve. However, if you don't realize and practice the realities of the profession, you'll soon be back to being bossed at a 9-to-5 job or sitting at the employment agency with a lot more time on your hands than you want.

## *Plan most, but not all, of your time*

Time travel through time planning takes you into your tomorrow. An important step in planning your time is to not overschedule yourself. What happens if you plan 100 percent of your day and then an unexpected crisis or opportunity arises? Whoops! There goes the whole schedule, and you'll never get back on track.

Don't try to plan every moment of every day. You can't. For one thing, you have to respect your prospect's time. What if she's running late? Automatically that means you're running late and there's that "whoops" again.

The schedule is not an end in itself, just a way to get where you're going. Allow yourself some flexibility. Most experienced professionals plan only about 90 percent of the day. Time-planning novices should start out at 75 percent of the day. Practice and experience will bring you up to the professional level in no time at all.

 A champion makes time to plan time. The action is a fact of life. Like the sun, planning comes up every day. It's never a chore, either, rather an exciting conclusion to an exciting day and a preview into an even more exciting tomorrow.

## *Use the Best Tool for You*

Now that you've figured out how to travel through time, it's time to get down to business. I firmly believe in planning your business where you do your business. You need to be near your telephone numbers, prospect files, reference materials, and other sources of information. Schedule a quiet 15 minutes with your time planner and your briefcase or your files and start organizing your business day.

You need an efficient planner, and many are readily available, such as DayTimer, Day Runner, and TimeDesign. Find one that you're comfortable with and that you will use. The planner is no good to you in the bottom drawer of your desk or tucked away and forgotten under the car seat. Your planner is a valuable tool, so choose it carefully.

Make the planning part of your day a ritual and always observe it. Whether working out of your home or office, don't allow yourself to get distracted from this vital task. Even if the kids are yelling, the other salespeople are wolfing down coffee and donuts, and the phone is lit up like a Christmas tree, find the time and place to plan your day. Without a plan, you just won't have a day that's as productive and satisfying as you'll have by planning it.

Think of the first day of the month as your first opportunity for time planning. Schedule all your family and social events that are important for you to attend. Note any important dates such as family birthdays or an important anniversary for a good client. Break down any large projects into manageable weekly and daily tasks so that you don't get overwhelmed by the size of the overall task.

Keep an accurate log of what you do during the day as you do it. No matter how busy you are, don't wait until the end of the day to fill out your daily record. Something can fall through the cracks and get lost: a phone number, a first name, an address, something important that you'll need later. Write down information as you go.

Some people write down a lot of unnecessary activities just so that they can check them off. This is make-work and not very productive, and you're only fooling yourself if you think it means genuine accomplishment. Dash N. Fidgette, the busywork executive mentioned in the earlier section called "If You Need To Get Something Done . . .", is a master of this technique. Do you want someone like that as your role model?

Also, just write down the important information. Nothing else is necessary. You aren't writing the great American novel, just key names, addresses, phone numbers, and information that you need to use.

# A pop quiz on your time planning for the day

Reviewing the day's events at the end of the day is a good idea. Recall your successes and setbacks, what you did right and what you'll do better next time, who helped you out and who got in the way, and how things went overall and in specific detail.

Following are a few questions to help in your evaluation, a fill-in-the-blank check list for your day:

❑ Accomplished all of my priorities

❑ Reached or exceeded daily goals

❑ Invested as much time as scheduled for persuading others

❑ Contacted every prospect on my list

❑ Amount of time spent prospecting

❑ Amount of time wasted

**Where and why?**

Could I have avoided any of that wasted time? How?

❑ Most productive thing of the day:

_____.

❑ Least productive thing of the day:

_____.

❑ Amount of time spent toward my own profit. Can I devote more?

❑ Was today productive for me? My company, too?

❑ All important paperwork handled.

❑ How many of the day's activities put me closer to my goals?

❑ Amount of time scheduled for my family.

❑ Amount of quality time invested with my family.

❑ I can improve quality time with my family by

_____.

❑ Took time for my own physical and emotional health.

❑ If I could live today over again I'd change:

_____.

❑ I feel really good about doing _____ today.

❑ Sent appropriate thank-you notes.

❑ Who or what wasted the greatest amount of my time?

# Go High-Tech

It hasn't been that long ago that top scientists were dreaming of the day when a computer would fit inside an average-size room. Today, we have computers that fit in the palm of our hand, and you see laptop computers everywhere. Fax machines and modems put us in touch with prospects, customers, and resources around the world almost instantaneously, and now you can make a personal call anywhere on the globe from 39,000 feet in the air. For more on remote prospecting, see Chapter 6.

We are living in the most exciting time the world has ever known, a time that has presented us salespeople with tools that are nothing short of phenomenal. One sure sign of it is the fact that in today's world the incredible has become commonplace. Hop on the high-tech merry-go-round. It's a great ride.

## You've got the car, now get the phone

Better than a car phone, get a small mobile phone that you can carry pretty much wherever you go. I don't see how an outside salesperson can operate these days without one. Portable fax machines are also very convenient and, like car and portable phones, are becoming more and more affordable every day.

Those of you old enough to remember Dick Tracy (the comic strip, not the Warren Beatty movie) will recall looking forward to the days of detective Tracy's wristwatch phone. Well, friends, the days of those dream-come-true communication devices are here. To paraphrase an old song, there's a high-tech train a comin' and it's time to get on board.

## Communications courtesy for high-tech times

The unexpected ringing of your portable telephone in the middle of an important meeting can destroy that meeting. The same applies to the beep-beep-beep of that beeper on your belt or in your pocket. Such interruptions don't make you look important, if that's what you think. They just show how little you think of your prospect and the value of her time. A high-tech intrusion is like leaving a meeting when an assistant steps in to say you have a call. Think how much more impressive you look when you instruct the assistant to tell the President and the Joint Chiefs that you'll have to call them back later.

Think about how important that makes your prospect feel!

The most important person in the world is your prospect or your customer. Turn off the phone, put the beeper on vibrate mode, and don't accept any interruptions to the job at hand.

You've heard the reports: Driving while using a portable phone is hazardous to your health. The number of traffic accidents involving the use of car phones while driving is on the rise. As convenient as this practice is, it's not safe. Driving while on the telephone endangers you, your passengers, and the other people in cars and trucks all around you. The smart way to use a car phone is when the car is at rest. If safety isn't enough to motivate you, call your local or state police. More governments are making the use of a handheld phone by a driver when the car is in motion illegal.

You can't prospect while getting a ticket on the side of the road, in traffic court, or in the intensive care unit.

When sending a fax, always include a cover letter and remember to include the total number of pages. Losing a fax in the operations of a company is amazingly simple. Individual pages can get bundled in with someone else's fax. Your last page, the one with the financial information and dotted line for approval on it, can languish for months on the overloaded desk of old Mr. Longtooth (our founder) who is on a three-month extended cruise in the South Pacific.

Calling the intended recipient or an assistant to verify that the entire fax got through is a good idea.

## *Make Your Paper Work Not Paperwork*

I recommend that you get to your paperwork the first thing in the morning and get it out of your way. If you wait till the end of the day, an emergency can come up, you can run across a time-consuming opportunity, or you can be just plain tuckered out at the end of the day and decide to put it off until the morning. What's happened then? That's right, now you have twice as much paperwork as before.

Train yourself to pick up paper only once. Either deal with it right away or put it aside for consideration later. Remember, keep only immediate concerns on your desk. Place all those distracting secondary papers in a paper tray, a filed-away folder, or even a stack on the floor across the room. The main thing is to keep those papers away from your wandering eye.

# Part VI
# The Part of Tens

The 5th Wave    By Rich Tennant

INTERROGATION ROOM

"He's a new breed of cop, Captain—smooth, cocky, a real salesman. He's getting names, addresses, contributions to the Police Benevolence Fund ... it's incredible."

## In this part . . .

The short chapters in this part are full of ideas and quick tips to help you be a better prospector. The pointers are great to review just before meeting with a new prospect.

# Chapter 18

# The Ten Biggest Prospecting Mistakes Everyone Makes

*In This Chapter*

▶ Talking too much

▶ Having the wrong attitude

▶ Being sloppy

*E*veryone knows about the great Babe Ruth's 60-home run season, but few people realize the staggering number of times he struck out to earn that record. Failure has happened, is happening, and will continue to happen to all of us. Failure is inevitable, but isn't something to fear. Fear of failure is one of the greatest causes of failure in the world!

I'm not saying embrace failure as a friend — it's not. However, you can learn and profit from the experience. This chapter gives you a brief look at the ten most common mistakes we all make on the bumpy road of prospecting. If you take the time to learn from these examples, they'll help smooth out the grade.

## You Don't Really Understand Prospecting

Prospecting is hard work. The subject is intimidating for many people and something they'd rather not face. But to be a successful salesperson you have to make sales, and to make a lot of sales you have to prospect.

Prospecting is fundamental!

I have the privilege of visiting a lot of sales operations all over the world, and I am constantly amazed at the lack of attention paid to the primary step in the universal selling cycle. It's as if people have thrown up their hands, saying, "Prospecting is difficult, frustrating, demands hard work, and constant attention, so we'll just skip it and jump right into step two." Did I use the word *amazed?* Shocked would be more appropriate.

Real professionals learn how to prospect. Professionals keep on learning and applying what they learn until they become real champions.

## You Expect Things to Get Better on Their Own

You've been walking door to door. You've worked the phone, mailed the letters, used the Internet. You're working really hard, and you're just not finding qualified prospects. Lots of people work hard. The world is full of salespeople who put in long, hard hours and who aren't even close to living up to their potential. It's sad but true that many of them will then blame everything but themselves and their lack of skills for the poor results.

> Well, it's the economy.
>
> This year's line isn't up to snuff.
>
> We need a new location.
>
> Things will get better. (Maybe, but nothing gets better on its own.)

The ability to prospect isn't a gift from that magic genie in the bottle. Prospecting is a skill that any one of you can learn as long as you have the drive to learn it and are willing to make the effort. If you are not living up to your full prospecting potential, I suggest the challenge is attitude. Become enthusiastic. Set some goals. Get some prospecting knowledge and then apply your skills and strategies.

That's how things get better.

## You Talk Too Much

The flip side of talking too much is that is you don't listen enough!

I admire people with the "gift of gab." I love to hear them tell stories and relate their fascinating or funny adventures. Spinning tales is great to do around the campfire, swimming pool, or living room, but it's death to the salesperson. You just can't buttonhole someone, turn on the charm, barrage them with friendly words, and think you're prospecting.

Prospecting is a skill that requires careful questioning so you can glean useful information while you listen. An interested introvert wins out every time over an interesting extrovert. Why? Because the center of attention for the introvert isn't himself, it's his prospect. He'll ask more questions and better questions, which means he gets more and better information. The interested introvert has the prospect properly evaluated and qualified while the extrovert is chasing his prospect away with every word.

## You're Killing Your Chances with the Wrong Words

What are wrong words?

The answer depends on the situation, the nature of the business, the people involved, and a thousand other factors. You have to play this one by ear every time you go out.

Several areas come to mind. A good example is overfamiliarity. Calling someone by their first name before an introduction would be the wrong use of a word. Cursing, even mild profanity, is clearly out of place. Referring to a woman as a "gal," using jargon the prospect doesn't understand, poor grammar, slang, and incorrect references to the individual's business are all examples of the wrong word in the wrong place.

Imagine the number of prospects who have been turned cold by "Hey, buddy."

## You Don't Practice What You Preach

You read and study skills and strategies. You rehearse them with your family and friends.

Finally the big day arrives and you "gear up" your mind, knock on that door and say, "You wouldn't want to buy a motor home would you?"

Bang! You're dead.

Prospecting isn't an inborn trait and it's not a fine art. Prospecting is a skill that you can learn. All you have to do is learn the principles and apply them. The techniques in this book have been tested, proven, and improved for decades, and not only do they work, they work very well. Trust them, use them as you're supposed to do, and you can become a master prospector.

## You Don't Ask for Referrals

This mistake is so fundamental that it hurts me to list it, but so many salespeople blow so many chances for referrals. Forgetting the basic tenet of asking for referrals is easy to do in the excitement of making a sale or during the fear of a cold call. Make yourself remember. If you forget, you're just hurting your own success. Somebody, sometime is going to close those very prospects you never bothered to get.

The best time to ask for referrals is right after you've closed the sale. Even when you're cold-calling and the answer is a polite "thanks, but no," you can ask if someone in the neighborhood might be interested in your product or service.

Getting referrals can be done. It must be done. Like lightning, it's elemental.

## You Lack Sincerity

I believe most people have some kind of built-in radar that helps them spot insincerity. Maybe it's a trait that goes back to the caveman days before we had fully developed speech. Who knows, but that radar exists, and it can be your friend to guide you into a safe landing or it can help shoot you down.

To buy from you, people have to like and trust you and believe that what you are saying is something to their benefit. If they see dollar signs in your eyes, they know immediately the person you want to benefit the most. I promise that with sincerity and a genuine commitment to serving the needs of your prospect, you will find more prospects, make more presentations, close more sales, and build a more successful and prosperous life.

I see two areas where insincerity is a challenge. One is when you get those dollar signs in your eyes. The other is when you try to interest someone in a product or service that you know is not for her benefit. The second one is really just a version of the first. I admit that some people may turn off their radar when your dazzling performance overloads their brain circuits. However, the majority can see through the act and you not only have lost a prospect, but you've created an enemy.

A professional is dedicated to finding the people who can truly benefit from his product or service so that he can sell them . . . and only them.

# You Don't Pay Attention to Details

Knocking on a neighborhood door cold-calling with your big, smiling face directly in front of the peephole is not called paying attention to details. Lack of detail includes handing out a business card without a "thank you" on it, reading your newspaper just for the news, and not checking those file cards to see if it's been about 30 months since Mr. and Mrs. Jones bought that car.

Sloppiness has no place in the professional world. Stalling on the phone while you look for the name of the person you just called or a misspelled word in a follow-up letter marks you as someone less than professional.

This lax attitude tells your prospect that you really aren't interested in his benefit, and that awareness can surely send him looking for someone who will.

Look around your office. Who's busy at the file cards or double-proofreading a follow-up note? Maybe I should have said, "Look over your shoulder."

# You Let Yourself Slump

Everybody has highs and lows, good days and bad days, moments when you can't even bite your tongue, and times when everything clicks into place and you can do no wrong. If you were to chart that cycle for a year it would look something like a wave pattern.

You can make similar charts quarterly, monthly, and weekly to measure your performance. Like an annual sales diagram, such a chart can tell you not only when to expect the highs, but when to anticipate the lows. For example, if you're really hot Monday and Tuesday after the weekend, but finish poorly at the end of the week, plan some activity Wednesday to recharge your batteries and avoid the Thursday–Friday slump.

Being able to see a slump coming gives you the time and opportunity to head it off. On the other hand, you can climb out of a deep slump after you've allowed yourself to become mired, but it takes a lot of pulling. Why not just stay one step ahead of the situation and avoid stepping into that hole in the first place?

## *You Don't Keep in Touch*

I met an advertising professional who produced an excellent brochure for a client. The brochure was a one-time project, and both parties were very happy with the results. Later, the client produced a series of radio commercials with another professional. The man who had produced the brochure asked the client why he had not been allowed to bid on the radio project.

"If I had known you produced radio too, you would have had the job," the client said.

The adman didn't follow up on other services the client might need down the road, and he lost a good job.

If you have asked the right questions you know what services your prospects are likely to need, even if it's not today. The key is to get permission to keep in touch when today is not the best day for them to get involved. Then, plan time to make three to five follow-up calls a day.

Mrs. Jones, this is Richard Row of The Richard Rowboat Company. We spoke last fall. I was wondering if you have given any further thought to that 10-foot, aluminum model I discussed with you and your husband.

A few seconds per call is all it takes. You won't even notice the time away from the rest of your schedule. Isn't a few seconds of your time worth a potential sale from someone who already knows you, perhaps even likes and trusts you?

Learn from the mistakes of others and don't be afraid to make your own. You will make mistakes, so you may as well learn from them too. Remember that even though Babe Ruth struck out more than any other baseball player, history forever will know him as the home-run king.

# Chapter 19

## Ten Creative Prospecting Methods

*In This Chapter*

▶ Using voice mail as a prospecting tool

▶ Showing your dedication to service, especially in bad weather

▶ Letting your reputation prospect for you

*Y*ou may not be able to connect the dots in a dot-to-dot drawing, paint the simplest little horsey by the numbers, write a ripping yarn, sculpt a bar of soap, or sing a note, but if you're in sales I assure you that you're creative. And talk about creative! Artists have sketches. Sculptors have models. Singers and musicians have notes, and the dot-the-dot people have all those darn little dots. You and I are the ones out there in front of an audience with just our nimble minds and little else. Prospecting is a creative challenge, and true champions make it a real art form.

Following are ten creative prospecting tactics developed by some of the most talented masters of the art of prospecting. Try them out, add your own creative touches, and use the methods again and again. As your prospecting confidence builds, you'll soon start writing, arranging, and singing your own tunes.

## Prospect by Voice Mail

Voice mail is a terrific tool for modern business. Unfortunately, many frightened corporate types also use this technology to hide out. The recipient doesn't feel obligated to personally answer the phone because the recorded greeting picks up the call. If this rather frightened or lazy person doesn't want to respond to your call, he can always use any number of excuses to prevent a call back. I've heard about salespeople who have dealt with such extended voice mail "answers" that the telephone had to be surgically removed from their ears!

You don't have to submit to this tactic — in fact, you can use the voice-mail system to your benefit. For the full skinny on how to get the most out of voice-mail contacts, see Chapter 6.

When you must deal exclusively with voice mail, speak as if you're talking directly to the prospect. In a very real way, you are. Adapt the following role play to your own style.

> Hello, Ms. Prospect, my name is John Doe with the John Doe Dough Company, manufacturer of quality prepared baker's dough. An associate, Mr. Richard Row, suggested I call you. The reason for my call is to see if we can get together at your convenience to see if our products can be of service to your organization. We will need only a few moments to explore the matter. I'll be available _____ or _____. My number is 555-5555. If I don't hear from you by (insert an appropriate date), I'll call you again. Thank you for your time and your interest.

Remember to include your area code if you're calling from outside the prospect's area code.

If your prospect doesn't respond, call back as you promised and keep calling back until you get a response from a real, live human being.

## Prospect Around Your Prospect

Whenever you get an appointment with a prospect, arrive early and stay late. Take note of the business environment around the office and see if any other prospects are within walking distance. Many excellent prospects have turned up on the floor above and below, and in the offices right down the hall. Sure, these prospects are cold calls, but you're in the neighborhood anyway and the effort takes only a few minutes per call.

As with the old TV game show *Let's Make A Deal,* you never know what treasure is waiting behind door number three.

## Get Out On a Dark and Stormy Day (Or Night)

Think about this the next time you see those old storm clouds rising, the bright explosions of lightning, and the heavens opening up. Opportunity is opening up, too. When are your competitors least likely to get out and about to call on prospects? That's right, in lousy weather. Why should they get wet and cold and miserable when there's that nice coffee shop right down the street?

Bad weather can also bring good things. The prospect has to be impressed that someone is willing to risk life and limb and cleaning bills to come see her on a day like this! Additionally, she's probably had a couple of canceled meetings due to the weather and just may have a lot more time on her hands to listen to your presentation than she would on a fair-weather day.

You can also consider the sympathy factor. Many a cold, hard-hearted secretary or receptionist, bound and determined that no one get through his protective barriers, may soften at the sight of someone soaked to the bone and trying so hard to bring the benefits of his service to others. It doesn't hurt either if the salesperson looks an awful lot like a wet puppy.

Bad days can mean really good opportunities. You can have the entire market to yourself while the competition is busy running up their cholesterol levels on those hot donuts at the coffee shop.

## Pick Prospecting Partners

If you adjust your thinking cap just a bit, you can probably come up with a number of fellow salespeople who are in a position to help you out, and vice versa. If you're selling stainless steel flanges and pipe fittings to the hydrocarbon industries, you probably have a friend or an associate who sells valves, fittings, pipe, or whatever to the same industries. Don't you think you may be missing a boat here by not getting together for mutual benefit? Make a professional agreement to swap leads and information about prospects.

In addition to new leads, you can pick up and share a wealth of inside information that can not only get you through the door, but help keep you in the boss's office long enough to make your presentation. Think about how you might use a friendly tip such as "he loves high school football . . . whatever you do don't dare mention mayor/governor/senator/president so and so . . . she is a master skeet shooter . . . they're planning a 4,000-square-foot expansion . . ." and other such valuable tidbits.

Clearly you have to play fair, provide as much information as you get, and never partner up with another person in the same niche of an industry.

## Become a Newsmaker

Publishing your own newsletter is a great way to stay in touch with your customers and prospects, especially those on your secondary lists. A newsletter should contain legitimate news about you, your product, and your company, again, with emphasis on benefits to the prospects and not yourself. The newsletter should look and read as a professional publication — neat, clean, well-designed, and easy to read.

A lot of newsletters arrive and go directly to the "round file," the wastebasket. I think that's primarily because they are produced as an obligation, something to crank out and drop in the mail by PR departments or advertising agencies that may be talented, but who lack the specific information of real insight and interest to the customer and prospect base. If you want people to read your newsletter, put real news in it. Forget puffed up stories, insider's jargon, and anything that says, "Hey, look at me!" You want to provide interesting news and information of value to your prospect. Remember: The *prospect* is the real heart of your newsletter.

Professional style and appearance don't necessarily mean formal and stuffy. Consider your audience. A mailing list composed of rural bass fishermen will respond to a folksy, low-key approach more than a group of young insurance salespeople just out of school. Don't misunderstand me on this. You never, never write down to your audience. Just remember that different people, different professions, different interests require different ways of writing.

You can find many printers, advertising and public relations firms, and freelance marketing people who can help you write and design a newsletter. You can also explore many excellent software packages on the market specifically targeted to helping the inexperienced publisher get published. The rule of survival in the academic world is called "publish or perish." That is, publication of a professor's written works vastly enhance career stability. You can say the same about people in sales.

## *Branch Out*

When dealing with large companies never hesitate to ask about the needs of any branch offices. If you're selling office supplies to an office on the west side of town, chances are that the branch on the east side needs the same materials. Your prospect or customer may provide the name of the appropriate buyer in the other branch. This rule applies equally to separate divisions of a company or even totally separate sister organizations under the same corporate umbrella. Listen carefully for talk of new branches or divisions about to open up. Such inside information can often put you on the inside track toward new prospects and greater sales.

You can even use this method with small companies that have only a single office. The owner or manager you work with probably knows of other businesses in his line of work that can benefit from your services. Ask.

## Write Before You Call

Right before you call, write before you call. You can frequently improve your chances of getting a prospecting appointment by writing a basic letter of introduction before you make an in-person or telephone call. Write to the specific individual you want to contact, not the company or "to whom it may concern." Make a couple of phone calls, long-distance if necessary, to get the right name and the correct spelling and pronunciation. These last two bits of information are critical. You can take a chance on writing or saying "Hello, Mr. Rascholnikovinski" without double-checking, but I advise against it.

Wait a couple of days, or whatever time you think it takes for your letter to arrive, and then follow up with a phone call. I think you will be surprised at the effectiveness of this simple courtesy in opening up important doors.

A letter of introduction should read something like the following:

> Dear _____,
>
> *Thank you for the opportunity to introduce myself and my company, XYZ Circuits, Inc. a manufacturer of high-quality circuit boards for the professional sound systems industry in the U.S., Canada, and the Pacific Rim.*
>
> *I would appreciate an opportunity to see if there could be a mutually beneficial relationship between your company and XYZ Circuits. I would like to meet with you at your convenience to discuss your present and future circuit needs.*
>
> *A few moments of your time discussing the benefits we offer could turn out to be a sound investment and to your benefit. I will call you within the next few days to determine when we might get together.*
>
> *Again, thank you for your time and consideration.*
>
> *Sincerely,*
>
> *Your name*

## Say Thank You

After your initial contact with a prospect, take a moment to send a brief thank-you note saying how much you appreciate the time and opportunity for the call. Your investment in time and supplies is minimal, yet the effect on your prospect can be substantial. This simple, easy-to-do courtesy often sets you well apart from the 101 other salespeople who also called last week.

A thank-you note should be short and sincere, something like this:

> Dear _____,
>
> *I just wanted to take a moment to express my sincere thanks for sharing your time with me this morning/ afternoon. I enjoyed speaking with you, and I certainly appreciate the opportunity. I'm looking forward to being of service to you and your company. Again, thank you.*
>
> (Your name)

"Thank" and "you" are two of Captain Kangaroo's magic words and they really, really are magic.

You're welcome.

## Ask for Help

If you've ever listened to a call-in show on radio or television you know that the host employs a "call-screener" to help select who gets on the air and who doesn't. Many owners and managers operate under a similar system. The call-screener may be a receptionist, a secretary, or an assistant who decides who gets in to see the boss and who gets to spend the afternoon on the bus back to Defeatsville. Often these people become fanatics at their jobs, believing sincerely that they know more about what's good for the boss than the boss.

When you've tried every trick in your bag and you still can't get through, make a sincere appeal to the call-screener's sense of decency and fairness. Try a brief presentation, something like this:

Ma'am, I really *need* your help. I appreciate the fact that (name of the great protected one) has to handle a lot of calls.

It's clear that you want him to receive only those calls that are of real value. I sincerely believe that I can be of genuine benefit to your company. (The great protected one) will know within a moment if my call is of real value. Perhaps he comes in early, stays late, takes lunch in the office, or has a brief period of time for a call like mine. When can I get a couple of minutes, and I really mean just a couple of minutes, to speak with him?

In the preceding example you have been polite, sincere, honest, and have demonstrated a genuine concern for one of the call-screener's major areas of responsibility — the boss's time. Sometimes that's all it takes to move from the outside to the inside of that mighty and seemingly impregnable protective barrier.

Now, you've earned your couple of minutes with the decision maker, don't waste a second of them.

## Call Early, Call Late

This technique works well with just about anyone, but can be particularly effective when dealing with a hard-nosed call-screener.

Think about the people within any business. The size of the company really isn't relevant. What happens at 8 a.m. and what happens eight hours later? That's right, the rank and file arrives in the morning and leaves, rather precisely, at the end of the workday. The rank and file generally includes the call-screener. Many companies are owned or managed by dedicated, hard-working people who do not "punch a clock," and a major part of their lives revolves around a quest for excellence on the job.

Many of these dedicated people arrive early and stay late.

Try calling up a half hour or so before most employees arrive or a half hour or so after they leave. Many large corporations, particularly those doing national or international business, maintain open telephone lines long past regular working hours in their particular time zone. The telephone operator on duty generally isn't a call-screener and probably will put you right through to the party you want. After all, the operator isn't on the job to protect anyone. His job in reality is to facilitate communication via the telephone, to help put person A in touch with person B(oss). Because the operator usually doesn't work directly for the manager or owner, there is little opportunity to develop a power trip or that sense of "I know what's best" found in overly protective secretaries, personal receptionists, or assistants.

In smaller businesses the boss or manager may just be the one to answer the phone.

Using this technique not only gets you through to the appropriate party, it puts you in touch at a time when there are virtually no distractions. Few people, other than your own wise self, will be calling in. The chances of the boss being in a meeting are slim because most people have gone home. For the same reason there is also a significantly reduced chance that someone important will knock on the boss's door and interrupt your presentation.

That's using the old noodle. Salespeople are among the most creative thinkers in the world. We're also among the most creative doers! You may never have a showing of your paintings at a local gallery, your sculpture may never grace the courthouse lawn, your words and music may not hit the Top 40 list or fill Carnegie Hall, but in the fast-moving, ever-challenging, exciting world of prospecting, you can become a real artist.

Play on!

# Chapter 20

# Ten Questions to Ask about Any List

. . . . . . . . . . . . . . . . . . . . . . . . . . . . . . . . . . . . . . . . . . . . . . .

## In This Chapter

▶ Considering cost and accuracy

▶ Checking out the minimum order

▶ Creating your own list

. . . . . . . . . . . . . . . . . . . . . . . . . . . . . . . . . . . . . . . . . . . . . . .

*D*irect mail, when used properly, can be one of the most effective ways to prospect, reinforce, sell, and just stay in touch with people you meet. The medium offers many proven benefits.

Direct mail may seem expensive on a cost-per-contact basis, but equally important is that you have little or no waste audience. Unlike mass media such as television and newspapers, which reach thousands of people who aren't your market, direct mail goes precisely to the individuals you want to contact.

Because you know exactly whom every piece went to, you can precisely measure the success of your mailing.

You can customize the piece to narrow segments of your market. For example, if you're a boat dealer advertising on television, you had better promote a broad range of products to attract the attention of the broad range of viewers. In direct mail, you can target your efforts to only those people likely to be interested in canoes, ski boats, yachts, or even accessories.

Studies show that once people get a piece of direct mail, they are receptive to receiving more from the sending company. You can easily become a known and welcome entity.

No matter how large your postage budget may be, no matter how brilliantly effective and creative your mailing piece, and no matter how much your product or service is in demand, it's all a waste if you don't use the right mailing list!

Following is a list of ten questions that can help you acquire the list that will deliver the goods.

# Is the List Vendor a Reliable Firm?

Asking for references — preferably from someone or some company in a similar industry or your same geographical area — never hurts. As with any other industry, direct mail has its share of top-notch companies and people, its share of fly-by-night organizations, and its charlatans. If you can't get any references there's probably a very good (perhaps a very bad) reason.

# How Much Is the List?

The amounts companies charge for their lists of names and addresses vary. They can range typically from 10 cents to 50 cents per name, depending upon the information you get with the name. Most companies can give you age ranges or geographic areas; sometimes they can break the list out by education level or income levels.

Investments for lists can vary company to company. Shopping around never hurts, but make sure all things really are equal. A lower investment means very little if the vendor has a poor delivery system and your list arrives the day after your sales event.

# What Is the Minimum Order?

You can always expect a minimum order and that, too, varies. Some companies may send you a test list of say 100 names so you can do an early mailing and see what type of response you get. Hopefully, the 100 names aren't all "plants" — people who get paid to respond.

I know someone who recently handled a direct-mail effort throughout the Southwest, but the number of recipients was fewer than 200 people. He actually mailed out 250 pieces knowing that 50 of them were a waste. Why? Due to price breaks in the costs of printing, postage, handling, and the list, it was actually much cheaper to print and mail the extra, wasted pieces than to mail only to his list. Be wary of trying to "pound the dollar" too hard. You may unnecessarily knock a few dollars out of your own budget.

# How Accurate Is the List?

Accuracy is everything. All your time, energy, creativity, and budget get wasted if the direct-mail piece doesn't get delivered to the right person. If you want to do business with the presidents of banks in your area, find out if the list directs your materials to that individual, to "President," to the bank's address or just to "occupant." Some of the more accurate list companies ask for any returned mail you get as a result of poor addresses, and they even reimburse you for your lost postage. The companies use the returns to keep their lists up-to-date.

# When Was the Last Time the List Got Updated?

The importance of this question depends on the stability of movement of the prospects within your target area — but, obviously, the more recently updated the list, the better.

# How Are the Lists Organized?

You can buy a list for just about anyone organized by zip code, municipality, state, business or industry, organizations, clubs, interests . . . well, you name it and there's probably a list for it. Just take the time to make sure that you find and purchase the list that corresponds exactly to your needs. Why buy the entire town, when you need only the west side?

# Does the List Company Offer Additional Services?

Many list companies sell only lists, but other list providers offer handling and postage services, pick up and delivery, and even a print shop. Again, look around, but also evaluate the convenience of one-stop shopping.

# What Formats Are Available?

Generally you can get a list in all kinds of formats, such as computer printouts or peel-and-stick labels. Some companies can actually direct-print the name and address on the envelopes. Printed envelopes are more effective than those with labels because they're more personal. Consider your budget, but also the impression you wish to make.

# Can I Create My Own List?

Building your own list of prospects and existing customers is a time-honored and effective direct-mail technique. The decision to build your own list versus going out-of-house requires you to evaluate both options in terms of cost, labor, time, efficiency, and convenience.

# What Can I Do to Make My Direct-Mail Efforts More Effective?

Pose the above question to everybody: your staff, public relations firm or advertising agency, copywriter, art director, printer, and even your letter carrier. You may be surprised at the free flow of helpful information and tips. For example, unusual sizes or shapes or even how you fold your direct-mail piece can affect not only the investment of time and money in design and printing, but also the cash-ola you expend for materials and handling for distribution.

You really don't buy a list, you rent it, usually for one mailing at a time. Never try to slip by a "fast one" and use a one-time purchase twice. Mailing lists are "salted" with the people representing the list vendor who are on the lookout for exactly that kind of activity.

Champions don't cheat. They don't have to.

# Chapter 21

# Ten Places to Prospect You May Not Have Thought of

## In This Chapter

▶ Approaching your prospects

▶ Getting a "line" on potential clients

▶ Turning the tables on salespeople you meet

*I*n today's society, people are generally cautious about talking with strangers. I blame the media for this. Of course, there are cases where stranger-danger comes into play. However, I still have faith in the general populace that most of them are kind and considerate people with a healthy curiosity about the situations of the other inhabitants of this great and wondrous planet. That's what makes a career in selling so much fun. It's part of your job to meet all kinds of interesting people everywhere you go.

## Prospect with the Cows

One of my students, Tracy Pierce, provided health insurance to small-business owners in Wisconsin. She called upon a family-owned dairy farm and made a prospecting call to the owner right on the spot. The spot happened to be inside the dairy barn. Tracy made her presentation, as she said, "among the cow anatomies" and their inevitable and odorous by-products. She made the sale because she wasn't afraid to go where the prospect was — neither was she afraid to get a little dirt (or whatever) on her shoes.

## Prospect in Scotland

Wherever you go for business or pleasure you can find people of all nationalities who may be very interested in your product or service. Striking up a friendly conversation with folks you meet can significantly increase your prospect list, whether you're overseas, across the country, or just down the road. I had the pleasure of finding an opportunity to play St. Andrews Golf Course while in Scotland on vacation a couple of years back.

While waiting for others to complete our foursome, a young man walked up, looked at me and said, "Tom Hopkins!" He was a fellow American and student of my training. As we chatted, the other members of the group became interested in what I do and have become clients as well.

## Prospect at 39,500 Feet in the Air

Well, if you're going to Scotland, Nova Scotia, or Scottsdale, Arizona, you'll probably go by plane. Sleeping, handling paper work, reading a good book, or just looking out the window are certainly worthwhile activities during the flight — so is making friends (and possibly business contacts) with the people in adjacent seats. I have made some excellent business contacts during flights.

Beware of telling your seatmate right away that you're in sales. If they believe the negative stereotype associated with average salespeople, you may find them retreating into a month-old newspaper rather than talking with you. Worse yet, they may ask to change seats! Limit your job description to one of "helping people" until you know their level of interest in your type of product or service.

## Prospect in the Middle of Nowhere

People out here in the Southwest do a lot of desert hiking. As this popular activity increases with the population growth, more and more hikers encounter more and more people out on the trails. Most folks are friendly and stop and chat for a moment or two. You can easily bring the conversation around to "what do you do for a living?" After you get a reply, courtesy demands that she ask you the same question. There's your opening. This tactic applies also to hiking in the hills, mountains, prairies, and grasslands, not to mention public camp and picnic grounds or even during a walk around your neighborhood.

## Prospect When Someone Is Prospecting You

Why not? If two people can be of service to each other, isn't that twice as good? After all, if you're taking a test drive in that new car or truck, you've got a captive audience. This is called taking advantage of the Law of Reciprocity. If I do something nice for you, you're bound to feel at least a little bit obligated to return the favor. Even if that person isn't a prospect, remember, she probably knows someone who is.

## *Prospect at Mother Goose's House*

A lot of fast-food franchises, and other establishments catering to families, provide so-called "kiddie-lands," playgrounds that usually go under fanciful, fairy tale, or nursery rhyme names. While the kids are busy climbing, bouncing and sliding, you can be climbing the ladder of success by meeting the other parents. Just walk up and say, "Cute aren't they? Which one is yours?" If you sell insurance or financial services, the next natural comment would be, "They grow so fast, don't they? Before we know it they'll be in college." Then, you can lead into discovering how this parent plans to pay for the child's college education and, hopefully, she will be interested in how you're handling it as well.

## *Prospect in the Mud*

So you're taking a mud bath to enhance the beauty and health of your skin. While you're sitting there, why don't you ease into a conversation with the other "mudders." This technique works equally well in the weight room, exercise machine room, gym, track, swimming pool, sauna, and locker room.

## *Prospect Where You Least Expect to Prospect*

If you take time to think about it, I bet that you've missed a lot of prospecting opportunities because you were out of what you believed to be a "prospecting environment." Let me tell you, *everywhere* is a prospecting environment. You just have to keep your mind attuned to the fact that opportunity is all around you all the time. Act on it.

## *Prospect in the Lineup*

You get to meet an amazing variety of people standing in check-out lines. There's nothing wrong with chatting with the other folks in line. What else do you have to do? Don't forget about Aisle Three either. Talking to people is easy if you can see a common interest, such as a food item, a book, cards, a video or audiotape, home furnishings, tools, computers, and so on.

## Prospect Over There

I don't know where "over there" is for you, but I do know a prospect is waiting for you. "Over there" may be just across the street where the new neighbors moved in. It may be in that office down the hall, up on the fifth floor, or in the new office park out by the airport. "Over there" may be thousands of miles away or just a few steps across the floor. Look up. Look around. Look for the opportunity, and you will surely, most surely find it.

A champion does know where to find the prospects. To borrow the title of a famous hit by The Beatles, prospects are "Here, There, and Everywhere."

When approaching people for the first time, the most important thing for you to do is to appear nonthreatening. What's the opposite of threatening? The word *friendly* comes to mind.

✔ Be relaxed, professionally dressed, and don't forget your smile, and you'll do fine.

✔ Approach people casually. Never rush up to someone. You don't want their first impression of you to be a startling one.

✔ It's often wise to sidle up to someone rather than approaching them directly in what may look to them like a frontal attack. I tell my retail sales friends to set their courses to cross the paths of new clients rather than approaching them directly.

For a closer look at how to approach prospects, see Chapter 5. A quick review of it prior to starting on the road to new prospects is a good idea.

# Index

# IDG BOOKS WORLDWIDE
# BOOK REGISTRATION

## We want to hear from you!

Visit **http://my2cents.dummies.com** to register this book and tell us how you liked it!

- ✔ Get entered in our monthly prize giveaway.
- ✔ Give us feedback about this book — tell us what you like best, what you like least, or maybe what you'd like to ask the author and us to change!
- ✔ Let us know any other *...For Dummies*® topics that interest you.

Your feedback helps us determine what books to publish, tells us what coverage to add as we revise our books, and lets us know whether we're meeting your needs as a *...For Dummies* reader. You're our most valuable resource, and what you have to say is important to us!

Not on the Web yet? It's easy to get started with *Dummies 101*®: *The Internet For Windows*® *95* or *The Internet For Dummies*, 5th Edition, at local retailers everywhere.

Or let us know what you think by sending us a letter at the following address:

*...For Dummies* Book Registration
Dummies Press
7260 Shadeland Station, Suite 100
Indianapolis, IN 46256-3945
Fax 317-596-5498

BUSINESS AND
**GENERAL**
REFERENCE
BOOK SERIES
**FROM IDG**

COMPUTER
BOOK SERIES
**FROM IDG**